Sir Neville Cardus CBE was born on 3 April 1888. He first earned his living as a pavement artist, and went on to sell papers, deliver washing, push a handcart and serve as a junior clerk. From this inauspicious and basically uneducated background, there grew one of the twentieth century's finest journalists.

Cardus joined the *Manchester Guardian* in 1917, for which he wrote ardently on his passions, cricket and music, until his death in 1975. He was knighted in 1967.

Donald Wright is a retired schoolmaster. He was educated at Cambridge and knew Neville Cardus closely for thirteen years. He now lives in Wiltshire.

CARDUS ON MUSIC

A Centenary Collection

Selected and edited by
DONALD WRIGHT

A CARDINAL BOOK

First published in Great Britain by Hamish Hamilton Ltd 1988
This edition published in Cardinal by Sphere Books Ltd 1990

Reproduced, printed and bound in Great Britain by
The Guernsey Press Co. Ltd, Guernsey, Channel Islands

ISBN 0 7474 0687 1

Sphere Books Ltd
A Division of
Macdonald & Co. (Publishers) Ltd
Orbit House
1 New Fetter Lane
London EC4A 1AR

A member of Maxwell Macmillan Pergamon Publishing Corporation

Contents

CONTENTS

Acknowledgements

I wish first to record my appreciation and thanks to the *Guardian* for its permission to let me photograph the writings of the late Sir Neville Cardus between the years 1927 and 1975, with a view to the publication of a selection from his essays and notices which he wrote about music.

Later I received assistance from the staff of the British Newspaper Library, from Mr Patrick Hodge of PDI Microfilm Services, and from Mr Edward Arias who kindly made available to me a large collection of Cardus material written since the second world war.

I also acknowledge with thanks the permission of *Punch* to include parts of an article entitled North versus South, which appears on page 20.

Amongst letters and messages of congratulations which Sir Neville received from friends and acquaintances on his 71st birthday (which he and they mistakenly took to be his 70th) I have chosen two, from the late Sir John Barbirolli and Mr Desmond Shawe-Taylor. I warmly appreciate the spontaneous agreement of Lady Barbirolli and Mr Shawe-Taylor to their publication.

I have received encouragement from many but, not least because they knew Sir Neville better and for longer than I did, I wish especially to thank Mr Michael Kennedy and also Mr Kensington Davison of the Friends of Covent Garden.

However, my warmest thanks are kept for three people. First for my wife, for reading the proofs, her cheerful interest, and her views and sureness of touch when I have often turned to her for both.

Secondly, for Mrs Betty White, my secretary in years past, for typing and adjusting the script with skill and precision.

And finally, for Miss Else Mayer-Lismann who was a close friend and associate of Sir Neville Cardus. Without her buoyant spirit, professional guidance and personal knowledge, this book might never have come to fruition. Her assistance has itself been for me a musical education, and one for which I thank her with respect and affection.

D.W.

A Career Note

Neville Cardus was born on April 3rd 1888 and died on February 28th 1975, aged 86. He was married in 1921, to Edith (née King), who died in 1968.

He had no formal training in either music or cricket. Music came to him naturally and gave him his first chance of getting into print. His autobiography and cricket books became classics in his lifetime. No compliment pleased him more than that his writing about either a concert or a cricket match made people wish they had been there.

He earned his first money as a boy as a pavement artist, went on to sell papers, deliver washing, push a handcart for a builder, and serve as a junior clerk. Then, in 1912, he was taken on as a cricket assistant at Shrewsbury School, where it was C. A. Alington, the headmaster, who first recognized his talent of mind. He made him his private secretary and gave him the run of the library.

In August 1914 Cardus volunteered for military service, but was rejected owing to extreme short sight. On Alington's appointment as headmaster of Eton, Cardus returned to Manchester, becoming a part-time employee of an insurance company.

Then in 1917 C. P. Scott, editor of the *Manchester Guardian*, invited him to join his staff as a reporter for 30 shillings a week, with 10 shillings for expenses. Three years later he became cricket correspondent and between 1920 and 1939 he wrote about 8000 words a week on cricket every summer.

However Cardus never wavered in his love of music as his first string. He wrote musical articles from his early years on the *Manchester Guardian*, acting as assistant to its great critic Samuel Langford. He succeeded Langford in 1927, and held the post until 1940 when – at the age of 50 – he went to live in Australia. There he worked for the *Sydney Morning Herald* as music critic, also giving regular weekly broadcasts on music which came to attract large audiences.

On his return to England in 1948 he worked for a year on the *Sunday Times*, rejoining the *Manchester Guardian* in 1951 to become its senior music critic in London until he died.

In 1963 Cardus was awarded the Bayreuth Gold Medal for his services to Wagner's art and to the festival; in 1966 the Hallé Society's Gold Medal; and in 1969 a Special National Press Award for outstanding journalism.

He was made CBE in 1964 and received a Knighthood in 1967.

Foreword

This centenary collection of Sir Neville Cardus's writings on music, edited by Donald Wright, is a remarkable document.

It gives not only a very clear idea of the thoughts on music of a privileged mind but also quite a precise impression of the accepted opinions which reigned in Europe throughout the greater part of this century. The combination of wisdom, genuine feeling and humour is indeed a rare one, and Sir Neville Cardus projects all these in masterful fashion.

I am sure it is a book that will appeal equally to those readers looking for deep thoughts as well as lovers of charm, wit and entertainment.

Daniel Barenboim
January 1988

"Genius is a miracle to be revered whether in fashion or not."

"As far as the spark is in us at all, it must be tended and fanned not to illumine any way of our own planning but simply for the sake of the light itself. This is the one lesson I have learned in my life about which I am certain . . ."

Neville Cardus

Introduction

It is nearly forty years since thought was first given to an "anthology" such as this. From the time Neville Cardus succeeded Samuel Langford in 1927, as senior music critic of the *Manchester Guardian*, until his death in 1975, he wrote over two thousand music "notices" for that newspaper. They became for him his pride and joy, and throughout the 1950s he was hoping a selection would be made and published – edited by one professional colleague or another. This was to have been an apotheosis of a lifetime, and a "legacy to all who come to music in search of beauty, art, and a deeper understanding of humanity".

That the opportunity has fallen to me has come by chance. I did not know of past hopes until many months after I had started collecting his work.

I am but one of that huge company for whom Cardus's writing bridged the distant and temperamental gap between platform, stage or orchestra pit, and the public he made for himself. It had come to seem obvious that a selection of all his writing should be made. This has been a very humbling experience, but one more absorbing and refreshing than I could ever have anticipated. He remains remarkable company.

But how was I to select from the complete collection, and then organize a selection? As to selection there *was* no choice: Cardus's best writing was about the music and its interpreters he most admired and enjoyed, from the inside; and he knew it. Many of these artists became his friends. However, organization of the material required a deliberate decision, one which would shape the book and the reader's response, yet also one determined by both the range and the quality of Cardus's immense output. He himself published a number of books about music, using miscellaneous articles of his own.

I have grouped his writing, only a little of it republished hitherto, into sections, taking advantage of its forty-five year span of time, 1927–1972. This is about half the whole period of English musical criticism and I hope its altering perceptions, so many contrasting with to-day's, will stimulate if not provoke. Of the nineteen sections, nine are given to composers and seven to conductors of the orchestra, the instrument which for Cardus was supreme and which has known most change. Within the sections each piece has its date and each usually, but not always, appears in the order of its publication. The reader's perspective therefore becomes increasingly kaleidoscopic. I hope this will add interest even if it may strain sometimes at chronological habits of thought.

Of course, I have had to leave out a great deal. The limiting constraints on selection have been tantalizing. Only exceptionally is Cardus to be found here writing from abroad; from Salzburg, for instance, or from festivals at home, or from the "Proms". Many renowned instrumentalists and singers have been omitted, while others have entered only by a "back door". Nor has it been possible to include pieces about music composed in his latter years. He would have been sad.

There can be few more vividly pictorial descriptions of any writer's early life than in Cardus's autobiography. In 1917, having been found unfit for military service three years earlier, he was invited by its great editor C. P. Scott to join the staff of the *Manchester Guardian*. In 1920 he was appointed its principal cricket correspondent. He had become one of Scott's "young lions". His musical awakening had begun when he was about fifteen and had become a torrent of interest four years later. By the time he joined the newspaper, cricket and music were in harness. He was thirty-two.

Neville Cardus was among the most persuasive and cultured craftsmen journalism has known. His writing had a compelling style. If, today, it seems expressed in warm colours he would not have been surprised. He remained in love with words and phrases, not forgetting the semi-colon, when he was describing, promoting or – most likely of all – just enjoying what came to ear, sight or mind. His pieces still live, while others have long since dulled, lying flat now on the page. His allusions and imaginative use of metaphor entertain, and sometimes he did not resist satisfying a mischievous (but never malicious) irreverence. Above all, his luminous insights remind us that "we outgrow many of the cleverest ideas but not the simplest emotions."

From Samuel Langford, Cardus used to say he learnt "to feel and translate", and that it was C. E. Montague, the *Manchester Guardian*'s drama critic, who taught him to bring "to the diet of sights and sound the wine of a journalist's temperament". He rebelled against what he called the dryness in human nature, and the parsimonious good-mannered use of English. Moreover he detested pretentiousness and "humbug" in all their manifestations; but he could excuse aesthetic vanity – provided its owner had something to be vain about. He was not above admitting to his own past misjudgments or his inconsistencies. Given the length of his experience, it would have been surprising had he not sometimes changed his mind. Likewise he repeated himself. Meanwhile he loved the spontaneous, the unpredictable and unexpected.

Cardus was writing during a half century of unprecedented development in the musical world: the coming of radio, of sound recording, the widespread and astonishing improvement in instrumental techniques, the arrival on the scene of immense numbers of accomplished musicians – to which the promise and brilliance of young soloists and youth orchestras all over the globe have been testifying – and the groundswelling increase of the music-loving public. He was among that small number who interpreted music with a flair which encouraged the very enthusiasm which led people to listen with more intelligence and insight; first from Manchester, then for seven years in Australia and, on his return, from London. He and his colleagues did much to make possible those more specialized interests and perceptions which their successor-critics can take for granted today. George Bernard Shaw, Ernest Newman, Neville Cardus – each was born to his time.

But although he was one of the leaders in music's expansion, and despite an extraordinarily active life as "Cricketer" also, one cannot say that Cardus quickened his own critical step. In his writing he painted the scene, savoured it, dwelt on it in proportion, and (at least until 1939 but less so later for frustrating lack of sufficient newsprint in a newspaper) then he took what space he needed. Always it was the music that mattered most. Language was his instrument. He wrote his notices, always in longhand and with few corrections, hot from the performance. He would have regarded a word-processor, for *aesthetic* use, as an outrage and a diabolical sorcerer. After all, his notices did come to be placed, alone and in the middle, on the back seat of a chauffeur-driven Daimler hired from Harrods, to be driven to the *Guardian*'s offices from the National Liberal Club. That would have seemed agreeable to his Faust, even if today Mephisto, centre-stage, considers it merely quaint. Just as he feared.

In his youth, from 1912 to 1916, Neville Cardus was employed at Shrewsbury School first as assistant cricket professional and later also as part-time secretary to the headmaster, Dr C. A. Alington. These were years of mounting national anxiety, then unprecedented human sacrifice. Young and old alike looked to their leaders as never before. In Alington, the whole school community found someone they could admire and follow. "I saw *decor* in him, and irony," Cardus was to write later. Alington had understood his cultural interests and curiosity and encouraged them. "Wouldn't you have liked to come as a boy to a school like this?" he asked him one day. "No, headmaster. No, I don't think so," came the reply. "You see, I should have been really rather bored."

In 1967, when I was its headmaster, Neville Cardus returned to the school as its principal guest. He talked to the boys and their parents.

"Ladies and Gentlemen," he began. "This is for me an extraordinarily romantic and sentimental occasion. As an obscure young man of twenty-three, who had some ideas, I first came to this school, where I had all its advantages without the disadvantages of an academic education." Later, turning to the boys, he said, "I very soon made up my mind in life that, whatever befell, I would not *work* for my living. Find something in your nature, everyone is born with something, and then enter into it body and soul, whether it's cricket, music, or the trade of a boot maker. Make the best pair of boots in the world, be an individual, you are isolated in the world, alone." Then he paused. "To this day," he then added, "I still go to concerts. The same old programmes I've been listening to for over fifty years. But whenever I go I always find something *new* . . . The only thing in life to guard against is mediocrity; I would rather be a nit wit than a mediocrity, because there are too many of them."

Neville Cardus would have taken for a nit wit anyone who spent months collecting copies of nearly all any one man had written about music. However, had he known what a delight it has been to collect and enjoy again *his* writing and to act as *his* part-time secretary, I think he might have smiled. Who knows?

Donald Wright

Coulston, Wiltshire
1987

I

CARDUS –
THE MANCUNIAN

Eighty Years Ago

1947

Manchester was good for a young man to live in during the years before the 1914–1918 war. The Germans had given the place a solid culture; they came to Manchester for trade and brought their music with them. Richter had played on Christmas morning when the Siegfried Idyll wakened Cosima as no other woman before or since has been wakened; at the Royal Manchester College of Music Brodsky was the Principal; friend of Tchaikowsky and Brahms. The Continental Restaurant was München in Lancashire. I one night saw Brodsky, Richter and Richard Strauss going in there together. I remember a week in Manchester when a new play by Galsworthy was given at the Gaiety Theatre on Monday; on Tuesday there was a concert of the Brodsky Quartet; on Wednesday a matinée by Réjane; on Thursday a Hallé Concert, with Richter and Busoni, and on Friday a production of Ibsen's *Ghosts*, connived in camera; for *Ghosts* was then a banned play in England . . . . All these exciting events were written upon in the *Manchester Guardian*; Montague almost breaking shins over his own wit and pregnant with metaphor; Agate already full of Sarah and the Goncourt brothers; while Allan Monkhouse, who grew to look more like Dante every day, kept the balance in prose as cool and judicious as any in the land. No city has known the equal of the *Manchester Guardian* as an influence for acute living. A little austere, maybe, but a passionate Puritanism. I often wondered who read it except the Jews and the Germans and the self-educated denizens of the hinterland of Manchester.

Autobiography

His "Sensitised Plate"

1947

Stendhal said that for him a landscape needed to possess some history or human interest. For me a place must have genius in the air, a sort of distillation of years, a pathos of perspective, a mist of distance. In a word, it must have *ghosts* of lost wandering life, now forgotten by the extrovert and contemporary world. Historical and archaeological interest is prosaic for me. I do not particularly wish to see the house in which the greatest poet was born; but to walk from Grinzing down to Vienna on a September evening, as twilight deepens and the lights of the city begin to twinkle, and to feel the sense of the past, almost to hear the vanished beauty and song whispering in rustle of leaf or wind, and in some hurrying footfalls on the roadside; to feel an awareness to all the hearts that have beaten here, the hopes and the strivings in these old houses, huddled in deserted gardens; birth and marriage and death; the comings-home at the day's end, the glow of candlelight and wine and fellowship that surely seemed perennial and everlasting; the security of life at the crest, and now not only dead but lost to a world that must for ever be up and doing – this for me is to live and "go places". Every great city is a palimpsest not of facts and events but of atmosphere and feeling, shaped by the irony of transition. That means I cannot enter into an unexplored land, a new land, where nature has not acquired an aesthetic and a pathos. Mountains and grand canyons and plains and mighty rivers are only so much geography in my eyes; mere mountain-maps built on a large scale. A sunset in the Indian Ocean once bowled me over because it was like the closing scene of *Götterdämmerung*.

Happiness, as the world seems to want or to know it, is a strange idea to me. There are few material circumstances that have the power to satisfy more than a part of me; usually there is a spectator watching from the back of my mind, a little bored. Only when I am entirely alone, enjoying a book or music, is he quiet. So I see to it each day that I spend six hours in solitude . . . My spectator – I can put my finger on him – can cause a feeling of discomfort that is almost as unpleasant as toothache. The feeling is at its most painful when I sense that I am talking to a nature of different texture from mine. And it is not a matter of opposed or dissimilar ideas. It is pure emotional reaction, affective. A scientific mind normally repels me, but I have been happy with at least one kindred spirit amongst scientists, because I have tasted a texture of temperament behind all the science, warming and approachable. Any extrovert is for me the last word in tedium; and the tedium of externality is life's most searching trial. The objective everyday universe is only so much material for sensibility or imagination to play upon; and sheer "play" it must be at times, as much as a more austere occupation. Humour is a necessary salt, and without a corrective of cynicism all seems foolishness and callow . . . .

A plain case of the "sensitised plate!" When, years ago, Ernest Newman applied this term to me as a writer on music I took it as a sort of compliment. I think he made too little of the fact that the plate was indeed sensitised. Even in those early days I had grown some fine and responsive antennae or cat's whiskers, developed after much adjustment and squeezing through narrow apertures and scarcely-opened doors. I could at once become absorbed into music; I ceased to feel that I was listening to it from the outside; I was drawn into the composer's mind, almost to participating in the creative process. In a word, I surrendered myself to music as a lover to his mistress . . . The true critic must collaborate in the creative act; he must be as much a man of imagination as of knowledge and judgment . . . The material of criticism, the evidence so to say, is the recollection in comparative sanity of what happened to one while under the spell. The critical credo is proved embracing or narrow by trial and error. The critical antennae are developed while groping in the actual territory of the creative artist.

In all this I am only saying in another way, "in anderen bischen Worten", as Gretchen puts it, that the critic should be a poet. Indirectly I am also saying – and perhaps not *so* indirectly – that I am myself a poet as well as a critic. It is not a boast; a man is not responsible for natural gifts, and can take no credit for having been born with them.

Autobiography

The Hallé Concert

(The first notice from the "M.G.", written by Neville Cardus following his appointment as the newspaper's senior Music Critic)

28th October 1927

The Hallé Orchestra has learned well the secret of playing Brahms and has found that in his Third Symphony fancy was bred in the heart and not merely the head. As we heard the great-hearted singing of the man last night, we found it almost impossible to believe that a few years ago this same Brahms was regarded as austere and cold. Such is the fate of the artist when his friends mark him out to carry the banner in the eternal battle of the schools. Brahms was used as a weapon with which to beat the romantics down, as though every great genius in the fullness of his humanity and culture is not romantic and classic by turn. Has not a classic senses, affections, passions? Has not a romantic organs, dimensions, eyes? Brahms was a full man; in his symphonies alone he seems to sum up all the cultural forces of music that were in the air of his period; he was moved by the moral grandeur of Beethoven and his sense of the invisible drama that goes on behind the outward show of things.

He was moved, too, by the rich outpouring of Schubert's and Schumann's songs, those sweetest songs that tell of saddest human thoughts, and those glad songs "with a lilt of words that seem to sing themselves". And so Brahms composed his Lieder, his violin sonatas, that adorable fifteenth of the piano waltzes, and the Third Symphony. He warmed his classical hands at romantic fires; he poured into the heart of romance the same cleansing reflectiveness of the true classic. In the Third Symphony the poet and philosopher mingle in one another's being. The mighty descending tread of the opening phrases of the first movement are gigantic and tell of a sublime, tough mind. But the opening melody of the andante puts the symphony as though into a

6

cradle, and our great giant caresses his art with the tenderest touch. Sweetness is always coming out of strength in his work; at one moment the music is granite and vast, and then, suddenly, we come upon some flower of grave and modest song – and we think of the quiet blossom sheltered in the mountainside, and the thought of it moves us as a like thought moved Goethe. How swiftly the symphony will abate a great sweep of grand rhythmic power and die down to that softness and solitude which is the very breath of romance. If we call Brahms a German Wordsworth we hope the point of this simile will not be missed altogether. His music is generally thought to be drab of colour – let us frankly say it is sometimes bald, adding, in Matthew Arnold's phrase, "But bald as the mountain tops are bald." Only in his moments of orchestral power, though, can Brahms ever be thought hard. The Hallé Orchestra now knows where to find the sweets of Brahms's scoring – in those meditative melodies, those dying falls of sound in which we can well imagine the composer saying:

> "The music in my heart I bore
> Long after it was heard no more."

Sir Hamilton Harty's finest contribution to our musical life is the way he has opened the big heart of Brahms for us. Last night the Third Symphony won more applause than we have ever before heard. The performance was sensitive at all points, and every affectionate touch and stress was made without hurt to the symphony's infinite rhythmical changefulness. The work in its technical aspects has a surface intricacy which might easily lead a conductor to turn, by want of a spontaneous handling, fancy into mere contrivance. Often in the past has the symphony come to us stone cold because of a deliberate exposition of its manifold ingenuities of design. Last evening the performance throughout combined firmness with delicacy, head with heart. The players caught the glow of the composer's deep love for the masterpieces, and at the end we could only bow the head before its beauty. The varieties of tonal ascent and descent in the last movement obviously delighted the orchestra as much as they delighted the rest of us. We can think of no composer whose future is safer and surer than Brahms's; every one of us can find a point of contact.

Sir Henry Wood in Manchester

THE VERDI REQUIEM

24th November 1933

Sir Henry Wood has never before conducted at a Hallé Concert. He came last night to his fresh laurels faced with a difficult task. The "Requiem" of Verdi is a work far removed from the English conception of the spirit and purpose of a Mass; the vocal technique, too, is at the extreme of the rolling contrapuntal technique which in oratorio has been for long (for too long) the basis of English choral singing. Verdi's "Requiem" is not contemplative; it does not soften the terrors of death, as felt by an almost medieval view of disillusion and the sepulchre. The "Dies Irae" has been described as a vivid glimpse into the "Inferno" of Dante; it would be better to say that it is a glimpse into the "Inferno" of Doré. The English idea of liturgical music is likely to be shocked by Verdi's very swift flashes of macabre realism, in which we seem to see the awakening swathed corpses, like so many figures out of a canvas by El Greco – though really the horrors of Verdi's imagination are never so gaunt as all that; he always had a fundamental virility; he saw into the grave from the vantage-ground of a great healthy and manly Italian.

Yet the external aspects of Verdi's emotionalism in this Mass are likely to strike English folk as so much theatre stuff. All in all, then, Sir Henry Wood's task was hard; leadership at the Hallé Concert under the circumstances was about as cheering as that of Uriah the Hittite. To his eternal credit, Sir Henry gave us a magnificent performance of the masterpiece. He reaped the good sowing done by him at rehearsals which the Hallé Choir will discuss enthusiastically for many a day to come. Sir Henry is a worker and has the faith that moves mountains – and the average choir is nothing less than a mountain. Seldom has the Hallé Chorus sung with more life and point than last night. The volume

8

of tone was capital, with apparently that power of reserve which counts the most in the end. One or two defects were possibly unavoidable. In this country it is the quaint custom to rehearse a choral work apart from the orchestra; in other words, the chances are that until last night the Hallé Chorus had not performed the work with the instrumentalists. The blend of orchestra and choir now and again lacked the rapid adjustments of attack and release which are demanded by the dramatic nature of the score. It is music which the imagination must *see*, not only hear. The beginning of the "Dies Irae" is spectacular; the rushing strings, the typical Verdi piccolos, the unaccented beats of the drum, the shuddering of the chorus at the words "Quantus tremor est futurus" – here we need not only vocal but histrionic art. It is too much to expect of English choralists a sudden and complete forgetfulness of the comfortable faith of countless oratorios, all resting in the Lord. Even the opening agony of Elgar's "Gerontius" has often gone beyond the average English vocalist's notion of the macabre.

The "Sanctus" is, one supposes, unthinkable to lovers of Bach, but not even the pedant will deny the delicate mysticism of the "Agnus Dei." At the opening of the "Libera Me" we are plunged into the thunder and lightning once more. An apocalyptical stroke occurs when Verdi calls back the horror of the "Dies Irae" in a charnel-house passage for the basses, with the menace of trombones thrown in to make our flesh creep creepier still. The fugue crowned an evening which was unexpectedly memorable for fine and musical singing. Sir Henry controlled the movement of the parts like a man who knew the score backwards; they all were vivid yet clear and invested with not an ounce more of the energy they needed. This fugue shows how superbly Verdi could bring scholarship into the forge of dramatic imagination. In "Falstaff" he shows also how the fugue can be expanded and humanized by the girth and juice of comedy. The Mass no doubt has its naïve accents; they must be taken as part of the composer's psychology and style. There is no a priori case for a metaphysical complexity. Verdi was not an abstract thinker; his Mass is emotional simply because emotion was his life's force, as well as his material as artist.

Sir Thomas Beecham in the Free Trade Hall

16th March 1934

At last night's concert Sir Thomas Beecham announced to a large and delighted audience in the Free Trade Hall that he had accepted the office of president of the Hallé Concerts Society. Also he suggested he would not regard the position as merely "honorary"; he hinted that a new chapter was about to begin in the history of concerts. He has already given us a splendid prelude this winter. For the second time in the Society's career he has come forward at a trying period of transition and stimulating new ideals and new life. During the war he held the city's music together by his own generosity and his own genius; at the beginning of the present experimental season his example and power made failure straightway impossible. There were people who gloomily imagined that without a permanent conductor the Hallé Orchestra would achieve speedy and terrible deterioration. The unmistakable fact today is that the Orchestra is more vital and musical than it has ever been in recent times. It was hard to imagine playing of swifter and surer attack than last evening's . . . . First the audience was won by the Handel music, large-hearted, manly, strong, yet capable of exquisite yieldings . . . . Then we were given a performance of the Fourth Symphony of Beethoven which caused the work to sound the loveliest and most spontaneous in existence. It was good to have Beethoven put before us for once in a way in a genial and approachable vein. But how remarkable is the introduction – to a symphony so lighthearted! The processes of the musical imagination are so free that they can go beyond the logic of the prosaic universe; the shaded solemnity of the Fourth Symphony's opening does not contradict the jolliness to come, yet there is no logic of the reason that can say why the symphony should begin with a moment so vast and mysterious. Sir Thomas conducted the introduction with a magnificent feeling for intensity and expansion; then he gave us a transition to the allegro vivace which was a masterpiece of instantaneous rhythmical release, subtle, headlong, but perfectly controlled.

After the interval the charming Fourth* Symphony of Dvořák was played with all its originality of fancy, as new as it was when the composer felt the birth of it in his mind and heart. This is Sir Thomas's secret; he knows how to come to a work and strike individual life out of it and get it performed as though for the first time. A work of art does not grow old; it is outside time and space; it is we who grow tired, because few of us possess the imagination that never submits to the blunting effects of routine and repetition. Sir Thomas loves every work he happens to be conducting; indeed, there is obviously for him no other music in the world quite so good. He enjoys himself, and communicates his enjoyment to everybody in the orchestra. His gusto is immense; for so instinctive is his technique that he has no need to think of it. His freedom of spirit is the measure of his technical command. His movements suggest tremendous animation; in any conductor less great they would be at times excessive. But he wastes not an ounce of his energy; no gesture is wasted. He is the very image of the music he is directing. The orchestra draws vitality from him – and joy. You could see the players revelling in their parts last night; the melodies were tossed from one instrumentalist to another with relish; this was true art, because it was related to true play . . . .

The Hallé Society will be wise to place the musical and artistic policy unreservedly in Sir Thomas's hands; to be bound to a despot so benevolent is to find the only freedom that matters nowadays – freedom to move and survive.

*Now renumbered the Eighth

The Conductorship of the Hallé Orchestra

HOW SHOULD THE VACANCY BE FILLED?

7th March 1935

The Hallé Concerts season is drawing to an end and people are wondering what the committee are going to do about the conductor or conductors for the future. Correspondence is breaking out in the newspapers telling of internal contention. The case for the "guest" system is easily stated: it makes for freshness and it appeals to the large section of the public who go to concerts not only to hear but to see. Few people really listen to music; the art of listening involves many years of constant experience. The Hallé Concert Society, of course, are not concerned wholly with the specialist music-lover; they have to look to the taste of the ordinary audience. But it is worth keeping the fact in mind that the Chancellor of the Exchequer has recently arrived at the opinion that the Hallé Concerts are affairs of musical culture, and not directed for the purpose of entertaining "the greatest possible number". In the long run, the Hallé Concerts will sink or swim in these difficult days according to the will of the comparatively few folk who love music with passion and knowledge; nobody else will make the necessary sacrifices, or keep the Hallé Orchestra in mind a week after the glamour of the last concert of the season has died away and vanished.

The Hallé, like every other fine orchestra in the world, was not formed and given its status under the guest-conductor system. Until a year or two ago nobody in Manchester dreamed of placing the orchestra in the charge of a different conductor week by week, or even month by month. The question is not only one of good performances. A brave orchestra must have a head, a master-authority. Programmes cannot be planned satisfactorily under the guest-conductor system. New music, or unhackneyed old music, will not often be heard, for the simple reason that a conductor who is invited to Manchester for one or two concerts will be tempted to take no risks with the unfamiliar; feeling that he is "on trial" with a strange orchestra, he would be foolish if he did not concentrate on well-worn works. There can be no widening of the orchestra's activities in the absence of a permanent chief; guest-conductors are in no position to develop an organization with which they come into contact only for a few days, and only by the hazard of fortune at that. On its merits, there is indeed little to be said in favour of the guest-conductor system, whether from a point of view of the style of playing, the arrangement of good programmes, or the cultivation of a larger field of activities for the instrumentalists. (And the last point is crucial.)

The average subscriber to the Hallé Concerts will naturally give ear mainly to the technical results which he can enjoy for himself in performance. Questions of the business side of the orchestra, and of the society, he will leave to the watchfulness of the officials. Most of us have troubles of our own, and we go to concerts not to add to them. The Hallé Concerts will prosper or dwindle according to the pleasure they give to those people who cherish music sufficiently to feel lost if they do not hear it frequently. Why should these people take the trouble every Thursday to go to the Free Trade Hall and leave their radios and warm firesides – unless they are given distinguished performances and not commonplace ones? This season the Hallé Orchestra has on several occasions attained an excellence of style not often reached in this country. Under the conductorship of Sir Thomas Beecham and of Mr Georg Szell, the playing has caused that enthusiasm which gives birth to fresh interest – and fresh subscribers. Alas! there have been disconcerting, if inevitable, fluctuations of form. Opinion on this matter is of course quite personal. But there are persons and persons; the opinions of those who are in touch with the best standards should count for rather more than the opinions of those who have other affairs in life to attend to than the study of orchestral style. To the man who seldom goes beyond the borders of his home-town, the home-town orchestra is the best in the world. Do the members of the committee of the Hallé Concerts Society keep themselves qualified to estimate the work of their orchestra by the comparative method, based on a close acquaintance with orchestral performances elsewhere? The present writer has this winter heard playing by the Hallé Orchestra which was fine enough to compare favourably with performances, recently heard, of one or two of the world's greatest orchestras. He has also heard playing by the Hallé Orchestra since the new year, which has fallen away astonishingly and alarmingly. No orchestra ever established can survive sudden extremes of the good and the indifferent; style is bound to suffer. Too many conductors in a season, even if all are first-rate, are certain to cause restlessness, confusion of outlook, and perhaps lack of discipline in the best-intentioned body of musicians.

It is fortunate at the present time that the Hallé Concerts can turn for guidance to Sir Thomas Beecham. For even the incredible energies of Sir Thomas do not assist him to be in two places at once; when he is polishing the technique of his own orchestra in London, or planning the Covent Garden seasons, what chance has he of keeping his attention riveted on the Hallé Concerts? He gives us half a dozen great evenings a year; he leaves his mark on the orchestra for weeks. Then the bloom of style goes, rubbed away by efforts of other conductors which vary – as they would be bound to vary if the conductors were Furtwängler, Toscanini, and Bruno Walter themselves.

The Hallé Concert Society owe it to Sir Thomas to appoint a reliable lieutenant, who will in his absence cooperate with his good work. Tastes will differ as to the right man for the job; the present writer would vote for Szell. But there is no denying that such a post is now vacant and urgently needs to be filled. Sir Thomas for six concerts next year, or, of course, as many as he is able to conduct; for ten a first-class artist, musician, and orchestral trainer, to be "on the spot" most of the winter. For the other three or four concerts the Society might wish to risk a gesture with artists of the rank of Furtwängler. Whatever the names none must be that of a mediocrity. We have had more than one or two this season, whose effect on the orchestra – temporary, thank goodness! – has been dull or even worse than that.

Ghosts of the Old Free Trade Hall

RECOLLECTIONS

17th November 1951

My memories of the Manchester Free Trade Hall go farther back than the first time I ventured to cross the portals of the imposing edifice which, as I was subsequently told by people privileged to look upon the building before the city's soot settled down thoroughly, possessed a facade in the Lombardo-Venetian style. This celebrated hall of song and harmony was mainly associated in the minds of Manchester boys forty or so years ago with the dissonances of politics and the abstractions of political economy. Free Trade! Tariff Reform! Long before barbarian ears attended to Richter they were willingly lent to Belloc and Victor Grayson; I heard them cheek by jowl, if not in actual debate on the same platform, the rapier and the bludgeon, or rather the toreador and the Bull of Bashan.

Other half-vanished impressions are of the organ in the Free Trade Hall, swathed in Union Jacks, playing not Bach but "Land of Hope and Glory" to herald the approach of F. E. Smith, who later in the evening with hands in his pockets, directed every eye in the multitudinous meeting upon some poor devil who had merely asked him a civil if awkward question. Horatio Bottomley came to the Manchester Free

Trade Hall one winter night and, for reasons which escape me at the moment, told us proudly that he hadn't been educated at Eton or Harrow or Oxford or Cambridge but "in the larger universe of the world".

In the new building, on the night of its public opening, shades of Bright and Cobden may well mingle with those of Sir Charles and Lady Hallé – Lady Hallé, who was known to her doting audiences as Norman-Neruda, the incomparable player of the Mendelssohn Violin Concerto. On alternate nights the Free Trade Hall accommodated many and diverse notabilities – Richter and Arthur Balfour; Handel (who was Balfour's favourite composer) was scarcely out of our ears before Balfour, calm and aloof, was discoursing, as though to himself, on Protection and Philosophic Doubt.

Inscrutable if not insubstantial was the back of Hans Richter as it presided over the Hallé Orchestra. He was impressive even seen in perspective from the rear of the Hall, where we huddled together in the few shilling seats at the disposal of the likes of us. But we preferred in those days to keep our heroes at a distance; consequently they grew in stature and dignity. Besides, Richter had come to Manchester with the weight of Bayreuth behind him. When he conducted Wagner we knew we were getting it from the horse's mouth, so to say; for had he not made the first copy of the original manuscript score of "Meistersinger"; had he not played on the staircase when Cosima was wakened one Christmas morning by the strains of the "Siegfried Idyll", wakened as no woman before or since? He conducted all the Beethoven symphonies and all Wagner from memory. In those days this was an impressive and rare achievement, for most conductors kept their heads in the scores. It was this same tremendous Richter, resembling Hans Sachs or Pogner in spectacles, who called a famous soprano to order, at a rehearsal of "Fidelio" (in concert version) because she stayed on a top note too long, justifying herself by explaining to Richter that she always held it that way – it was one of her famous notes. In his curious but expressive English Richter replied: "If Beethoven 'ad wished pau-se he would 'af wrote. He 'as not wrote, so we do not make." And this was spoken in the heyday of the prima donna, when she reigned supreme and tyrannically. She has long since been deposed; in her place the conductor holds sway, and often enough he too "makes" what Beethoven "'as not wrote".

Simple gospel-truth observance of the holy writ of the score gave to a Richter interpretation an impersonal objective sense of sublimity. The method did not suit all composers and he was wise to know where not to venture. Young rebels in Manchester tired at last of his mainly German or central European outlook and territory. They petitioned him and asked why he wouldn't play some modern French music. "Zhere is no mod'n French musik," he is reputed to have replied. Ernest Newman, who round about 1905 was critic of the "Manchester Guardian", opened fire one morning, after Richter had conducted the "Romeo and Juliet" of Berlioz, by beginning his notice something in this strain: "It was fairly obvious last night that Dr Richter was not thoroughly acquainted with the score." Considering Richter's fame and authority then, I imagine this sentence of Newman's is the most courageous ever written by any critic, alive or dead.

Richter was high priest of the Hallé for years. But from behind the scenes a rare power for good emanated over many more, though conductors might come and conductors might go. Policy was moulded by Gustav Behrens, and ideals were scrupulously guarded by this great citizen of Manchester. We are accustomed these days to economic strain and disruption; we have grown flexible. There had been no rehearsal at the outbreak of the war of 1914–18 for adaptation. When the test came and tradition was suddenly imperilled, when even the name of Schubert became suspect in certain quarters and Wagner's anathema, Gustav Behrens, anonymous but uncompromising, kept his head and a firm hand on the Hallé tiller.

Free Trade didn't end with political economy in the Manchester Free Trade Hall of my youth. After Beethoven and the "Ninth" Sousa could be heard there with his band, not in the same programme naturally enough. I heard Kreisler for the first time in the Free Trade Hall, playing the solo part of the Elgar Violin Concerto, and seldom since has he equalled the gold frame of melody he lavished on Elgar. His "playing" wrote Samuel Langford in these columns, "is in every sense highly strung; it is taut to the last degree. His chordal playing . . . had the sound of miniature horns." It is well for us to bear in mind this description of Kreisler at his best; he was not all charm and honey. Of all the impressions that remain of the old Free Trade Hall on Thursday nights that of Langford is strong as any, sitting in his seat, head bowed, as he read a newspaper during a dull piece. He seldom carried scores about with him.

There will be a cohort of ghosts tonight when the Hallé Orchestra returns again home, not the least haunting of them Hamilton Harty, who created the concerts afresh and brought to them a range of style not consistently there before. Harty followed Beecham, who was pilot of the orchestra through the troublous seas of the first war. In our present day we all know what Sir John Barbirolli has done for the Hallé; we know of the vision of the committee in council at the crisis a few years ago; we know of the inspired SOS sent in wartime to Sir John in New York, and we all know of the miraculous salvage restoration. The story has been told many times, but not for the last.

The Post-War Homecoming of the Hallé

A GREAT OCCASION AT THE FREE TRADE HALL

19th November 1951

There were tumultuous and moving moments when the Hallé Orchestra at full strength returned home to the Free Trade Hall last night, with as many harps as they could hope to boast in heaven itself. The occasion, of course, was more than a concert; as Sir John Barbirolli said in a speech at the end, a reunion was symbolic of a ray of life in these parts and proof that we can get most things we want even in this world, if we want them hard enough, whatever befall. Less than ten years ago the Hallé Orchestra all but foundered. Only the funnel and bridge were discernible in the tidal wave of the world. No players, hardly; the hall destroyed. But faith remained strong, so the miracle was possible, even in a period not of local but universal shipwreck, and now the miracle has become, in the naïve language of the scientists and materialists, a fact.

There is a time for criticism and a time to refrain from criticism, as C. E. Montague might say. It is not the custom to look a miracle in the teeth and consider if it has been well contrived. Few people in the audience were able to sit and attend in detachment; emotion swayed the scale of values. Imagine, then, the case of a Manchester man, returning from exile after years to the place where he first heard the music, where he learned all that a man need know of music, returning to the place he had thought lost for ever, and not only returning by an incredible swing of the great wheel to any sort of Hallé concert, but to the Hallé Orchestra on the night of resurrection in the desired paradise.

The programme itself included a performance of the Viola Concerto of William Walton, who was born less than an hour's journey away to his native Lancashire town. Finally we heard the "Symphonie

Fantastique" of Berlioz, which received its first English performance, I believe, at a Hallé concert . . . .

The playing of William Primrose in the Concerto is likely to go down in the permanent annals and legend-lore of the Hallé concerts; it was inspired by a Paganini sort of tradition of virtuoso witchery, challenging to imagination and senses and nerves alike. I cannot remember viola playing as brilliant yet as musically full and round of tone as this. The viola most times sounds like a spinster of the string family, a violin that has never really been in love. The concerto explores the viola through and through, from bottom to top, veins and tissue and bloodstream. Mr Primrose's fingers touch the strings as a pianist touches a keyboard, seeming to evoke the music even before his bow has incarnated it. The range of tone, the blending of registers, the syntax of his phrasing, and the point and significance he gives to small groups of notes without over-emphasis or forgetfulness of the embracing living line – this is all as firm as any representative musical art of the present time. Sir John Barbirolli and the Hallé Orchestra made an admirable setting for Mr Primrose . . . .

The "Symphonie Fantastique" crowned the evening, and it is astonishing that this work, a hundred years old, is still capable of a challenge to a modern orchestra's resources of technique, dynamic, and also to its powers of dramatic expression. Occasionally in the first movement instrumental ingenuities seemed dwelt on for their own sake, sections revealed to us as though under a magnifying glass, so that a page as a whole was heard as though outside the circle of full illumination. But the playing expanded, grew in momentum, as the work went on. One of the four harps was played by Mr Charles Collier, who played with Richter. Sir John has come into his own, and the audience's acclamation let him know, and everybody else, that they honour him and appreciate his value.

The Hallé Orchestra Pension Fund

HANS RICHTER'S INNOVATION

13th May 1953

Since Hans Richter proposed to the chairman and executive of the Hallé Concerts in 1903 that something should be done for orchestral players in old age the economic welfare of most instrumentalists has vastly improved everywhere. Not half a century ago the rank and file of the Hallé Orchestra were receiving round about twenty or thirty shillings a performance with less than fifty concerts a year. If it is argued that an English pound sterling went further then than today's currency, the mass of people of the period did not especially notice it.

"Such a fund," wrote Richter, "would greatly strengthen the bond which unites the musicians of the Hallé Orchestra and would make it easier both to obtain and keep talent of the highest quality." The unity desired by Richter has been obtained mainly because standards of playing have risen to such an extent that none but a permanent orchestra would command public support. The Hallé Orchestra in Richter's period was "permanent" only for a part of the year; in summer time it was dispersed by winds blowing to the seaside piers of Blackpool and New Brighton. The strain on skill and physical endurance which is put on the orchestral player of 1953 is severe indeed; he and she must submit to constant and highly disciplined rehearsal. Also there are the rigours of perpetual travel from place to place, not only from town to town in the British Isles these days but from hemisphere to hemisphere. To make music is an exacting profession technically; also it carries unusual social responsibility. The musician's lot is not, however, as precarious as once it was, but not yet is the orchestral player recognized in this country with the respect, and financial aid, that is shown to other professions which, if they are more utilitarian, do not obviously contribute to the "great cause of cheering us all up".

Richter laid stress on the fact that talent must be "kept". There are temptations today not known to Richter, luring first-class instrumentalists away from our finest orchestras. The public does not realize how much personal idealism and loyalty are needed to maintain a permanent orchestra in 1953 . . . .

The Hallé Orchestra Pension Fund at the present time has accumulated £52,378, but this amount is not enough to ensure the limited benefit of £102 annually to individual members as they in turn become eligible. A special effort is being made to present a Jubilee Pension Concert tomorrow worthy of the occasion . . . .

The name of the Hallé Orchestra stands higher today than at any other time, in most parts of the civilized world. Long memories try in vain to settle the question so often asked: "How does the orchestra compare with the Hallé of Richter?" In Richter's day there was no means of measuring the Hallé with the world's greatest orchestras. No other orchestra played often in Manchester; some of us never heard any orchestra other than the Hallé. There were no gramophone records or radio to provide us with reliable standards. Merely as a personal opinion formed in young enthusiastic years, I should describe Richter's Hallé as a very authoritative symphony orchestra which, at the conductor's prompting, aimed at characteristic rather than a beautiful or finished tone. The Hallé of 1953 is perhaps more versatile and intimate in style than in any period since Harty, and, thanks to rehearsals not enjoyed by Harty and to the devotion of the conductor who is both artist and musician, it is probably more trustworthy and polished in technique than ever before. Hallé players have always given their best in skill and service. They deserve annually a prosperous Pension Fund concert; more than that, the Fund should not be forgotten after the musicians have contributed their services tomorrow night in aid of it.

North versus South

5th July 1961

For the purpose of my share in this argument (in the North we say, "I am not arguing – I am telling you"), I take it that the term "South" means London. For Manchester is not as provincial as Potter's Bar or Ealing; besides Manchester has never heard of either of these places, so therefore admits no animosity, or suspicion, towards them. London, as a fact, is hard to locate, even by a Londoner. It is a geographical or a cartographical expression . . .

County boundaries, county character, are eliminated by London's sprawling bulk. And in the North of England, in Manchester especially, it is character that matters first, certainly not "culture". When I lived in Manchester the word "culture" was seldom pronounced. Even if we had heard it spoken on the Irwell air, we wouldn't have known exactly its meaning. "Kultur?" Yes; we vaguely had heard of "Kultur", connecting it with Kaiser Wilhelm – in those days as remote from Manchester as Primrose Hill or Poplar. True, there were numerous Germans living in Manchester in the years of my youth there. But the climate generally assimilated them. Climate in Manchester is thicker than blood or water (i.e. rain); even C. P. Scott and C. E. Montague, though born in Bath and London respectively, Corpus Christi and Balliol, were taken in to Manchester's seductive, carbondioxidized atmosphere, so much so that they would have had to produce birth certificates to prove (to posterity) that they were not born in Manchester.

C. P. Scott, on his bicycle from Manchester University, a Manchester spectacle and possession. Brodsky who first played the Tchaikovsky violin Concerto, Charles Hallé, Lord Rutherford (originally from New Zealand), Tout, Flinders Petrie, all Manchester men by birth or assimilation! London, having no compact concentrated character, does not likewise absorb Northerners, or any sort of foreigner, to a point that these lose county or regional identity. A Scot remains a Scot, even in Fleet Street. I have myself lived in London week by week for more than a dozen years, and though my Lancashire accent is leaving me, I am in psychological texture – a jargon picked up in London – to this day as Lancastrian as Albert Square and Throstle's Nest . . . . But I have always found that the average untroubled Londoner is not easy to get on to my Northern England wavelength. It is, I think, at bottom a matter of humour. I have met wits in London now and again (yet none as witty as Sir Thomas Beecham, Ernest Newman or James Agate, all three of the North).

A self-conscious manner is imposed on Londoners by the fact that they grow up knowing that they live in the world's greatest city, historically, culturally and in every other way of human accomplishment. Such a self-consciousness is naturally crippling. London is the spectacular stage on which its people appear – in profuse ensemble. Puppets of cosmopolis and the latest fashions! London simply dare *not* be out of fashion. London's long-run must be re-dressed time and time again. The consequence of a perpetual awareness of the greatness of London – which, as we have seen, annihilates a county identity – encourages Londoners to assume attitudes of sophistication, attitudes often involuntary and habitual. Nobody with Lancastrian humour could go to a cocktail party anywhere in London between Dover Street and St John's Wood and not risk expulsion on account of his raucous, irrepressible laughter. An unusually intelligent Londoner *might* share a Lancastrian's awareness of the ridiculousness of London's social and rather suburban poses, but he would show and express it in terms of a rather sour and superior cynicism. Wit is a form of intellectual snobbery, unless it is leavened by humour. Unadulterated humour is probably provincial, because it does not respect social divisions, breeding, or taste (real or put-on) and, most important, because it doesn't know itself how funny it is.

The following incident will illustrate and characterize Lancashire humour. Some years ago, during the period of war rationing, I went to Rochdale on a bitter winter night to give a lecture in a cold, gloomy schoolroom. An audience of a hundred or two had braved the weather; and they sat at my feet ill-clad. But they laughed, saw my points in advance. At the end of the lecture a man in a scarf and cloth cap came from the audience to the classroom at the back of the platform and, shaking me by the hand, said "Hey, Mr Cardus, that were a grand talk. Ah left a warm fireside to come and hear you. And Ah paid one-and-six to come in. And Ah've reight enjoyed miself, that Ah have." He paused, then added "Mind you, Ah wouldn't do it again!" I doubt if this brand of humour is comprehensible in the King's Road, Chelsea, or in Hampstead Village . . . .

This Lancashire humour – not a laughing matter, remember – is the main thing dividing North from South of England and rendering the North preferable in the sight of God . . . . And the difference between Yorkshire breadth of human nature and Lancashire Lowry-ish leanness is the difference between woollens and cottons . . . .

From Lancashire, in our own time, blossomed the lovely girl Kathleen Ferrier, the most poignant of all singers of the music of Gustav Mahler, most un-English of composers. From Lancashire James Agate forced his aggressive way out of the primordial slime to embody raffish cosmopolitanism, without hurt to his essential provincial concentration of Ego . . . . Ernest Newman, though unfortunately born in Liverpool, a place not renowned as generally Lancastrian by Manchester folk ("Manchester men – Liverpool gentle-men") remained an "outsider" (like myself) to London. He worked in the capital for the last forty years of his long life, nonetheless he died a man of the North. Fashionable circles of the South . . . have not exorcised from Sir William Walton and his music a Lancastrian downrightness and humorous disregard of the "latest" musical movements. He could, if he liked, compose atonally to a length, or rather to a brevity, which would astonish even Mr William Glock. Alan Rawsthorne is as rooted to Manchester as the Hallé Orchestra itself.

Frank Sladen-Smith would not be drawn to London. He was producing in a Manchester slum, where he changed a top-room in a factory to a "Little" theatre of style, plays by O'Neill and Anouilh some time before Sloane Square had advanced beyond Shaw, and before the West End had thoroughly digested Noël Coward. Sladen-Smith was one of the few Manchester men of my acquaintance who had more of wit than humour . . . . We were once discussing "honours", "knighthoods", and I asked Sladen-Smith if he would accept a knighthood if one were rightly offered him. "Of course!" he replied. "Not to accept a knighthood is a sort of inverted snobbery. Of course I'd accept: I'd accept anything. Would you?" Then charmingly he added: "I beg your pardon – *will* you?" . . .

Forty years later, in January 1967, Neville Cardus received a knighthood, the first music critic to have done so. In a discussion which subsequently followed and was published in *The Times*, he contributed a letter to the Editor as follows:

Sir, – I am not in the class of the famous literary names that have been so far mentioned regarding the distribution of Honours. But, speaking for my humble self, I would like publicly to state that I accepted my particular award for two reasons: (1) because I was pretty certain I'd enjoy being a knight, and (2) because it is not for the likes of me to go counter to the pleasure of Her Majesty the Queen and (to adapt the language of Doctor Johnson) indirectly "bandy civilities with my Sovereign."

Yours truly,
NEVILLE CARDUS.

112 Bickenhall Mansions, W.1, January 11.

Samuel Langford's Column

16th May 1963

This year of 1963 is the centenary of Samuel Langford, born in Withington, Manchester. And who was Samuel Langford is a question I can well imagine asked today. He was the most searching, most thoughtful and wise writer on music of his time.

The fashions in music-criticism were different then. He wrote, and was expected by his editor to write, a column about every Hallé concert. I, who was his assistant, was once called over the coals by C. P. Scott because I dismissed a not very engrossing Hallé concert in half a column.

Langford would come into the office at 10 o'clock after a concert and, in a scrawling fist, compose his thousand words in little more than an hour. He wrote no books, though publishers tempted him often enough. He would not be disturbed at his work if somebody came into his room, interrupting him by talk. I have known him put down his pen and discuss a variety of topical subjects, the latest Test match, a parliamentary row, or a case in law, then continue his article, which most likely would proceed with sentences like the following:

"Busoni (playing the 'Emperor' concerto of Beethoven) has still an abundant fund of energy but he no longer seeks to conquer by its means, finding his strength in those fallings away and vanishings which are the most wonderful part of Beethoven's spiritual power. One might almost call it the sole aim of Beethoven's music to give us such intimations of immortality. If he gathers strength, it is not for its own sake, but to have those diminuendo and pianissimo effects in his power with which he surprises us and makes us ask what kind of being we must be to feel ourselves so much touched by the mere passage and vanishing of sound."

Those last few words – "the mere passage and vanishing of sound" – a whole aesthetic of music, an ethic of music, are in them.

At times "S.L." would write about a singer or an instrumentalist as though he were examining or discerning them under a glass – in fact, under the magnifying glass he carried in his capacious pocket to read with, continuing to use it after the glass had left the frame and broken in half. He was not only the imaginative analyst but, given the spur, he could be vividly (but always relevantly) descriptive. Consider this:

"Rosenthal while playing wears a look of almost pained fastidiousness, and in the expression of playing this fastidiousness is never relaxed. His use of the sustaining pedal is more scrupulous than of any other player in the world. In the long tarantella movement which closes Chopin's B minor sonata he uses this pedal throughout with an almost staccato shortness, allowing the bass only the most momentary thrill through the harmonies; and this reticence in the use of the pedal is characteristic of all his playing . . . . Only rarely and deliberately did he use the left pedal to help the flashing and glistening pianissimo, the diamond clarity of which is the chief ornament of his technical style. These renunciations laid an enormous burden on his fingers."

"These renunciations" – what memorable language in a perishable morning newspaper! And I must again quote the sentences which are perhaps "S.L's" most memorable. Of the late quartets of Beethoven –

"As the work of a deaf man, these quartets assert triumphantly the imaginative nature of musical art, and the heritage of this proof musicians may well prize in an age which is apt to associate music not with the cleansing power of the imagination but with external things . . . . One cannot speak justly of the short dance movements of these later quartets without regarding them as Elysian in their nature, and as removed by their ideality from every contamination of the world."

He was a dumpy man, small of inches but fairly round; and he wore his clothes with an elephant's looseness of fold. His face resembled a mixture of Socrates and Repin's portrait of Moussorgsky. He had a wonderfully domed forehead. His walk was a shamble, soles of feet flat on the earth. In wintry weather he would go bump down on the frozen pavements, then get up, apparently undisturbed in his meditations.

He was, I think, made of intellectual and temperamental and natural constituents left over after God had created Goethe and Dr Johnson. His wit could be swift and scorching, but he seldom used it in a music article. He had great respect for artists, even those he did not think much of. He once chastised late-comers at a concert – not because they caused discomfort in the rest of the audience but because "they showed disrespect to the performers."

He was a lovable man, once he had "proved it" with his tongue. He loved his garden. In fact he loved life all round . . . .

"Of all ground basses, surely the bass of this movement (of the Sanctus of the B minor Mass of Bach) is the most original and the most sublime . . . . The notes in their octave leaps are like vast pillars not sunk into the deep but embracing in their height and depth an imagination of heaven and earth, and if we add the sea, the combined images will not complete what one feels from the music. Such music, indeed, fulfils all those ideas in which music becomes a symbol; we see in its laws, as in a glass, a divine equipoise which is our ultimate conception of the universe itself."

That was Samuel Langford in a daily newspaper, that was!

C. E. Montague

A KREISLER AND HEIFETZ PERFORMER ON
THE ENGLISH LANGUAGE

1st January 1966

C. E. Montague, born a century ago today, was for young "M.G." men of the C. P. Scott dynasty the inspiration of all of us who hoped to live up to the paper's reputation as one for which, first of all, we were expected to *write*. One morning, passing each other on the stairs of the office in Cross Street, Manchester, a reporter might say to another, "Good stuff yours today". A compliment didn't involve quick news-gathering or anything so utilitarian as all that; it was a recognition of an article couched in good, personal, allusive and all-knowing English.

The chances are that it had been written not with an eye on the "Manchester Guardian's" readership but in hope of pleasing C.E.M. Not that Montague ever went out of his way to instruct or influence his 'prentice acolytes . . . .

But the indirect sway of him on our aspirations! – he somehow awakened our half-formed desires, longings and impulses to be "Guardian" men. One morning he sent me a note, liking something I had written about Pavlova, who in her last years danced on an improvised platform in the Manchester Free Trade Hall. It had a loose board, which you heard when everybody except Pavlova was dancing. I risked in my piece a metaphor about angels dancing on the point of a needle. Montague liked an image or an allusion. "Don't keep your nose to the factual grindstone," was one of his rare instructions. Even in a notice of a pantomime (a column long, 1500 words) he would give his pen its virtuoso head:

> "When and where principal girls should be pert and when and where refrain from pertness; how close they should come to being minxes and yet how they should differentiate themselves from minxes in the eyes of the experts; to how many affairs of the heart they should make lyrical reference while adhering like gum in their prose passages to their respective Sinbads, Prince Charmings, and Little Boys Blue – all these are deep and hidden things, for ignorance of which, let us trust, we shall not be rebuked, as à Kempis says, at the day of judgment."

Can't we see the sub-editor of our present day with his blue pencil hovering above this passage, a vulture after his prey?

A young scribe of our current age of enlightenment has honestly stated that he now finds Montague unreadable. I imagine that C.E.M. would, employing the retort courteous, confess to a similar response to much of today's type-written blank prose. He, who was a shy puritan in everyday walks of life, nursed under a neat donnish suburban apparel an intense romantic nature, revelling in and ravishing our language, sucking red blood from the entire corpus of literature, so that, whatever the cue, the long leader on Financial Reform, on the latest Army Estimates, on the week's play in the Manchester Prince's Theatre, or on the "Top of the Bill" at the Hippodrome, whatever the occasion Montague's spirit and all his senses would liberate themselves, leaving his earthy and respected physical vessel temporarily vacant: "George Robey will come on the stage first as that veteran theme the middle-aged toper in a black frock-coat, tieless and collarless, leering with imbecile knowingness, Stiggins and Bardolph and Ally Sloper in one, his face all bubukles and whelks and knobs and flame o'fire." Montague loved a hidden quotation. The young lions of the "M.G." emulated this vanity and archness, though not often were we modest enough to conceal our cultural sources . . .

Montague, as I say, was not directly accountable for the aesthetic athletics of those of us on the paper who went leaping from literary branch to branch like so many imitative monkeys. The rare fact is that the "M.G." did not (to change the metaphor!) clip our wings. There was always the omniscient eye of C. P. Scott fixed on us with the rod of punishment ready for any straying from accuracy and grammar. Montague's example, to be seen in print every day, was our perpetual spur. He, aware of it or not, made us want to write. He was not only a writer himself but the cause of writing in others. As a man and colleague he had a courtesy which belonged to an epoch pretty well vanished, in journalism at any rate. Yet he somehow suffered short-circuitings in his flashes of companionship. James Agate said that nobody seemed to get to know Montague any the better after twenty years. Myself, I got as close to him as was, I think, possible (outside his family) one afternoon on the cricket field. He frequently turned out for the Manchester Guardian XI. We actually played one day on the historic turf of Old Trafford, then recently trodden by such as McLaren, Spooner, Tyldesley. That afternoon Montague hit a six, and was bowled next ball. After he had returned to the pavilion and was taking off his pads, he said to me, out of his heart, "You know, Cardus, I *love* cricket, but – but, damn it, I can't play it!" I doubt if ever he swore under the German fire of the 1914–1918 war, for which he had once joined up, dyeing his whitening hair black to diddle the recruiting officials, and thus inspiring Nevinson's famous tribute: "Montague is the only man whose hair, through courage, turned black in a night."

C.E.M. was a fiery particle by the fashioning of his intellect and imagination. He rationalized his senses and sensitized his keenly acute mind. We could say of him, in the language of Goethe (which wasn't, I fancy, his cup of tea), that he saw with an eye that felt, and felt with a hand that saw.

A Writer's Craft

1947

I suppose it is no longer fashionable for authors and journalists consciously to "*write*". No longer do we insist on a distinction between good talk and well-written prose. For my own part, I am incorrigibly out-of-date. I was brought up as a journalist on the "Manchester Guardian", under the eye of C. E. Montague, who was a virtuoso in words. His young men searched for the decorative or the witty phrase, as self-conscious of our cleverness as a cage of monkeys.

But simplicity in writing is hard to come by – I mean simplicity that does not fall into flat dowdy English. Those of us trained in the old school which encouraged a risky flourish of words find it difficult to conform to the telegraphese of to-day.

A lifetime's habits continue to persuade me to hunt for the word which, simple or not, isn't just plain and as battered as current coin. I believe – I still believe – that at times there is a *certain* word a writer must continue to search for, even though a dozen words should spring to his mind all meaning the same thing – according to the dictionary. And the paradox is that a writer only quite loses self-consciousness when he absorbs himself in words, in feeling them, rolling them over his palate, matching them, and getting them with child. While words remain in the dictionary they are sterile. Words are rather like Yale keys. They are of use only to a particular owner. They fit keyholes of his own workshop, and nobody else's.

The style – if I may make a platitude – reveals the man. The natural style comes after, and never before, we have learned by hard practice to handle our words instinctively; when we have lost awareness of all except our writing self; by long immersion in a theme or subject.

It is another paradox that an artist is thought usually as being egotistical; yet only by surrendering the "I", and only by subduing not merely his hand but the thinking and feeling whole of him to the material he works in – only then can he hope to produce vital personal stuff. That is what a writer is telling you when, on those rare days, the miracle happens, and he is lifted above heaven and earth, and says: "It came by itself."

You can pay your money and take your choice. You can have this – about music:

> "The ruminations of Bruckner, in his adagios, inspire key relationships unprecedented at the time of their composition. Never do they interpose between us and the raptness of expression. They are not exploited demonstratively; they lift veil after veil on the deepening note of trustfulness. The argument is not easy to follow. Like religion and matrimony, Bruckner needs faith."

Or you can have the other more fashionable stuff, the jargon turned out in reams after a few months of technical study.

I prefer the harder way, which involves first the knowledge, the power of reception, then the instinctive gravitation of the writer's mind to the right word. With some writers, myself included for certain, it takes years and years to know where to find it – for one writer's vocabulary might easily be another's Tower of Babel.

2

MOZART AND SCHUBERT

Mozart the Unparalleled (1756–1791)

1957

The great miracle of Mozart's achievements, most of them a separate miracle, is that though bound to his period's "absolute" patterns of music, undramatically shaped, he composed opera which in 1957 we can see, now that the Wagnerian mists are clearing and we can dwell on other peaks in the range, as unparalleled for breadth of characterization in all phases of human activity, from the ridiculous to the sublime, from Papageno to the Countess, from the rogue picaresque to the traditional romantic seducer, from Leporello to Don Giovanni. He can embody in a melody which an infant can sing the vivacity of a Zerlina, or the awakening ardours of the boy Cherubino. By a few chords in the trombones Mozart can evoke the shape and presence of the majestically spectral; in simple notes for a bass singer, almost displaying the lowest spectacularly, he wrote for Sarastro the only music which, as Bernard Shaw said, we might decently conceive coming out of the mouth of God. The "Non mi dir" air in "Don Giovanni" is none the less expressive and in character even if it does end in virtuoso vocal embellishments.

Mozart had no need to invent leading-motives to identify his characters; all the music each of them sings is nearly always in character. I cannot explain – and nobody has enlightened me – why "La ci darem" comes naturally from the mouth of Don Giovanni though really it is the most childlike of tunes, ideal for performances on the chimes which on sunny afternoons at Salzburg evoke feelings of awe and majesty, of solemn temples and the insubstantial pageant; yet they are strains of a harmony scarcely going beyond the stage of study reached by a first-year pupil coping with "elementary inversions". Other composers, Bach and Gluck for example, had composed dramatic

33

music before Mozart came to the scene, using forms not fashioned or evolved from a dramatic intent or impulse. But they had been obliged by the limitations of the dominant musical patterns to confine themselves to a general and not particular dramatic suggestiveness. Mozart, with much the same material and moulds, created a whole "Comédie Humaine". This was the wonder, the miracle, of him. His instrumental works, his "absolute" compositions, are for all their perfection of style and diversity to be explained in terms of a flowering to genius of an eighteenth-century musical culture. By means of forms and tones not yet associated with precise expression, not yet rendered dramatically significant and plastic, he breathed life into figures which in their different libretti are more or less the lay stock puppets of the hack theatre scribbler.

Mozart was the least consciously expressive as he was the most comprehensively ranged composer. He contributed to every kind and shape of music, secular and sacred, opera and symphony, all manner of chamber combinations, all manner of concerted pieces, all manner of "occasional" pieces, including a composition for a musical clock. He seldom went to work directed by an aesthetic theory. No sweat of notebooks for him. "I made it a little long on purpose," he writes to his father of an aria he had written, "for it is always easy to cut down, but not easy to lengthen." If the tenor engaged to sing in *Don Giovanni* is unequal to "Il mio tesoro," well then let him try "Dalla sua pace". If Elvira wants another "number" perhaps she will be placated by "Mi tradi". And if "Mi tradi" does not quite fit into the context, heard only with the ear of logic and dramatic sequence, the Mozartian style will in time reconcile the irreconcilable. All is changed in the twinkling of an eye from earth to heaven. Shaw compared Mozart as a dramatist to Molière, and he was right to think of him as a being essentially informed by the Comic Spirit. Whether the characters in Mozart's operas are living vitally in laughter, or suddenly softened by pathos, or possessed by the daemonic or harried, like Elvira, by jealously outraged pride and contumely which are ironically a proof of the love that is a constant wound to the self, no matter how often these people may strike home to our ordinary hearts, yet we can never come truly to know them, any more than we can come to know Mozart. They are aloof, masked like their creator, who surveys his work as though "sub specie aeternitatis". Mozart transcended the comedy of Molière; and he brought to it a Platonic ideality and finality.

He would be moved to astonishment and perplexity if he could revisit and learn that he is safe with the greatest of those who have illumined and transfigured existence here below. His attitude to his art was almost professional; he composed much as craftsmen making Chippendale. He described himself as "soaked" in music; he composed habitually. In the last year of his life he composed "La Clemenza di Tito" and "Zauberflöte", the Requiem, the E flat Quintet, an adagio for harmonica, a work (K.617) for harmonica, flute, oboe, viola, and 'cello, three pieces for a mechanical organ, his last piano concerto, the clarinet concerto, the beatific "Ave verum corpus". In six weeks he composed the E flat, G Minor and C major symphonies.

"I gave to-day to the mail coach the symphony which I composed in Linz for Old Count Thun, and also four concertos. I am not particularly happy about the symphony, but I ask you to have the four concertos copied at home, for the Salzburg copyists are as little to be trusted as the Viennese . . . ."

This is another passage in a letter to his father; and the symphony he thought of little value, tossed off for the "Old Count", is as near to perfection as human genius can reasonably hope to approach. Sometimes Mozart's inexhaustible gift to compose had inevitably to nourish itself on notes and ingenuity. The flawless execution happened as instinctively as the weaving of a bird's nest, which of course is one of the wonders of creation. He remains the most enigmatic and inexplicable of composers. That a Mozart was born once, and once and for all, is a happening and consummation which beggars understanding and all known science, all psychology, physics and metaphysics, and all cosmogony whatsoever.

Genius

17th November 1927

What is a critic to say of Mozart at his most felicitous? The purer the music the less there is to be said about it. In the chamber music of Mozart we come upon the well of music pure and undefiled. Not that we are not moved into deep moods. Where in all music is there anything more poignant than the slow movement of the G minor Quintet? But

Mozart does not fertilize music by a common emotion, in Wagner's phrase; rather does he seem to open some vein of emotion belonging to the music's own being. The quietness of the slow movement of the Quintet, the intentness, the sense we have as we listen, that music is drawn to some secret place within itself, leaving us and the rough world behind – surely Mozart here is the very spirit of music, just as Bach is music's great sane head, and Beethoven its storm-tossed heart. One of Mozart's finest critics has complained that the finale of the G minor Quintet lets the work down, because of its lighthearted chatter. His argument is that, as the slow movement descends to some tragic abyss, an affirmation of the spirit was demanded in the closing movement. For our part, we do not see the need for music to be an argument, spiritual or other; nor do we think the slow movement has any significance which can be described as tragic. It does not even enter our human – all-too-human – world; only by cutting free from those passions of ours that "spin the plot" may we share its beauty. The careless chatter of the Quintet's finale, so far from being inadequate, seems to some of us one of those very touches that make Mozart's art so lovable, modest, and winsome. He does not strike the poetic attitude; he never assertively declares his joys, his griefs. Happiness and sorrow play like sunlight and shadow through Mozart's music, swiftly, innocently. A happy turn of melody comes, and we are made happy, too. Then, as suddenly, pathos surprises us, steals out of the serene air, and – here is the crowning pathos – not only overcomes us but, surely, Mozart himself.

The Requiem Mass

5th October 1934

Verdi's Requiem is marvellous melodrama; it fails when spiritual consolation needs a voice. Verdi belonged to the earth; Mozart in his C minor Mass makes all other music almost vulgar – all music save parts of the B minor Mass of Bach, the last quartets of Beethoven, and one or two gentle pieces by Schubert. The convinced sceptic becomes a believer for so long as the strains of Mozart's setting of "Et in Spiritum Sanctum" are entering his heart, music whose secret is not only joy but peace.

Astonishing that any human being should have written music for the angels: "Shall Christ of Cain forgotten be, out of a baseness beauty born?" . . .

The work was composed over one hundred and fifty years ago at Salzburg. And now to-day by the incredible wheel of circumstances it has been heard at Leeds in the heart of a civilization the nature of which Mozart would find inexplicable. Yet we of the hard-bitten and unbeautiful twentieth century are moved to our foundations by the music; we are, temporarily at any rate, purged and purified. It is the Mass and its loveliness and holiness that live on and on; it is we with our pitiful imperfections that perish.

Schubert, The Man to Cherish (1797–1828)

19th November 1928

A hundred years ago to-day Schubert died in Vienna in his thirty-second year.

Sentimental biography still perpetuates the legend of Schubert the constantly poverty-stricken and illiterate peasant. He was educated at one of the best secondary schools of his day, and his father had a sound if narrow culture. Throughout his life Schubert drew his friends from the ranks of Vienna's artists and poets. The best houses of the city were open to him. Schubert, were he alive to-day, might have to walk far through the centre of Manchester to find his superior in culture and taste. Vienna did not let him starve, week by week. In one year, 1826, six different publishers brought out his works, issuing in all 106 different compositions. Between 1820 and 1828 his income from music has been estimated at £575. Schubert's earnings in the last eight years of a young life can safely be calculated in modern cash values at more than £350 a year. At the age of 19 he cut free from the drudgery of schoolmastering and for the remainder of his days he devoted himself to composition, declining the routine of music teaching. On one of his summer jaunts through Upper Austria he writes a letter saying that his songs are known and sung everywhere.

Even the musical critics recognized his genius . . . . Reviewing the first performance of "Rosamunde" in 1825 the "Wiener Zeitschrift" spoke of the "genius of this popular master". At the age of 22 his first opera was produced; at 19 he had the knowledge that one of Vienna's greatest singers was interested in his works and introducing the songs to the city's most distinguished places. When we deplore Schubert's income from music we must remember that in his period the public vocal recital was almost unknown. In his lifetime Schubert gave only one concert; it attracted a crowded audience, the largest ever seen in the hall of Musikverein. The pathos of Schubert's life was not the product merely of a slender purse. From the portraits of the man we might indeed gather that he was one of a very respectable and comfortable community. His sadness, when it came upon him, was a thing of the imagination; had he been as prosperous as Croesus he would still have written his greatest music out of his moments of, to use his own word, "suffering".

Modern criticism has not hesitated to accuse Schubert of over-indulgence in pleasures not exactly noble; it has even been argued that he tended to dissipate his creative powers by allowing himself to be "led away" too easily by his friends. The fact is that as artist and man he lived a pretty full life, according to the middle-class aesthetic and social fashions of his day. Consider the extent of his output, and let it then be asked whether his genius during a brief lifetime could have been better served by the more thrifty habits of certain modern composers: six full Masses, over 600 songs, thirteen or more piano sonatas, the Impromptus and Moments Musicaux, eight symphonies, fourteen string quartets, the "Trout" Quintet, the C major String Quintet, seven trios, and the Octet, about a dozen operas and singspiels, and a heap of other music in various forms – here is only an incomplete outline of his output.

In one year, 1815 – he was then 18 – he wrote two symphonies, four piano sonatas, an adagio, twelve dances, ten variations for piano, two Masses, a Stabat Mater, five large dramatic pieces, and 146 songs. It may be true that he ought to have blotted many more pages than he did, but that is a point of view which does not recognize that lyrical genius must trust its impulses in and out of season, and risk the mishits of the spontaneity which is the first condition of its being. Schubert, at the end of his life, was thinking of taking lessons in counterpoint. It will be sensible for us to applaud the instinct which, while he was young, led him to hold back from placing his muse in the grip of more science than the spirit of pure song craved after. Had he lived longer, his intellect might conceivably have hardened and sought to use music as a serious criticism of life. The C major Symphony and the String Quintet in the same key tell of a bigger Schubert than the singer of the world's sweetest songs. But who of us to-day can regret that Schubert composed as he did compose, profusely, sometimes uncritically? A Schubert with an art of half of Bach's masterly formalism would be a Schubert so much the less lovable than the man whose centenary the whole world is now celebrating . . . . God almighty alone has the right to ask whether Schubert made the most of his gifts; the rest of us must thankfully take our Schubert as we find him.

If he had never written a single song and only his instrumental works, our view of the nature of his music would be much as it is to-day. All that he composed lived in a ceaseless current of song. He was indeed the first great composer to warm music through and through with the homely poetry of the folk. Beautiful though the melodies of Mozart are, they live in an air of eighteenth-century refinement; their pride is aristocratic. There is no landscape in Mozart, but the music of Schubert is full of landscape. Though Beethoven had his movements of pastoral relaxation, it was the relaxation of a giant who came down for a while from austere and sublime heights. Schubert made music familiar; he took the art on happy jaunts through the meadows; he let it linger over the rustic bridge and watch the busy stream, with the trout flicking its tail in the running water; he gave music an ear with which to listen to the mill-wheel and the call of the post-horn; he gave it also a heart simple enough to beat with the heart of the lover who waited for a letter from the beloved.

Schubert made music kindly and humane. For even his chamber compositions have the urge of his own nature; their themes seem to ask to be sung rather than played. He seldom wrote music which was instrumental in the sense that the music of Mozart is instrumental. Melody in Mozart is never so charged with the lyrical impulse that it threatens to run away with Mozart the superbly poised symphonist. Mozart's tunes – even in his operas – lend themselves freely to the plan of classical instrumental form; they do not move with the heart and blood pulse of familiar song – song so instinctive with a human spontaneity that its transitions cannot always be anticipated. The true instrumental tune is easily subjected to the requirements of formal logic; it will mingle with other tunes on equal terms in a symphonic scheme: it will gladly serve as simply one strand amongst others in a symphonic web. But pure song is tyrannical; it lends itself to statement and repetition – not willingly to development. That is why folk-song has so seldom provided a basis for a symphony . . . . Schubert loved to sing a tune over and over again because it was in itself complete and well worth repetition. This is not to imply, of course, that Schubert did not know a magical way of his own whereby to carry along an instrumental work. Because of his transitions of melody, his chromatic alterations of harmony, he is classified to-day as the first of the Romantic composers. But these mutations were the outcome of his own poetic sensibility; they had nothing to do with the sequence and logic of the classical forms. At his greatest he created or envisaged form of his own and the transitions of it can often be fully appreciated only in terms of the workings of the spirit that moved him . . . .

Schubert wrote much music from sheer habit, true; then he was a mechanical worker in the tricks of the trade of his day, "lacking," as someone has written, "the cerebral power which is the necessary concomitant of the highest artistic achievements." Here is a typical attitude of mind of much modern Schubert criticism; it overlooks the fact that Schubert made most of his music at a time of life when, with all his genius, he could not possibly have come to the intellectual mastery needed in the creation and filling of new and big instrumental forms. While still a boy Schubert perfected the song for voice and pianoforte; his imagination was old enough then to take the measure of a moderate-sized canvas. At the age of 31 he had grown large enough in imaginative sweep and power to compose the C major Symphony. While it is true, then, that a vast amount of Schubert's music is mild, even trivial, in conception and technique alike, criticism will do well not to base on this routine output a judgment which leaves out of account the Schubert of the year of his death.

In 1828 he wrote, besides the C major Symphony, the String Quintet, the "Schwanengesang" settings, which include the grim, hard-headed "Doppelgänger", and the piano sonata in B flat. Faced by such works, the epitaph of Grillparzer comes to mind: "Music has here entombed a rich treasure, but fairer hopes." Fairer hopes! In that year was the advent of a graver note in his music a certain sign that Schubert's mind was indeed becoming tougher with the stuff of what Matthew Arnold called "criticism of life"? Or was this graver note nothing but the deepening of the original lyrical impulse? Were Schubert's solemnities like the solemnities of his life – accidental and secondary? Schubert's pathos steals in swiftly and goes as swiftly; it seldom hints of the tragic sense, the philosophic habit of mind.

Fancy, who leads the pastimes of the glad,
Full oft is pleased a wayward dart to throw,
Sending sad shadows after things not sad.

But nobody other than the critics will pause in this year of Schubert's cen' nary to ask whether Schubert died before his time with a master piece in him of even bigger mental span than that of the C major Symphony. The world at large will be satisfied to cherish the Schubert who during the brief life that was his portion gave to the world the loveliest music it has ever known.

Abundance

30th August 1968

It was when the E flat Schubert Trio was attacked that the genius of the evening came to a glorious consummation. And it was indeed grandly attacked and taken to heart. The fingers of Istomin flashed over the keyboard, sunshine on a running brook of melody. He was absolutely proportionate in his strong handling of plunging arpeggios and chords. Soft playing or loud was always calculated and related to structural whole. Stern's violin and Rose's 'cello shared the string melodies with reciprocated joy.

The performance of this Trio made us, more than ever, believe that of all composers Schubert is the most lovable-spontaneous, extravagant, and fragrant. Overwhelming the trellis of sonata form, or any other musical form revered in his day, with abundant wild flowers, all of them wild and gracious as the Wienerwald, not one of them cultivated in a hothouse. Schubert is repetitive because he delights in song; he echoes a strain, plays with it, passes it up and down the piano's and the fiddles' range. Then, suddenly, he is visited by solemnities, and stays in his course contemplating the advent of them, the mystery of them. He is apparently unaware of his own subtleties of abrupt transition, of his own genius to compose an ample and glowing musical texture from three instruments only. He is also unaware of his own prolixity and is unable to come to an end. But in the finale of the E flat Trio he does indeed arrive at a heart-easing and heart-satisfying, and by remembering, in all the movements' marching, striding and dancing energy, the haunting 'cello song of the andante.

3

BEETHOVEN
(1770–1827)

"A symphony is as much a part of Beethoven as the voice and mind, heart and humours, of my best living mortal friend."

The Full Man Himself

25th March 1929

Beethoven's imaginative world was vast and multitudinous. In this respect the Centenary Concert must have done some excellent service, for centenary criticism of Beethoven has tended to make the average man think that the composer lived utterly in a shadowy realm of introspection, and that he even standardized the expression of his tragic isolation. No symphonic writer could thrive if he were less than a full man; the symphony itself is a universe for the musical imagination to fill or else not enter at all. The extent of Beethoven's emotional experience was so immense that to this day writers, poets, and philosophers seek in vain, after the manner of Schopenhauer, to find in his works a sort of first principle giving a hint of the meaning of the world "as in itself it really is". It is Beethoven's range, indeed, that has led many of his admirers to call him Shakespearean. But that description rather runs counter to Beethoven's essentially personal way of experiencing emotion and giving expression to it. A Shakespeare mingles his genius with the passing show of things; like Childe Harold, he says, "I live not in myself, but I become Portion of that round me." Beethoven's art is not protean in this sense; he did not project his imagination into the external world, but rather drew life into his own consciousness and made it part of himself. We can all find points of contact in Beethoven; we can all pass through, by means of his music, most of the moods and emotions known to man. But we must worship Beethoven always in his own image; he is not Hamlet today, Antony tomorrow, Prospero the day after. His music is the full man himself; as we hear it we hear his voice and nobody else's; we can even see the godlike shape of him through all the sounds that fall on our ears. His marvellous power of making a synthesis of what he lived through elevates personal and

45

particular emotion to the realms of the universal. In this sense he is the most democratic of composers; every man jack of us comes into his world and finds there some echo of the music we have at one time or other tried to make for the purposes of self expression. Every man jack of us, that is excepting those who are passion's slaves. There are perhaps fewer hints of sex in Beethoven than in any other artist.

Beethoven tore joy out of the storm in the Fifth Symphony; after the neighbourly liberating finale of that colossal masterpiece he rarely again, if ever, had to struggle desperately and against odds with the demons of doubt. The Sixth, Seventh, and Eighth Symphonies are all, as Nietzsche would put it, "Yes – sayers" to life. "Ach Gott," wrote Beethoven to his "Immortal Beloved," "do but look upon beautiful nature and gain strength to face the inevitable calmly." He little brooked the "inevitable" at any period of his life and it is interesting to find Mr Ernest Newman arguing brilliantly that Beethoven was, as an artist, very much in the control of "unconscious" forces. One has usually thought of him as an artist who had to hammer out his beauty by the energy of a giant; the victory won in the closing movement of the Fifth surely came only after a mighty battle with the hosts of dread and doubt. And the joy and strength achieved here belong to that "nature" of which he wrote to the unknown "Beloved". The symphony ends in a riot of folk-melody. Critics have complained that the coda is commonplace. True, the closing twenty bars contain little else save the common chord. The music is a piece of real "community" instrumentation. But think only of the music that has gone before in the other movements; think of its turmoil of imagination and technique, its countless modes of energy, its superhuman grasp of form (why, the first movement may be said to develop from beginning to end without a single bridge-passage!) – think of these marvels of conception and execution, and then realize the magnanimity of the genius who could crown the world's master-symphony with song the simplest hearts may comprehend.

Aristocrat in Intellect and Democrat in Sympathies

1962

Today, more than one hundred and thirty five years after his death, Beethoven's music remains close to the consciousness and feeling of ordinary humanity. Time hasn't diminished its significance or its power. On the contrary, it comes home to us more urgently than ever before. The clash of man's ideas, ambitions, and vanities, the struggle between the individual will and the irresistible massed stupidity of instinct, the littleness of the ego in the face of the tidal waves of the changing years – Beethoven has told us of the mysterious immensities and fluctuations which since the revolution in his own period created the nineteenth-century, setting into motion forces that have caused the greatest upheaval in civilization of all . . . .

At the present time Beethoven is neither to be claimed by the "new" or the "old". He is neither of the "right" nor of the "left". He himself was a rebel, but one who didn't run away from the past. "I have never believed in the *Vox populi*", he once said, yet in the finale of the Ninth Symphony he strove to embrace the "millions". He was, in fact, aristocratic in intellect and a democrat in sympathies. He was perhaps not the most truly and wholly musical of all composers, the most *suffused* by music. This distinction is Mozart's. But Beethoven was the greatest man ever to live and find a way of life in music.

Like every other genius, Beethoven has his legend, which is half a lie. He is often thought of as a grim, perpetually heroic, fate-driven Prometheus, setting himself against the order and propriety of the ordained gods of music. And it is the fact that Beethoven rudely disturbed the idea of a self-contained, "absolute" music, content with

47

formal beauty and to be itself. It is true that he shattered the immaculate palace of the eighteenth-century symphony. For consider – the G minor symphony of Mozart was composed in 1788, and not eighteen years later the "Eroica" symphony emerged. In no other art has a more terrific step forward than this ever happened. Mozart conveys to us profound enough matter in the G minor symphony, God and heaven knows! But the significance of it all comes indirectly out of the poised classic outlines. Beethoven dramatized the classic patterns and procedure. And he made the symphony for the first time an organic single-minded, single-purposed whole. In the maturer Beethoven symphonies, each movement is related to the thought-process and style of the others. You could exchange a finale, say, of one Haydn symphony for another. I don't think that any great harm would be done to the "Jupiter" symphony of Mozart, as a work of organically composed music if the finale of this masterpiece were exchanged for that of the E flat symphony. The discrepancy, at any rate, wouldn't go deeper than the externals of style, key-relationship, and the rest. But imagine the finale of Beethoven's Fifth, or any movement of any Beethoven symphony substituted for another! Beethoven made each movement of a symphony as important in itself and psychologically as much related to the rest as the acts of a play or drama.

Beethoven changed the face of music. Sir Thomas Beecham, who wasn't a Beethoven man without reservations, used to say that Beethoven was the cause of all wrath later to come in music – the subsequent discordance. Beethoven was certainly the cause, or he gave the lead to, Wagner and his fertilization of music by drama. He was never a note-spinner, never a maker of music for music's sake only. Throughout his works, even in the more "absolute" forms of chamber and piano music, we constantly are coming upon marks of expression, labels, descriptive titles – "Lamentation sinking into exhaustion", "Devout thanksgiving to God on recovering from sickness", "Reviving little by little", and so on. He wouldn't have shared the peculiar views, still circulating in 1962, that music cannot "mean" anything by itself, cannot express a "human" idea or emotion. He thought of music as a language. He believed and demonstrated that to compose music and to write poetry (for example) were the result of exactly the same imaginative creative processes.

If the Hammerklavier piano sonata was intended by Beethoven to appeal to no other faculty in our mental make-up than the musical faculty, we could justifiably question the purely musical credentials of the composer! Carl Reinecke, the old German musician, had a saying – "It is the nature of song to go up and down; repeated notes are ineffectual in it". The famous repeated notes, the poundings in the first movement especially, obviously have an extra-musical significance. "One must have suffered oneself," wrote Vincent d'Indy, "to dare attempt the execution of this adagio in F sharp minor." When Beethoven repeats his notes or rhythmical stresses, he is not engaged with tonal abstractions. He is hammering out something of human and spiritual importance.

But we can overdo the notion of Beethoven as a sort of Prometheus. He could unbend and laugh and make himself at home with peasant and prince, preferring no doubt the company of the peasant at times. Where are melodies more genial than those of the "Pastoral" symphony, the Opus 90 and 54 and 28 piano sonatas (I mention these at random); where is wittier music than the finale of the Eighth symphony? Still, for all his wide variable humanity his essential nature was daemonic, noncomformist, rebellious, against the Establishment. "An utterly untamed personality", said Goethe of Beethoven. He was afraid that the daemonic power in Beethoven the man might even disrupt Beethoven the composer. And it is true that Beethoven as a force of living creative nature was too big to be contained in music or, if it comes to that, in any art. It is when the life force in Beethoven broke musical and aesthetic bounds that he composed works in which here and there there is a miscarriage, a short-circuiting between conception and a wholly musical execution. Busoni was very proud, when after a lifetime of study, he thought he was able to distinguish between "good and bad Beethoven". The wires of strict musical communication sometimes fused when Beethoven the humanist ethical visionary put too great a pressure, a too highly voltaged conviction on the artist and composer. Parts of the choral finale of the Ninth symphony, for example, might fairly be described as good ethics in music rather than good music itself.

The mind of Beethoven, the entire mental make-up of him was forward-reaching, forward looking. He was a "Modern" in his day. He is still a "Modern" in ours. Where was he leading music in the variations of the Opus 111 piano sonata, with its mysterious trills and transitions moving upward and onward, in an upper ether and light? Here the scientific music-maker and the prophetic poet work hand in hand. It is pretty certain that if Beethoven were alive today he would be investigating and making use of all the latest "atonal" and "serial" discoveries. But he wouldn't have employed these discoveries for any "abstract" purposes or ends. He would have drawn them into his own creative forge, endowing them with a living identity, unmistakably Beethoven, embracingly human and humane.

4

GOETHE'S FAUST

A Production of Goethe's Faust
in Manchester

13th January 1933

This week the Manchester Unnamed Society will tackle the loftiest of their enterprises so far, the production of Goethe's "Faust", Part I. The translation is Bayard Taylor's – good enough as far as sense-values go, and, in part, the metrical values, but as far from the poetry as every other extant translation. Shakespeare reads and plays magnificently in German; Goethe has still to find his Tieck or Schlegel here.

In this country little is ever heard of Part II of "Faust", and the narrative of the first part of Goethe's drama is, to say the truth, not very different from Gounod's, only it is told "in rather different words" – as Gretchen herself might remind us. This first part will be preceded, in the Unnamed Society's production, by the Prologue in Heaven, which Goethe composed with his eye on the vaster intellectual horizons of his Part II. Unless we, also, keep in our minds the philosophical reaches spanned in the second part, the Prologue in Heaven will seem so much ado about nothing.

The Lord of Creation and Mephisto wager for the soul of Faust. Obviously the test was to be a severer matter than Faust's ability to withstand the attractions of the first simple Mädchen that came his way. Not even a German professor needed to summon up the Spirit of Evil to get an introduction to a Margaret. The wager between the Lord and Mephistopheles involves the question of the staying-power of man's creative activity, his power to begin each day anew and keep disillusionment at bay. The first part of "Faust" is merely an episode in the whole; it shows us the "little world" of the passions; in Part II we are shown the world of philosophical and aesthetic conceptions. Goethe, as he grew older, lost much of dramatic intensity, and gained more in breadth of humanity. This is why there are many inconsistencies in "Faust"; he outgrew the old legend, and in the end he not only redeemed Faust and Gretchen, but even played with the idea of a "redeemed" Mephistopheles.

The wager made in Heaven, then, is of an ethical rather than a dramatic significance. There can be no struggle between the Lord and Mephistopheles, unless we postulate a dualistic theology, with the Evil Spirit a free agent. But is the Mephisto of Goethe ever free? As soon as he appears before Faust he describes himself "Part of that Power, not always understood, which wills the Bad, and always works the Good." In the wager scene the Lord tells Mephisto: "Du darfst auch da nur frei erscheinen." Every translation known to me makes this statement read as a positive statement that Mephisto is absolutely free. But surely there is a conditional ring about the "darfst", the "nur", and the "erscheinen". If Goethe had wished to let us think the Lord was only encouraging an illusion of freedom in Mephisto he could scarcely have used a more suitable terminology. Anyhow, Mephisto himself . . . is at bottom altogether sceptical about his powers towards utter negation; he knows he is part of a cosmic process, a necessary spur to Faust's creative energy. He is, in the Lord's words, the goad given to man, to keep him out of "unqualified repose"; who must excite and provoke and criticize, "as Devil". But Mephisto's knowledge of the ultimate futility of his own satanism does not render him less interested in the part he must play. He has no use for the moral ends towards which Faust and the world are striving; he disbelieves in everything. But he takes an intellectual enjoyment in the idea of negation and futility. And here we hit on the superb irony of Goethe's conception of Mephistopheles. There is no snarling pantomime devil about this Mephisto; he is the arch-laugher, the urbane man of the world, grown ironical through his vast age. Many times has he looked on the show of life; has passed, in truth, beyond good and evil. The philosophical sceptic is neither sinner nor saint; he is an ironist – an artist, in his way, with humour as his mind's light and food. Goethe no doubt saw Mephisto in some such saving aspect: hence the idea of "redeeming" him . . . .

The tragedy of Gretchen is merely a moment in Faust's career, a necessary part of his education, during his regained adolescence. Irony and pity come into the tragedy because it means so little to Faust and so much to Margaret. It is the most poignant love tale in dramatic poetry. Croce gives us the proper interpretation of the part – "an affirmation of idealism in a creature who is entirely instinctive and natural." It is a hardened audience that can look on without emotion at the overwhelming of Gretchen's tidy, gemütlich home by the ruthless invasion from the sophisticated world, brought to her by the advent of good and evil mixed up beyond her comprehension in Faust and his travelling companion.

Love does not bring peace to Gretchen, as she thought it would do . . . . Now she too has fallen; but she does not condemn or justify. She says only the incomparable heart-piercing lines –

> "Yet – all that urged me so to do,
> Dear God, it was so good, so dear, so true."

The Gretchen tragedy reveals Goethe as an artist fit to stand at the side of Shakespeare.

Faust in Music

3rd April 1954

To the majority of people Faust is known only as he is presented in Gounod's opera. In it, old Faust, still a voluptuary and, worse than that, a tenor, sells his soul to the devil to wallow again in the pleasures and lusts of life. In Goethe's tragedy the point and moral are exactly contrary to this; Faust will surrender his soul to Mephistopheles if he is ever again sensually satisfied:

> "Quieted on a bed of ease,
> Then let that moment be the end of me!
> If ever flattering lies of yours can please
> And soothe my soul to self-sufficiency
> And make me one of pleasure's devotees,
> Then take my soul . . . ."

It is creative spirit that defeats Mephisto in Goethe's "Faust", the power of man to renew himself and to realize that fulfilment has no use for egoism. That is why, when Faust is falling under the innocent spell of Gretchen, Mephistopheles's gibe is terrible and searing.

"Du übersinnlicher Sinnlicher Freier,
Ein Mägdelein nasführet dich."

("You transcendental sensualist, a minx is leading you by the nose.")

In Germany, Gounod's opera was denied the title "Faust" and called "Margarethe" instead. The distinction, pompous and Teutonic, does less than justice to Gounod, who now and again relates his music closely enough to one or two of Goethe's finest strokes. The first entrance of Gretchen is true to scene and psychology; the "King in Thule" is not to be belittled, even if it scarcely conveys the enraptness and legendary pathos of the "Chanson Gothique" by which Berlioz sets the same words and mood. Where Gounod fails deplorably, of course, is with Faust and Mephisto. They are conventional opera figures, Mephisto a snarling "Ha Ha"-ing demon not related to "meine Muhme, die berühmte Schlange;" no, definitely not even related to the celebrated snake, but to the lurid genial gentleman who comes up from a trap door in a Christmas pantomime. And as soon as he has suggested in a few bars of monotone something of the essence of Gretchen's nature, Gounod disperses it by committing the enormity of transforming the girl into a simpering prima donna with her mirror and jewels; we are now far removed from the Gretchen who half in delight, half in fear, touched with a childlike envy, sees the case of ornaments and gew-gaws and cries out: "Wenn nur die Ohrring' meine wären!"

Berlioz departs greatly from actual dramatic sequence in Goethe, but he penetrates to the heart of the matter. The lonely world-tired Faust is audible and breathes in the address of Faust to nature, a transformation into music of Goethe's sublime "Erhabner Geist". Berlioz also gives us the sense of the impersonal evil of Mephisto, not only in the obviously satanic serenade but in the baleful music of enchantment to the "Voici des roses" scene, with the trombones alluring but menacing. Gretchen in Berlioz is too firmly and finely drawn: she remains Margaret throughout. Her "Romance", based on Goethe's "Meine Ruh' ist hin", is one of the most beautiful and haunting melodies in existence, and the transitions and shaping of it, in orchestra and as a lyrical and dramatic vocal scena, are consummate. But this is not the girl who, when she realized her sin, could say,

"Doch – alles, was dazu mich trieb,
Gott, war so gut! ach, war so lieb!"

We see Margaret in the "Damnation of Faust" through the eyes and mind of Berlioz; the music indeed is his conception of her and his imaginative grasp of all that her tragedy means in a romantic transcription of life. Likewise does Hugo Wolf make Goethe's "Mignon" more than life size, great though the Wolf settings are of her songs. Goethe's genius for expressing naïveté, unaware of the tragic texture of its environment, has never been equalled. It needs a German composer to approach closely to the simple secret of Gretchen.

Schumann evokes the image and the flavour of her in his "Scenes from 'Faust'" and, naturally, he fails with Mephisto; there was no diabolism in the psychological make-up of Schumann. But he copes with Faust finely enough, not only with the lyrical passionate Faust, but also with the old Faust of Goethe's second part. He even tries to rise to the mingled pathos, poignant nobility and macabre scene of climax when the signal falls, and the Lemurs take Faust's body.

Liszt, in his "Faust" Symphony, portrays Gretchen with a reticent purity of melody not usual in his music; it is the musing Gretchen of the chamber and garden scenes, awakening to love; we hear the echoes, in the orchestra, of "I would I knew who he may be" and the flower-plucking episode. This middle Gretchen section follows the turbulent Faustian first, and is followed by perhaps the most convincing evocation by any composer of the Mephisto spirit, as far as Goethe's conception can at all be suggested in music by force of long association of certain tones and rhythms with literary and dramatic ideas. Liszt was unwise to tackle the closing scene of Goethe's second part . . . .

Mahler, in his Eighth Symphony, aspired to the heights, metaphysical and poetic, of the "Alles Vergangliche ist nur ein Gleichnis." ("All that is fleeting is but a symbol" – untranslatable maybe, but this will serve): and Busoni, in his gigantic piano concerto, calls in an invisible chorus to intone the same verses. I cannot but think that Busoni was, consciously or not, preparing for his "Doktor Faust" while composing the piano concerto. The brooding solemnity of the opening of the first of the five movements conjures up visions of Faust in solitude; the second movement, the fantastic cadenza followed by gnomic rhythms, stirs the imagination with a sense of Mephisto calling on his host of enchantment; the slow movement is elevated enough in its invocation to recall "O mighty spirit, All that I asked you gave me" – and what is the significance, qua music in a piano concerto related in its end to Goethe, of the terrific Tarantella, if it is not an allusion to Walpurgis Nacht?

In Busoni's "Doktor Faust" he went back beyond the Goethe for the general burden of his libretto; but he was the most Faustian of musicians and men. For how many more years shall we need to wait for a production of "Doktor Faust" in an English opera house? In the "Faust" Overture, Wagner hints to us of the music-drama he might have given us had he dwelt longer on the theme; I doubt, though, if he could have shown the naïve art of Gretchen, without changing her to an Elsa.

Goethe's "Faust", once a source of inspiration to composers of stature, is not likely nowadays to produce even indirectly any amount of music, great or little. Its theme suited a view of life which set aspiration and negation in a creative clash or antinomy, from which dissonance could be resolved into a spiritual harmony. Nobody amongst contemporary composers seems to believe in such a dualism. It is the day of the "Geist der stets verneint" – the spirit of denial. Mephisto is occupying the foreground if not the centre of the stage:–

> "Der kleine Gott der Welt bleibt stets von gleichem Schlag,
> Und ist so wunderlich als wie am ersten Tag."

5

BERLIOZ
(1803–1869)

A Composer of Rare Power
and Significance

24th October 1932

Berlioz, essentially a solitary spirit, a little austere for all his external diablerie (who is so lonely and austere as the devil himself?), has never wooed the impressionable senses, never sung of Mädchen or Nachtigall to the accompaniment of sensuous thirds and sixths. The world loves a sentimentalist, and the curious fact about Berlioz is that, grandiose and bombastic though his music can be in periods of objective dramatic painting, it is never fulsome in sentimentalism when it is expressing sorrow or longing. Take the Romance from "Faust", the equivalent of Goethe's "Meine Ruh ist hin," known to the world in Schubert's setting.

Here, I believe, we have one of the most poignant, heartbreakingly beautiful airs ever written. But the pathos is dry-eyed; this Margaret of Berlioz sings out of an aching loneliness, her sadness is not exhibited; it hardly comprehends its own ache – that of a heart which has lost all the world's warmth. I know of only one other piece of music which shares the secret of Berlioz's solitary, withdrawn, and *patient* pathos, and that is the cor anglais air at the beginning of act iii of "Tristan". It is the same with the love music in "Romeo"; Berlioz does not parade his passion in the manner of Wagner, the great voluptuary. Berlioz was a lover of Virgil, and in his love music there is always the sense of tears restrained, of a reticent bareness of emotion which for some of us is moving beyond words simply because it does not protest too much. But the German 19th-century composers rather hindered, by their rich and often "treacly" idioms and colours, a taste for the sparse, almost gaunt, romanticism of Berlioz. Again, Berlioz seldom writes love music which does not ask for the collaboration of a quick, sensitive understanding of

61

the poetic ideas behind his music. Wagner once said that Berlioz placed obstacles in the way of a full appreciation of his art by often withholding the poetic clue. In Schubert, Brahms, and Schumann a love lyric is entirely musicalized – if an ugly but expressive word may be used. With these composers melody and rhythm and harmony are ends in themselves, to be enjoyed wholly as so much beautiful sound. You need not know the verbal text intimately. But Berlioz uses music as means to an end, more so even than Wagner, who for all his arguments and attitudes as dramatist was really symphonic in his methods of composition.

Berlioz was a subtle blend of literary and musical poet; and to get the full beauty out of his most expressive music the listener too must be a poet and a musician. Even the more obvious effects in Berlioz – the macabre instrumentation of the "Ride to the Abyss", for example – become more significant if you hear them with the imagination well inflamed with the particular kind of picturesque romanticism of the literary tradition of the age in which Berlioz wrote his "Faust". It is not Goethe's "Faust", but rather a mixture of Gerard de Nerval and Byron. But the Mephistopheles of Berlioz occasionally strikes the right note of Satanism, and when Faust sings the "Invocation to Nature" we hear the authentic boom of the earth which Goethe gives us in the great lines beginning "Erhabner Geist". The "King of Thule" setting, too, is transmuted Goethe; the music has over it the golden mists of distance, the note of far away balladry. And the idioms are marvellously Gothic; to this day they seem new and original. Astonishing to think that "The Damnation of Faust" is over a hundred years old.

Berlioz's instrumentation is still fresh and seminal; he had an acute sense of how composers would be writing for the orchestra a hundred years after his own period. The old talk about the "colour" of Berlioz – which usually implied that he had no idea of line and design – was nonsense. The chief technical interest in a score of Berlioz today is a subtle vitality of line; he seldom at his best splashes indiscriminately the orchestral paintbox over his instruments. Thickness of texture is already going out of music in place of a more individual treatment of line and rhythm and instrumental timbre. Berlioz sounds not half so old-fashioned to the present writer as sometimes Strauss does nowadays. The pity is he never fully realized and collected together the various parts of his genius, half literary, half musical – the whole a potential synthesis of rare power and significance.

Sir Hamilton Harty came very near the secret of Berlioz when he once said: "Viewed from a purely musical point of view, Berlioz has no right to the title of great, or even good, composer. Whether he was conscious of it or not, his object was not to write great music but to be a great poet to whom music would serve as an extra illumination of certain emotions and moods." The statement's extravagance is only one of emphasis; Berlioz was certainly a great composer, but a composer who had to feed his art on the stuff of the poets.

The Requiem Mass at a Hallé Concert

14th November 1930

The Requiem Mass of Berlioz was given last night with an eloquence convincing enough to place almost entirely in the world of the imagination a work which does not consistently emerge from a style that is experimental. Berlioz did not always artfully conceal his art, and even in a work of most solemn intention he seems too often to exploit curious instrumental combinations – trombones and flutes, for example – for their own sake. And it is bad art whenever our minds are distracted from a contemplation of the aesthetic ends and instead are directed to a very conscious interest in the technical means. Eloquence is hard to achieve in music that itself has temporarily forgotten eloquence because of a preoccupation with a new device of expression. In the "Agnus Dei", of all places, Berlioz suddenly gives us not so much music as an unpublished page out of his Traité de l'Instrumentation. The held chords in the woodwind are echoed in the divided strings – and we can see the composer enjoying his "discovery". Imagination for the while is displaced by invention. Only by the utmost sincerity of performance were we kept from the flat lands of the prosaic during these momentary miscarriages last evening. The singing was always letting us know how carefully the choir had been prepared; and Sir Hamilton Harty's conducting drew attention to those aspects of Berlioz's genius which are even yet not wholly appreciated by musicians at large – his sublime uses of restraint at times, his austerity.

Restraint and austerity are not words which are generally applied to the music of Berlioz; he is usually, and quite unintelligently, discussed as though he never struck any but a theatrical and rather gibbering attitude. The truth is, that compared with other great composers, he can be exhibited as a writer who was persistently turning his back on the more demonstrative tricks of the trade. His melody has never the ripeness of sentiment of a Brahms; his harmonies, heard after the luscious Wagnerian harmonies, are stark, even forbidding. His rhythms do not fall into easily measured quantities; they are, as often as not, supple and far-flung. Sir Hamilton's interpretation of the Requiem did honour to the Berlioz who, if romantic fires did burn perpetually in him, let them be kindled in his brain as warmly as they were kindled in his blood. There were silences in this performance which were as sublime as anything in Beethoven – sudden visitations of awe, when the imagination of the whole work seemed to hold back from a descent into the unknown.

Berlioz uses detached or broken notes as though they were things of terror for the art of man to handle; they were sung with exactly the right heartfelt tone and attack. Here and there we felt an insecurity of pitch in the soprano's bearing, but this was a fault hard to avoid – because Berlioz occasionally asks his vocalists to enter and find their tonality straightway from very precarious instrumental groupings or timbre. The basses were superb in their resonance and strength of rhythm, especially during the cantus firmus of the "Dies irae". Toward the end of this section there was a failure of tone in the tenors, and as a consequence their restless quaver figure was not sufficiently audible. The brass instruments in the "Tuba mirum" were admirably controlled; the attack was stupendous but not brutal; the weight of tone achieved the composer's lurid purpose but did not render impracticable the task of the bass voices to bear up against the instrumental sonorities. The "Offertorium" was a tribute to the composer's intensely musical sensibility – a sensibility absurdly challenged to this day by those critics of Berlioz who, not satisfied with his undeniable faults, must needs also close their ears to a quiet nobility which to some of us is as apparent as Bach's or Beethoven's most Godlike periods of spiritual release.

"The Damnation of Faust"

29th May 1933

The production as an opera of Berlioz's "The Damnation of Faust" was, on the stage, not impressive. The setting was only adequate and the singing and acting . . . lacked distinction and sometimes intelligence. Sir Thomas Beecham and his fine orchestra compensated for everything; after all, the music is not really of the theatre. Those folk who imagine Berlioz was constantly a man of inflated romanticism would have their minds improved by listening to Sir Thomas's treatment of the finest moments in "Faust" – which are not the "Hungarian March" or the "Ride to the Abyss", but the Marguerite music and the music where the enchantment is put upon the sleeping Faust. Purer music than this has never been written for the theatre. Last night it sounded somehow too self-contained for it, too isolated in its fineness from all the show and traffic of objective presentation either in the theatre or out of it. We could feel the noble loneliness of Berlioz, yet also could feel his independence; the man who was able to write such music, Virgilian in sadness and purity, was not born to write for the theatre. Strange that Berlioz, one of the most aristocratic of composers, one of the few poets who have used the orchestra for a medium, should so frequently be regarded as a strutting, windy romantic because of a few inessential gestures and attitudes. The finest parts of the "Faust" score are so complete in themselves, so withdrawn to a world of Berlioz's inmost heart and sensibility, that it is easy to think of the music as never wanting a public performance, never in need of any material extension in Time and Space. It is a secret show of pathos at its best. But imagine a Wagner music drama with no audience! The man of rhetoric has no meaning when he speaks to himself . . . .

Like Goethe himself, Berlioz threw his "Faust" together, section by

65

section. First of all he was attracted by the surface pictorialism of the Faust drama. Not until the work is far gone do we feel the music taking the measure of Faust's world-weariness, his sublime disillusion, his mystical nature-worship. The great boom of the earth is heard when Faust sings his Invocation; this music is fit to serve as a prelude to Goethe's own "Wald und Höhle" scene, with its symphonic "Erhabner Geist". Marguerite, too, is close to Goethe's Gretchen in the music which introduces her; the strain is psychologically true and moving in its suggestion of frail mortality.

Berlioz never falters in his presentation of Marguerite. His setting of "The King of Thule" ballad is a model of distant enchantment . . . . The love scenes between Faust and Marguerite do not always avoid a commonplace romantic climax, but they are usually sweetened by that sense of mortality which makes all the love music of Berlioz incomparably tender. In Berlioz love music is never braggart or swollen; Berlioz sees Faust and Marguerite, Romeo and Juliet, hedged around by menace; bliss is shadowed by the hurtful world. There are mis-hits in "The Damnation of Faust"; nonetheless, a range of the imagination which could give us the sweetness of Marguerite and the Gothic power of the Mephisto conception was obviously one of the greatest imaginations. Unfortunately, Berlioz played fast and loose with his idea of Mephisto; the serenade is a marvel of sharp-edged irony; there is a bodeful suggestion of control over things evil in the Elbe scene. But Berlioz did not take pains to see that Mephisto was consistently drawn; occasionally we are landed in or near the roseate underworld of the Demon King. There are elements of a great study in Satanism in Berlioz's sketch of Mephisto; a thousand pities it was never worked out. Berlioz saw things vividly but could not get them into an embracing sequence. No other composer has come near Berlioz in all the numerous attempts which have been made to get Goethe's spirit of denial into music . . . .

This production was the first of the work as an opera at Covent Garden but not the first in England. Sir Charles Hallé gave it on the stage of the Court Theatre, Liverpool nearly forty years ago.

Les Nuits d'Été

17th April 1970

There are concerts which give us good, or not so good, performances; and there are concerts which go beyond performance and become experiences of the mind and imagination, remaining there and enriching our aesthetic consciousness. Such an experience occurred last night, in the Royal Festival Hall, when Janet Baker sang in the "Nuits d'Été" cycle of Berlioz, with the London Symphony Orchestra, conducted by Daniel Barenboim. This was much more than good singing; Janet Baker seemed to embody, to incarnate, the wonderful music, which we could almost *see* passing over her face. She missed not a poetic *nuance*; she pierced the heart of the poetic pain of the cry "Sur les lagunes" – "Ah, sans amour s'en aller sur la mer!" A cry from the heart as poignant as Isolde's "Nur einmal, ach, nur einmal."

Barenboim and the LSO responded sensitively to every subtle implication of the evocative scoring of Berlioz, filigree yet potent. There was real ache in the woodwind beginning "Le Spectre de la Rose" . . . .

The entire cycle enshrines the essence of 19th century romanticism purified by a genius classically rooted. Janet Baker conveyed all the exquisite longing of "Absence"; and was as responsive to the gush of melody in the "Villanelle" and "L'Ile Inconnue". She also modulated perfectly to the quasi-recitative needed for the broken notes in "Le Spectre," at the line "Mais ne crains rien . . . ."

It is remarkable that within the last few decades, two English singers have penetrated to the core of two absolutely un-English composers: Kathleen Ferrier with Mahler, now Janet Baker with the Berlioz of "Les Nuits d'Été". Imagine any English composer writing out of his temperament, his heart, and inward parts a song so laden with the beauty of regret and melancholy, so heart-wounding with the sense of the impermanence of beauty, as the setting of Berlioz of "Absence" and "Sur les lagunes". And the music, vocal and orchestral, of this cycle is much more "modern" in its shaping, diction, rhythm, and relevant harmony than the newest of Stockhausen and fraternity. The subtleties of rhythm and accent in "Les Nuits d'Été", indeed, can easily cause Stravinsky's "Le Sacre de Printemps" to sound, in my ears, as naïvely rum-ti-tum as the next emanation from the Beatles. I recommend this cycle as a work advantageously to be studied by every present-day English composer, most of whom apparently feel capable of producing a whole opera but are unequal to writing one memorable song.

6

WAGNER
(1813–1883)

Like His Own Wanderer . . . .

FROM "THE TEN COMPOSERS", 1945
(REPUBLISHED AS "A COMPOSERS' ELEVEN", 1958)

So we come to the great irony of Wagner's life. He was au fond musician. But he followed Beethoven, and it was necessary that somebody should complete Beethoven's work – the fertilization of music by drama. Beethoven found music mainly an objective art, an art of patterned tone. Through eighteenth-century forms of instrumental music, Mozart marvellously drew *his* men and women: Don Giovanni, Donna Anna, Leporello, Susanna, the Countess, and the Queen of the Night. The formal limitations of the music of his period kept Mozart's genius within the ordered scope of comedy; the shadows were thrown from his temperament; tragedy *crept* in, to echo Dr Johnson's remark. He transcended a medium which not yet had been drenched in the dyes of mortality. With a few chords, two or three simple inversions, Mozart created Sarastro, true; but the sublime style had been implicit in music from the beginning. Beethoven stirred music with the sense of pity and heroic frustration; Dionysus succeeded unto Apollo, or rather Beethoven re-created music after the image of Prometheus. Nonetheless, he left music still in the empyrean of the sublime. There is no sex in Beethoven; his world is governed austerely by an ethic; Leonora, in his only opera, is not a woman so much as a symbol of the "Ewig-Weibliche".

To ravish the fair body and mind of music, the fates chose Wagner. He steeped the art in Humanity; he taught it love sacred and profane, acquainted it with good and evil. Like his own Wanderer he came down to earth and polluted the godhead of absolute music to beget human children.

DER RING DES NIBELUNGEN

Covent Garden Opera

"DIE WALKÜRE"

4th May 1933

A music critic's life is hard when he is compelled in order to get his work done in time to leave a performance of "Die Walküre" at the peak of magnificence. Tonight I found myself in the squalor of Bow Street just after the end of the second act and the contrast of reality with the splendour of Wagner's remote world was too great to bear. Still bereft of ordinary senses I wandered about the maze of Long Acre and Drury Lane until I woke up and discovered myself a mile from where I ought to have been. The true reality, of course, was not Bow Street but Wagner's teeming universe.

"The Ring" performances began yesterday with a competent presentation of "Das Rheingold" in which Fritz Wolff gave a wonderfully subtle interpretation of Loge. He is a singer with almost enough brains to endanger the vocation of a tenor. "Die Walküre" plunges us into the centre of Wagner's great smithy, where he seemed to see and feel the primitive stuff of nature red hot and molten. Wagner gives a tongue to the elements, to fire and air and devouring waters. His gods are stricken with pitiful mortality. His humans are exalted to gods. We see Siegmund and Sieglinde driven on the wind of the passions of ordinary frail men and women; we see Wotan losing his divinity and taking on the load of common frustration, limitation, and perplexity. And the orchestra is the continuous creative force, calling up spirits from the deeps, shaping the ends of earthly desire and ambition, and cancelling fatally the assumptions of the gods.

So much for the dramatic power of Wagner: anybody can experience it who has heart and imagination. But only the insight of long musicianship can hope to understand and appreciate the art of Wagner as composition, as inevitably growing and shaping form. The man wrote with a thousand eyes, a thousand hands, a thousand ears; he weaves his orchestral tissue with countless shuttles. He looks back and forward at the same time, a swift binding strand here another there, a sudden gathering up of a skein, a miraculous unravelling of it, the needles flash ceaselessly. But the simile of a tissue will not do; it is not dynamic enough. Rather let us think of the forces of growth themselves, the seminal energy of earth, beginning from the first upheavals which threw up the mountains and at the same time achieved the quietest flower and the peace of a spring night.

Wagner in "Die Walküre" is not always crashing the hammer in the world's forge; he has consummate and moving condescensions. The strings when Sieglinde bends over the weary Siegmund in Act I is in the style of the miniature, perfect chamber music. Then there is the magical moment of the opening of the door of Hunding's house. Until now the orchestra has been gloomy and bodeful as the pit. With a single touch Wagner sends the healing light of the moonlit woods over his orchestra; the man's strengths breed his sweetness. His art is so powerful that occasionally we are persuaded against our better reasoning. After all, what is the significance to us of all these gods and legendary men? Where comes, in the criticism of life, the metaphysics of all this pantomime? Wagner gives us no time to think; he takes us by the scruff of the neck and hurls us into his wood. Mozart does not use this violence; he invites us with a gesture of courtesy to share his secrets. Nietzsche called Wagner the "rattlesnake". No man but Wagner could have persuaded us that the "Ring" is a masterpiece and real. The tale is long drawn out, unwieldy, a sequence of mock philosophy and nursery fables, with dreary argument about it. The proof of his genius, the most audacious and dominating ever known, is that we do indeed go on attending to the worries and words of Wotan. We cannot help ourselves. Is it bad taste for an artist to protest so much? We might as well protest at the bad taste of volcanic eruptions.

Four great singers were responsible for the splendour of Act 2 of "Die Walküre" tonight – Lehmann, Leider, Olczewska, and Schorr. Four evenings ago Lehmann gave us the Marschallin of "Der Rosenkavalier", a study in poised and powered pathos, ironic and cultivated. Tonight she was the natural woman, the tender bearer of life, the impulsive beloved, close to the earth and closer to heaven. Lehmann's every inflection was at one and the same time music and poetry; she looked fresh and young, and her voice was not mere singing but the expression of her whole heart. Her acting is as fine as her singing. Opera becomes convincing and rational when Lehmann is in charge. Wolff sang well as Siegmund, but in Act I his want of significant gestures compared badly with Lehmann's exquisite shading. In Act 2 Schorr and Olczewska achieved a remarkable beauty and veracity in the scene between Wotan and Fricka – the scene which usually is merely an affair of endless verbiage. This was an eloquent Fricka, not a Mrs Grundy of Valhalla but a true woman with a point of view, a view of morality which in her eyes is the pivot of the whirling cosmos in which she and her lord have to live. Nobler singing than Olczewska's is not easily to be thought of. Leider was a lovable Brünnhilde, proud and warlike, yet young enough to melt and throw off her dignity with her armour and feel laughter and sadness. Hunding was admirably sung on the whole by Philip Bertram, but we could have done with a nastier snarl.

Robert Heger must be praised warmly for his conducting and the London Philharmonic Orchestra played superbly on the whole. It is easily our finest orchestra despite the unreliable horns, which are capable of bad and beautiful work in the space of the few same bars.

Covent Garden Opera

"SIEGFRIED"

10th May 1935

This evening we have arrived at "Siegfried" in the performances of "The Ring". As soon as Wagner gets to work with his magic we are enslaved. Before the event we groan at the prospect of having to sit through Wotan's endless excursions into pseudo-philosophy but the moment he strides into "Siegfried", disguised as the Wanderer, and the moment we hear the world-weary harmonies of "Wand'rer heisst mich die Welt; Weit Wandert'ich schon" we bow the head.

By far the most reliable and musical point in this year's performances of the "Ring" has been the playing of the orchestra, and Sir Thomas

Beecham's conducting. Praise of Sir Thomas's work is becoming mechanical. Criticism does him an injustice by treating him as though he were the prima donna who said "Praise is good enough for me." Not every conception of the "Ring" is likely to be satisfied by Sir Thomas's treatment of the score. The Germans would say – and they do say – that he gives to the music a fineness of style that reduces the stature of the work as a whole; they prefer a weightier harmony and a less fluid and nervous rhythm. Also they wish for a handling of the orchestra which is so consistently restrained that the singers are never compelled to strain in order to be heard in a climax. But a great conductor has a right to feel music in his own way: the test is not the objective score – which is an abstraction – but the convincing pleasure he gives us once his point of view is granted.

Nobody has ever made Wagner in the "Ring" sound a more artistic composer, a more musical composer, than Sir Thomas. As we listen to the lovely shades of orchestration, the flowing melody, the transitions of harmony, and the onward and easeful rhythm, we are at a loss to understand how Wagner ever came to be considered, even by people who do not like him, a turgid and prolix writer.

It is true that Beecham thinks up the "Ring" in terms of the orchestra. It is true that here and there his love of great instrumental crescendo and of his own splendid orchestra cause him to forget that vocalists are only human, and therefore limited in their lung power. But perhaps too much has been made of Sir Thomas' fondness for orchestral sonorities in this year's interpretations of Wagner. It is true that he exaggerated the climax of tone of the passage where the lovers meet in Act 2 of "Tristan", it is true that he urged his orchestra to a fury that drowned the Valkyrie in Act 3 of "Die Walküre". It is true nonetheless that in the first act of "Die Walküre" on Monday night and in the first act of "Siegfried" tonight the conducting was a model of skilful balance between instrumentalists and singers.

Sir Thomas is at his happiest in the opening scene of "Siegfried". He revels in the rhythmical opportunities given during the Mime music and the forging music. His instinct for the picturesque is fired by the vivid orchestration during Mime's description of Fafner and his efforts to play the fat boy in "Pickwick" when he gibbers to Siegfried about the terrors of the forest at night. And Sir Thomas's handling of the "Siegfried" music is a joy in its lyrical ardour and litheness of rhythm.

Wagner himself thought his music occasionally became rhythmically monotonous. It seldom does so when Sir Thomas conducts. Only

Wotan, and nobody else, suffers from Sir Thomas's impulsive yet stylish handling of the score. Being a man of wit, he can scarcely be expected to see the point of a bore, even though Wotan is a noble and tragic bore. Sir Thomas is at bottom an artist who loves the delightful, the vivid and the variegated pageantry of the world, the poise and culture of civilized men and women in the drawing room of life. The marvel is that he can turn from comedy to Wagner's mixture of legend and metaphysics and do rare justice to both.

Tonight in the first act of "Siegfried" the London Philharmonic played for an hour and a half without a single mistake or lapse from proportionate and finished musicianship. Melchior was in good voice. He gave the right heroic turns to "Siegfried". He is not satisfactorily poised during the lyrical passages though tonight he enjoyed one lovely moment of reflective song at the exquisite passage "Sonderlich seltsam muss das sein!" Hans Fleischer was an admirable Mime; he contrives, as few German singers do, to let us understand that the part is not only grotesque but that Wagner expressed the grotesque of the part musically, and not merely by means of a series of barks and snarls. Fleischer was clever in his suggestions of Mime's private and cunning communings with himself when he began to ponder on the riddles to be put before the Wanderer. How marvellous the music is at this stage. How vividly the woodwind chords tell us of a primitive mind, searching in its own darkness!

Covent Garden Opera

"GÖTTERDÄMMERUNG"

14th May 1935

Tonight a performance of "Götterdämn.erung" has concluded the first of the season's cycles of "The Ring". It has not been so finely presented as a whole since the war. One or two uncertain points were inevitable in a production more or less got together to meet the needs of an annual event. Opera in this country depends on the energies of a few devoted individuals who decline to be discouraged in spite of the lack of a constant tradition and the more important lack of a machinery of production that is always at hand and running smoothly. Continental singers come to Covent Garden at the last hour, so to say, and they have to adapt standard German views of Wagner to the different views of our greatest conductor, who is the last man in the world to treat any composer in a well-worn way. By force of his genius Sir Thomas has achieved an ensemble in the "Ring" this year governed by the reactions of his own intense and lively musical nature – a nature much more in love with Latin clarity than with Teutonic portentousness.

One or two of the vocalists may have found an occasional climax of Sir Thomas rather disturbing to their habitual spaciousness; they will be better artists for the experience – quicker in sensibility. The German tendency is to exaggerate the typical longueurs in Wagner; Sir Thomas seeks to alleviate them. He will not allow even Wagner to be dull (though probably the sublime style is none the worse for a certain tediousness here and there). Sir Thomas has no use for the so-called metaphysical significances in the "Ring". He is quick to see the dramatic and picturesque points in the score, and, above all, he sees the fine opportunities Wagner gives to the orchestra, and misses not one musical moment. I have seldom if ever before heard the instrumental tissue of Wagner woven as beautifully as I have heard it in this cycle of the "Ring". If we have missed the deep and weighty harmony of the times and consequent solemnity and bodefulness, we have received in exchange the compensation of a rare beauty of musical shapes in which power has been grand enough at the right moments, but never or hardly ever out of proportion.

I have insisted much in these "Ring" notices on the playing of the orchestra and on the conducting of Sir Thomas. It may be thought the vocalists should be discussed at greater length. But in the "Ring" the orchestra can make or mar the best singing. This season's performance of the "Ring" has had a unity of style which has come from Sir Thomas's personal conception of the music dramas. This conception calls for considered discussion – not for the mechanical praise given to it day by day by a large section of the London press that seems to think of Sir Thomas as a fretful prima donna who must be humoured at all costs.

The remarkable fact about Sir Thomas's reading of the "Ring" is that the quality of it has been achieved in spite of his congenital dislike of Wagner's music; he has by musical imagination conquered the prejudices of reason and taste in the abstract. Musical imagination and instinct have won a mastery within limitations imposed by a fundamental want of sympathy with Wagner's theory of music, a theory that involves a long-windedness quite alien to Sir Thomas's view of art and culture. He has concentrated on the melody and rhythm of Wagner; he has seized on the drama and pageantry of the "Ring" and has let the more ponderous significances emerge by the way. That is why the harmonic content has sometimes sounded less tremendous than it can be made to sound in a handling of the score which risks a certain rhythmical monotony. Richter possibly would not have agreed with Sir Thomas's treatment of the "Ring". It is certain that Sir Thomas would not agree with Richter's. Cosima Wagner, by the way, once stated that Richter's tempo in Wagner was too square, too heavily syllabic.

Tonight in "Götterdämmerung" we have had playing which has indeed gone a long way to cause us to revise the opinion that Sir Thomas feels the melody of Wagner before he feels the subtle harmonic chemistry. The music is of course harmonically more magical in "Götterdämmerung" than it is in any other part of the "Ring". The transitions are marvels of changeful instrumental colour. In the Hagen music – in fact, throughout the terrible scenes which depict the ensnaring of Siegfried and the shameful betrayal of Brünnhilde – the art of harmonic mutation is used with a psychological power, nay a witchcraft, that has no equal in music. During these passages there was no want of mysterious horror in the colours which Sir Thomas drew up from his orchestra, and in the scenes of the first act where Brünnhilde and Siegfried emerge from a cave and have their raptures before parting the playing was gorgeous. It was here that Frida Leider almost brought tears to the eyes with her proud womanly "Ein einzig Sorgen lässt mich saumen; dass dir zu wenig mein Wert gewann," or, in Mr Ernest Newman's perfect translation, "One passing care yet holds me captive – that all too little my love is worth." We may well take great pride in the contribution made to Covent Garden this year by an English orchestra and by an English conductor.

The "Ring" at the Vienna Opera

"DIE WALKÜRE"

14th September 1935

Nobody in Vienna pretends that the opera is what it used to be; if Mahler could return to conduct he would probably curse heartily and set himself to the job of beginning again. But no opera in the world at the present time can survive the comparison with its past for the simple reason that there has everywhere been a sad falling away in singing. There is not to be found at the moment a great Tristan, a great Leporello, a great Isolde, a great Otello, a great Kundry, a great Don José, a great Carmen, a great Donna Anna. The Vienna Opera House is more fortunate than most in its happy possession of the Philharmonic Orchestra which is still masterful and beautiful. Without a day's rest, the players travelled from Salzburg – after a month of exultant slavery under Toscanini – and began a new Vienna season with a performance of "The Marriage of Figaro". Now they embarked upon the "Ring".

The great point about the Vienna Opera's performance of "Die Walküre" was the poetic insight of the musical interpretation. The conductor, Dr Felix Weingartner, astonished me with his strong yet flexible control, his sensitive phrasing, his constant high-mindedness. Possibly he expects much from his instrumentalists; he certainly does not overdo the job of giving "the leads". But the Vienna players by this time of day need no conductor to tell them where to come in; Dr Weingartner concentrated on form and rhythm, and so finely did he attend to these matters that they seemed, as they should always seem, one and indivisible. I have never before heard "Die Walküre" sound so full and rounded in its teeming musical life; I have seldom before heard it sound so great as composition – that is, as organized and inspired music independent of the dramatic significances. Here, we could realize, was a musical mind as original and big and resourceful as Bach's or Beethoven's; here too, we were made to feel, was a nature as deep and sympathetic almost as Shakespeare's.

Friedrich Schorr is still the most moving of all Wotans; Bockelmann no doubt gets closer to the impersonal god with his less impulsive vocalism: but Schorr pierces to the heart of Wotan, and time after time he shakes us with the suggestion of a burdened divinity, of a struggle within, which might resolve itself less by philosophy than by tears and suffering. Our sympathies were with Wotan in the scene where he puts Brünnhilde to sleep. And here the Brünnhilde of Konetzni achieved an uncommon beauty, because she made us realize that this was not the hour of Brünnhilde's punishment; not the hour of loss of her glory, but indeed the hour of her achievement of true and full womanhood. It was a superb piece of acting and singing by Schorr and Konetzni – and with the orchestra playing fit for Valhalla and all the gods we were sent into the quiet and lovely streets of Vienna happy and blessed and grateful.

As I looked at the vast audience sitting under Wagner's spell, an audience ranging from men and women of culture to a small boy in the standing-place who would not go home after the curtain fell, but applauded the lights out – as I saw this great crowd in a city which is still one of the few places of culture left in the world, I realized how silly is all the chatter we hear in the caucus of Bloomsbury about the "reaction" against Wagner! It is the crudest provincialism, and if you were to breathe a word of it to any Viennese musician he would merely shrug his shoulders.

To hear the "Ring" played by the Vienna Philharmonic Orchestra is to be reminded of the truth that Wagner is an unnecessarily noisy composer only when he is conducted by men who do not understand him. Wagner seldom abuses his great powers; he can make the softest and most intimate music. At no point of these "Ring" performances were the voices overwhelmed in moments where detailed and eloquent expression is needed. The interpretation put Wagner before us in a way not often heard in these times – as a composer for whom style in the best meaning of the word was never forgotten. The loveliness of the strings in the Sieglinde and Siegmund music of Act I of "Die Walküre", the grandeur of the brass and horns (eight of them); the vivid double basses in the prelude to "Die Walküre", the attack and crack of the timpani at the entrance of Fafner and Fasolt – but it is useless to pick out single instances of the art of the Vienna Orchestra, which is under no obligation to observe pedantic preciseness.

Gramophone Music

"DIE WALKÜRE"

4th May 1936

The first act of "Die Walküre" has been recorded so beautifully by HMV that the company must be urged to finish the good work and give us the music drama in full with the same conductor and the same orchestra in charge. Finer playing than that of the Vienna Philharmonic Orchestra in Wagner could not easily be imagined and the conducting of Bruno Walter exposes the brutality of the average Wagner conductor who invariably makes the composer noisy and rhetorical – the fact being that of all opera composers of the nineteenth century Wagner was the most stylish, the most musicianly, the most thoughtful about balance between voice and instrumental mass, and the most proportionate in texture. Bruno Walter lends to "Die Walküre" the right lyrical impulse combined with the most scrupulous observance of Wagner's tempi instructions; Walter knows that rare secret of the conductor's art: how to keep time and, within the correctly directed line, obtain those nuances which mean the difference between living rhythm and dead time beating. At a hundred points Walter delights us by some imaginative stroke which lightens a whole page of the score – and how quickly, like a lovely mettlesome steed, does the Vienna Orchestra respond!

The singers are Lehmann as Sieglinde, Melchior as Siegmund, and Emanuel List as Hunding. Lehmann is at her most melting, most womanly; we do not only love singing of this perfect kind; we love the artist herself. Her art is better than ever in inflection and treatment of the subtlest significance in the music. There is one moment where Lehmann compels us to catch our breath and moistens our eyes – the exquisite phrase from a love scene where Sieglinde says: "Hush! Let me listen to thy voice: I heard it as a child." Wagner suddenly quietens the music mysteriously; it is a marvellous expression of memory throwing back to some romantic remoteness. The voice of Lehmann falls almost to silence as she sings "hört ich als Kind"; we can feel the woman's mind listening within itself for old forgotten tenderness; then Lehmann gives a quick little gasp of ecstasy and her "doch nein" knocks us over, as they say; the great artist's whole personality, all her sweetness, come through the gramophone as warm as life. We shall not hear Sieglinde's music sung better than this.

Wagner wrote no music more beautiful than Sieglinde's. What a thing it is the enemies say of Wagner? – that he composed all the neurotic, the perverted, love music! (As a fact, Wagner is the only opera composer who taught the austere lesson that the love-obsessed man and woman, who run against the world's balance, are doomed inevitably. In all operas but Wagner's love is glorified for the moment's magic – never in Wagner. His lovers are always set against an inimical background, and they are usually brought to earth tragically.) The music of Sieglinde is curiously "pure" in its passion; with unerring dramatic instinct Wagner drew out of the woman the sweetness of mother and sister love; in her most passionate moments Sieglinde is never out of character; Wagner seldom committed a stroke that was untrue to psychology. In "Die Walküre" he is at his greatest. Here all the elements in his red-hot crucible mingle and fuse; the music is dramatic and visual and yet always musical; poetry and drama melt into rhythm; action has ears which respond to the allurements of sound; eyes are given to music, making the most abstract of arts a vivid, concrete protagonist in the vast world of Wagner's conception. It is beyond analysis that Wagner can paint the scene without crude imitation. The storm at the beginning of Act I is not realism, even though the rhythms and the forked lightning suggest, or begin from, imitation. The entire picture and action are taken into the dimension of music, which, as I say, is given eyes. We can see Siegmund stumbling into Hunding's house; we can see the glances exchanged between Sieglinde and Siegmund; we can see the door swing open and the spring night asleep outside; we can see Hunding's every gesture; we can even see into his mind as he makes his sinister aside – "How like to the woman!" Yet it is all glorious music, bound together with the strictest musical art, quasi-symphonic, a self-subsistent thing.

To hear this music, perfectly done, is to feel coming back to one's mind some words written more than 36 years ago by Ernest Newman; he has written nothing more true and beautiful: "The Muse of Poetry seems to have dipped her wings into the lucid stream of Music, disturbing it with suggestions of a world it had never reflected before, deepening its beauty by closer associations with the actual world of men. This was the brain of Wagner. There is none like him, none . . . ."

Covent Garden Opera

"SIEGFRIED"

14th May 1936

Once again, on a summer afternoon, Covent Garden was crowded at half past five, all of us more or less bound by Wagner's spell to sit in darkness for hours, not always enchanted – frequently, in fact, inclined to scream at the thought of yet another announcement in the orchestra of the Sword or the Valhalla motif. Wagner's system could have been carried through only by a colossal genius; the mechanism of the representative theme is inexorable; besides, it is at bottom a prosaic idea, based on a naïve appreciation of correspondences or identities. But how marvellously Wagner used his cumbrous engine, and how ruthlessly it has ridden over and flattened out every other composer who has tried to drive it!

The defects of Wagner's "Ring" music are being pointed out to us at the moment by the post-war critics; these critics need the sort of help that Sir Walter Scott gave to the university don who wrote to him pointing out a number of errors of fact and anachronisms in the Waverley novels. Sir Walter thanked him for the corrections and emendations, and then added "an additional list of errors which apparently have escaped your attention". There are faults of style in the "Ring" which can be seen and heard at sight by any fool; no genius could create the cosmos of the "Ring" and remain stylish. But "Siegfried" has long stretches which, considered as strict musical composition, are as consummate in craftsmanship as any symphonic movements in existence. We have left the purely lyrical and dramatic world of "Walküre"; a curiously static, almost classical quality can be felt in the music of "Siegfried": the characters have ceased to act dynamically; they appeal to the imagination now as figures in a bas relief. Even the lyrical urge of "Siegfried's" young life is somehow fixed by Wagner's art, which has at last achieved pathos that is not self-conscious. There is also the world-weary sadness of Wotan-Wanderer expressed in chromatically alternated harmonies which are the most Prospero-like sounds outside Shakespeare, mysterious and wise, and as old as creation – Wagner had to shed skins and purge his emotional life with suffering and pity before he could enter this kingdom. One of the miracles of poetic imagination is the way Wagner interrupted his work on the "Ring" in "Siegfried", turned aside from it, and composed "Tristan" and "Meistersinger", and then picked up the colossal bulk and began again where he had left off. Admirers of "Siegfried" have maintained that scrutiny is baffled to discover the exact place in the score where the interruption occurred, so skilfully did Wagner gather up the discarded texture and begin another weaving. But there are surely in the third Act clear signs that Wagner has lived through the strengthening sunshine of "Meistersinger"; formal shapeliness of melody, based on easeful sequences, takes the place of the old intense sensibility; the music suns itself at the end in the C major of confident day – what a tragic and ironical preparation for "Götterdämmerung"!

The subtleties of the score of "Siegfried" must always try hard the finest conductor and orchestra, for a synthesis or balance must be made of the hero's strenuous Nietzschean vitality, his awakening tenderness to the mother who died when giving birth to him, his dawning sense of an heroic love for the sleeping Brünnhilde, and his kinship with the natural life of the woods – these characteristics in Siegfried have to be blended with Wotan's tragic resignation. Wagner gives us the synthesis, the resolution of apparent antinomies – but he asks much indeed from his artists and performers. For the conductor the problem is at bottom a matter of rhythm – a flexible, urgent one for Siegfried and a spacious, almost timeless one for Wotan; the two must seem to be related, in spite of their independent places in the score's structural curve. A comprehensive musical vision is needed in the conductor, an instinctive, not a measured or thought-out rhythm.

"Siegfried" Conducted by Furtwängler

26th May 1938

At Covent Garden the "Ring" goes its annual way, and the conducting of Dr Furtwängler smooths the course perhaps fastidiously, though the musicians in the audience are bound to be refreshed by a handling of the score that is not noisy, one that does honour to Wagner as a composer. Yet we have a price to pay: Dr Furtwängler's sense of detail and balance of periods lessen the rhythmical drive of the orchestra. As a consequence we feel, more than we ought to feel, the mechanism of Wagner's sequential bridge-passages. Also the motifs are introduced almost with a bow – and we are reminded of Debussy's taunt about the visiting-card. The tedium is a defect in the construction of the "Ring", and each year's performances, no matter how good they may be, seem doomed to emphasize the defect. Even Wagner could not solve the problem of a continuous and organic musical tissue of four hours' duration and more. He came close to the achievement in "Tristan", where his text was easily reduced to lyrical moods or, as he put it, stuff of music. In the "Ring" there is argument, almost controversy. "Siegfried", the most musically homogeneous score of the cycle, contains the boring exchange of riddles between Wotan and Mime. Last night I felt once or twice an impulse to rise in my seat and protest at the eternal recurrence of the "leading" themes. The Wagnerian method of transformation of motif occasionally recalls the quick-change artists of the old music halls – out of one door in whiskers and in at the next with a Tarnhelm instead of a hat.

The treatment given to the music by Furtwängler tends, as I say, to reduce the vitality of its movement onwards. As compensation we are granted not only an orchestration of the rarest clarity and finish; also we are able to hear the singers and even their words. One or two of the artists in "Siegfried" were unfortunately not at their best. Melchior's voice sounds fuller than in other years, but apparently he will not sing legato; he must needs emphasize two or three words in each of his sentences. He acts naturally and looks the part – as far as any tenor could look the part. Though Bockelmann is a fine vocalist, I have never found satisfaction in his Wotan. He lacks philosophy, and as the Wanderer his weariness was, I thought, physical rather than metaphysical. And Anny Konetzni's Brünnhilde, though frequently brilliant, missed the proper rapture – it was an external performance, a performance rather than an interpretation.

Alberich and Mime were admirably served by Adolf Vogel and Erich Zimmermann, who instead of wasting their time in damp, gloomy caves and crevices, should have opened a school in the district for the study of declamatory singing in Wagner. Mime snapped and yelped at times, as, of course, he was expected to by the composer; but there was usually a hint of tone in his voice, and at any moment he could have sung Siegfried to sleep with a cradle song by Brahms. And Alberich probably sang "Elijah" in the Nibelheim Three Choirs Festival. It was a joy to hear at the beginning of Act 2 an Alberich who did not bark like a dog. Adolf Vogel, in fact, almost won our sympathies to his side; and of course Alberich was grossly swindled and robbed – there was strong justification for Alberich's "Be off, out of the way! Be gone from hence, shameless thief!" Edith Furmedge was an excellent Erda, and Stella Andreva sang the bird-music accurately and sweetly.

Over everything was the style set by Furtwängler; he did not hurry, but in the end, despite over refinements, he conveyed the suggestion of gathering doom and twilight. Even the raptures of Siegfried and Brünnhilde seemed ill-starred, heard in their context in a reading of "Siegfried" which looked back to "Rheingold" and forward to the closing scene of "Götterdämmerung".

Thoughts on Wagner

4th June 1955

Thanks to the BBC it is today possible for thousands of people living outside London to hear the annual performances at Covent Garden of the "Ring". But it is a grievous thought that countless lovers of music might easily spend a lifetime at home and never once have a chance to see and really get to know the "Ring". And the "Ring" has to be seen to be believed. The Wagner spell has not at all been broken. It is amazing still that an enormous public all over the world, all over this hurrying modern world, will submit to Wagner's extortionate demands. "You must give up your evening meal, hurry from office, desk, workshop, sit in the dark for hours, giving ear not only to my music but to my words, my words, words, words, as I tell over and over again my story. From eventide till nearly after what you English poetically call closing time, I command you to remain silently where you are, hungry, exhausted, possibly bored, I don't care."

What is the abiding secret of Wagner in this monstrous masterpiece sprawling over four nights? It is mainly the appeal of it to simple elemental emotions and fancies; superficially it is a tale of gods and dwarfs and giants, with human lusts and ambitions, all brought to ruin by a denial of love. And into the vast welter of storm, and fire and flood, are thrown all sorts of strange creatures, irresistible to our inborn pantomime senses – a dragon, toad, water nymphs, a bear – not forgetting Grane, the faithful steed of Brünnhilde, never seen alas on the stage nowadays – and vividly and affectionately, even onomatopoeically, embodied in the music. I imagine that as far as this country is concerned, only a small proportion of a "Ring" audience have read the libretti word by word and are in a position to appreciate more than a few of the finer points of correspondence in Wagner's orchestration and treatment of harmonic changes. The public and general interest is chiefly visual, with perhaps overmuch attention to the singing qua vocalism. An admirable feature of this year's "Ring" is the conducting of Rudolf Kempe, who has on the whole controlled instrumental tone and drive on a plane on which good but not in every case great singers have been able conveniently to survive. The precision and lucidity of Kempe's conducting has, in fact, concentrated the average listener's attention on the stage, according to the modern aesthetic of opera, which is returning to the old view that the singer and the action are "the thing".

There seems at the moment a pervading notion that in the past all Wagner performances were bombastic, noisy, with no subtlety of nuance. It is a nonsensical notion. Nothing in this year's production of "Siegfried" holds comparison in memory with Beecham's lyrical unfolding of the score: he sunned himself in the music, letting us realize and glory in the knowledge that Wagner has been living through and in the general air of "Meistersinger". The many felicities of Kempe's treatment of the "Ring" cannot altogether compensate for a certain lack in it of epic largeness and urge. The orchestra is the "Ring's" encompassing energy and First Cause: it is the forge of Wagner's power of creation. The personages taking part in the cosmic process – singers, fiddlers, scene shifters and stage hands, one and all – must perish if they are not fit to survive. The plain truth is that the "Ring" calls at times imperiously for great as well as for intelligently cultivated voices. In this year's "Ring" the voices are seldom imposing, having richnesses to spare. Hotter's Wotan is in the authoritative manner. Harshaw seems likely to develop into a first rate Brünnhilde. The Siegfried is mediocre vocally and histrionically. The Hagen in "Götterdämmerung" is without the evil eye or the evil tone. Apart from Hotter – and he missed the world-weary note of Wotan's Wanderer – only Peter Klein, of the men, is matching standards of Covent Garden's quite recent past. Klein's Mime is a superbly subtle study in singing and acting. Much as I have enjoyed this year's "Ring" at Covent Garden – and more than ever marvelled at Wagner's genius to change a motif and nearly but not quite leave it the same thing – I fail to understand the generous verdict of those of my colleagues to the effect that Covent Garden's "Ring" is now the best in the world or words to the same purpose, a rather provincial appraisal.

Certain points in the production have bothered me. Gestures in the "Ring" are important. ("All his music is gestures," wrote Nietzsche.) When Brünnhilde is wakened by Siegfried the violins stretch upwards, a magical suggestion in tone of limbs finding freedom from the prison of sleep. Brünnhilde's arms should stretch upwards to these liberating phrases. Miss Harshaw sat on the rock as though awakened all right but waiting for her morning cup of tea. In "Götterdämmerung" the Norns sang competently enough, conveying by their placid actions that they were not winding the rope of fate but knitting diligently at a sewing guild; when the rope broke no sense of a tragic ripping and tearing of destiny shattered the action: I merely felt that the third Norn had dropped a stitch. Several maladjustments, a want of consistent correspondence between gestures on the stage and gestures in the orchestra, strengthened my suspicion that the tendency grows to ignore Wagner's written directions to his actors and singers and producers. Why did not Miss Harshaw wave Siegfried away down the Rhine? The music waves gorgeously enough; and Wagner explicitly tells us, in stage directions, that "she makes ecstatic sounds". We cannot expect producers to take Wagner's written instructions to the letter, yet I would love to see nowadays a truly realistic realization of just one or two of his instructions at the end of "Götterdämmerung". Brünnhilde has "leaped on the horse and now urges him on to the leap. With one leap it takes her into the burning pile of logs. The fire immediately blazes up . . . . The Rhine swells mightily and rolls its flood over the fire. When at last the glow is at its brightest there becomes visible the interior of Walhall, in which the gods and heroes sit assembled. Flames seem to seize upon the hall of the gods. As the gods become entirely hidden by the flames the curtain falls . . . ." But no scenic or visual arts, past, present, futurist, or surrealist, will match the protean wizardry of Wagner. The praise we can safely give to Kempe and the Covent Garden Orchestra is that they unfold to us a musical mime as original, resourceful as Bach's or Beethoven's, with a nature strong and drastic yet capable of the tendernesses which can come from none but a full and humane imagination. After all the "Ring" is not entirely peopled by abnormality, not entirely by Wotan, Alberich, Hunding, Hagen, and the like. Even Brünnhilde is not the most lovable of the "Ring's" inhabitants and denizens. In "Götterdämmerung" she is for a while corrupted (by Wagner not by Hagen) to the grand-opera level, of a vengeful dramatic soprano – until the "Immolation" scene. The hate, deceits, and betrayals in the "Ring", the baleful poisons of ambition and cunning, the fury and frustrations, are really purged by Sieglinde. It is a merit of Kempe's conducting of the "Ring" that he brings us close to her, so that even after she has passed from the scene, some melting sweetness of her heart seems to remain as a catharsis, to purify.

"Das Rheingold"

KEMPE'S FEELING FOR ORDER AND PROPORTION

27th September 1957

Covent Garden Opera House was packed floor to ceiling on Wednesday night for yet another unfolding of the "Ring", Wagner's colossal tetralogy depicting the everlasting conflict between godlike aspiration and Plutonic itch for power, between the growing moral law which must break or get round its own ordinations if a higher life and order is to be evolved. In "Rheingold" we are shown the beginnings of things in a primal world of urgent forces moving and multiplying. From the first E-flat chord of the prelude, continuous and expanding, rising from depth to height, everything emerges. Here in the orchestra is the harmonic matrix of the whole, the first cause of all the wrath, exaltation, and doom to come.

The "Ring" takes its being from the orchestra. The orchestra is, in Wagner's own words, the fructifying seed of the whole purpose. Rudolf Kempe, who is Covent Garden's conductor of the "Ring" in apparent perpetuity, once again made the music sound unusually clear, unambiguous and civilized. I have not heard a more articulate performance of "Rheingold". The singers were never in danger of losing audibility: they were given time to measure and flavour every word and accent; and the details of the orchestra could be counted almost, none of them lost or groping in a dark and backward abysm. Kempe's "Rheingold" was discreet, tasteful, finely balanced, entirely presentable. Strauss once ironically said that his "Salome" should be conducted to sound like Mendelssohn. Kempe's smooth, evenly distributed prelude to "Rheingold", in which instruments increase and multiply from a primal womb of harmony, indeed almost related the music to the "Hebridean" overture of Mendelssohn.

We had to pay a certain price for Dr Kempe's many musical excellences: grandeur and expansion from depth to height was conveyed to us on a smallish scale. This was a beautifully translucent Rhine at low tide. Even the descent into Nibelheim, with its marvellous and vivid orchestral onomatopoeia, was conducted with the nicest feeling for order and proportion: we were taken into no sultry subterranean realm of evil and greed: the smoke on the stage did not get into the orchestra. The orchestral interludes in "Rheingold" are symbolical and dramatic in their contrasts of ascent, descent, and again ascent. Dr Kempe, superb though his treatment of the score was as a whole, seldom rose to a climax, simply because he established a tonal scale of surface on which little rise and fall was possible. Kempe's fastidiously musical concern for vocal clarity is no doubt a change from many discordant barbarities on the part of Wagner conductors of the past: and it is a fact that taste and interest today is returning to the pre-Wagner conception of opera, in which the singer was the first attraction. But the Wagner opera aesthetic insists, especially in

"Rheingold", that the word-tone should emerge from a germinating river-bed of harmony. In "Rheingold" Wagner presents types, elemental beings, or godlike embodiments: he has not yet come to the more individually portrayed beings, with Wotan himself ennobled in his fettered godhood by human, all too human, intimations of mortality. But in "Rheingold" orchestral harmony is the essential element, every expanding chord or tonal change symbolic of the act of a "becoming". We should always feel in "Rheingold" that dread inexorable happenings are shaping, taking form, instinct, impulse, will, out of a timeless obscurity. In every way except grandeur of conception this was a superb performance with not a single loose end. It was a performance likely to please anti-Wagnerians and Wagnerians equally. Hotter as Wotan has no equal today in the part: already, in "Rheingold", he hinted of the tragic dilemma soon to raise him to a nobility and martyrdom not dreamed of in the Valhalla hagiology. Otakar Kraus, as Alberich, achieved the right stature to stand up to Wotan: after all, Alberich, of all the major characters in the "Ring", is as honest as the rest. Kraus was especially good in the scene where he is released from the bonds in which Wotan and Loge have tied him and expresses in withering irony that he is free. We know by now that the shackles of fate and conscience are already tightening round Wotan himself. Georgine von Milinkovic was a sympathetic rather than commanding Fricka. The Loge of Erich Witte, first-class generally, needed a sharper edge to his final comment – "I am ashamed to deal with these futile creatures". Peter Klein, as Mime, foreshadowed the memorable and fully realized Mime he presents to us in "Siegfried". The Fasolt of Kurt Boehme also rose to the proper vocal stature: this was truly Wagnerian singing, and the same can be said of the very eloquent Erda of Maria von Ilosvay. The Rhinemaidens were sung variably. They now dance and gallivant about the Rhine floor as though from the next ballet. I always thought they wore tails.

"Die Walküre"

BIRGIT NILSSON

9th October 1957

"Die Walküre" given on Friday to a crowded audience was notable for a very musical performance of the score and also for the appearance of a Brünnhilde fresh to London. Birgit Nilsson has a clear, natural voice sometimes a ravishment to the ear: and she is comely to look at. With more experience she will no doubt colour her lower tones with shades expressing a deeper meaning than she can always command at present. Already she is capable of considerable eloquence, as in the great scene of Brünnhilde's punishment by Wotan. There was the right unself-conscious pathos in her "O sag Vater sich mir ins Auge" and a touching rekindling of pride in her soft heart-felt "Du zeugtest ein edles Geschlecht," where Brünnhilde reminds Wotan that it was he himself who created the heroic Walsung race he has now tried to destroy.

Rudolf Kempe again conducted with a fine sense of proportion, always letting us hear the singers, always keeping the orchestral texture transparent. But the first act was too low in temperature and voltage, lacking impulse and magnitude. By concentrating on the voices and the melodic line, Kempe certainly enables the singers to make the most of their chances; and his treatment of the score reveals the finest skein in the orchestral weaving. But it is a treatment which tends to reverse the Wagnerian conception of the place of song in music-drama.

"Harmony," wrote Wagner, "is the most essential element in the womb." Melody in the "Ring", even in "Walküre", most lyrical of the four music-dramas, is not the dominating factor in the musical organism. Often melody in the "Ring" is borne from the orchestral earth-tone; often it is an extension or transformation of a chord, calling for imaginative control and cadence on the part of the conductor.

Melody in the "Ring" individualizes the human element, the particular and temporal; and it should always be related to the fundamental world or womb of the orchestra. The orchestra in the "Ring" is the timeless unseen destiny of the whole. We have no need to wait until "Götterdämmerung" to know that the Norns are spinning the fate of the drama; every instrumentalist in the "Ring", from "Rheingold" onward, is a Norn himself, at work on his own shuttle. As soon as Hans Hotter came before us, the performance expanded to the right stature. He brought to Wotan, and to the evening as a whole, dignity, range of emotion, and the god like gesture. Wotan's frustration in "O heilige Schmach" was terrific. And in less spectacular and subtle moments he was as superb, not missing in his narration to Brünnhilde ("Als junge Liebe"), the exquisite throb in the phrase in which Wotan tells her that the world's wisest woman bore her . . . .

The evening increased in blood pressure after a disillusioning first act of which something must be said on the pointlessness of one or two arrangements in the production. A great moment in this act is when, if Wagner's instructions are obeyed, the door of Hunding's dwelling swings open and the moon shines on the spring night outside, sending a beam on the lovers. "Ha, who passed?" asks Sieglinde, and Siegmund says, "No one passed. It is the spring smiling in the room." There is no visible door to Hunding's dwelling in Covent Garden's production. A green light is thrown from electricians working above. We do not see the forest peaceful under the moon, a moving contrast to the dark, sinister interior of Hunding's house and the awakening love of Siegmund and Sieglinde. Consequently one of Wagner's most beautiful and thrilling events runs to waste.

Another falsity happens after Hunding has retired to his chamber, followed by Sieglinde. Wagner instructed that Siegmund should sink on the couch before the dying fire on the hearth. A glow cast by a flickering flame falls on the spot on the ash tree indicated earlier by a glance from Sieglinde. The light of the fire fades, shadows darken the room, and Siegmund fancifully thinks he has seen on the tree the lovely gleam of Sieglinde's glance. In the Covent Garden production Siegmund does not sink on a couch; he remains standing, stiff and unemployed. The electricians aloft send down a light that reveals the hilt of the buried sword so obviously that it could be seen half a mile distant.

There is a case for clearing away from the "Ring" some of the old realism in favour of the symbolism now practised at Bayreuth. There is no case for substituting in place of Wagner's relevant realism a realism that is irrelevant and stupid. Also there should be some way of animating the movements and gestures in this act of Hunding, Sieglinde, and Siegmund. Each stood still waiting for the orchestra and their cues. Apparently there was no accommodating seat for anybody, though Wagner, regardless as ever of expense, ordered wooden stools and a table. Hunding has had a good shave and haircut since we last met him. Without his beard he was clearly not himself. For all the effect he seemed to have on Siegmund and Sieglinde he might have been wearing the Tarnhelm.

Götterdämmerung

7th October 1957

This was a generally superb performance of "Götterdämmerung" . . . . Rudolf Kempe's view of the "Ring" as a whole is proportionate, with the end foreseen in the beginning. We could realize, from the climax he gave us in the closing scenes of "Götterdämmerung" that his rather small scaled treatment of "Rheingold" was preludial, and that he was restrained in parts of "Walküre" only to leave room for the clinging apotheosis.

The gallant orchestra at Covent Garden is not to blame if, during "Götterdämmerung", there were insecurities among the brass before the long evening was done. We cannot in this country afford the Continental luxury of bringing fresh-lip players in for Wagnerian third acts. Kempe modulated very finely from the bright rapture of Brünnhilde and Siegfried at the music dramas outset to the dark tragic air and habitation of Hagen and the Gibichungs.

We say farewell to the true Brünnhilde and to the true Siegfried when the hero sets off on his Rhine journey. Henceforward until the transfiguration and catharsis we are plunged into corruption. Brünnhilde and Siegfried betray each other; Wagner betrays both. And Wagner is not always happy with his music now. He is reduced to brazen choruses, outmoded operatic "oath" and "revenge" numbers, which come into the score as though Wagner as a composer had atavistically gone back to operatic conventions he himself tried to render obsolete.

It is a paradox that Wagner when it came to the creation of an evil character, lacked the honest, lovable Verdi's genius. Wagner's Hagen, though harmonically evocative, is only an expression of evil from the outside. Much of the music by which he is represented is not more than mimetic. Wagner was not capable of the sinuous, seductive subtlety whereby Verdi embodied Iago; he did not know the secret philtre out of which Iago pours his poison into Otello's ear when he tells of Cassio's dream.

Not until Siegfried is released from the spell of Hagen, and not until Siegfried's death has released Brünnhilde from worldly woman's passion and bitchiness (a dreadful thing to say, but Wagner makes play that way for a while), does Wagner return to musical grandeur and to his own easeful mastery. The second act of "Götterdämmerung" not only shows us Siegfried and Brünnhilde traduced; also the true art of the Wagnerian music is traduced – thank goodness, only for a while. The recovery is Herculean. Kempe missed not a point of the transfiguration. The Death March was terrific in attack, sublime in arch, and profoundly moving in its tender sequences. Birgit Nilsson sang Brünnhilde's music with the voice of a century, now radiant, now vehement, now noble. She needed only the spiritual note in the last phrases of the "Immolation".

Windgassen was as good a Siegfried as any to be found today; his dying exordium was fine and touching acting as well as eloquent singing. There was dignity and pathos in Herman Uhde's Gunther; and Elizabeth Lindermeier sang Gutrune with the right frail line and tone. The character is pitifully shadowy.

Kurt Boehme's Hagen had ample resonance and spacious hints of expertise at dirty work. As Waltraute, Maria von Ilosvay dominated her one scene and sang with a dignity of vocal diction rare among Wagner singers of our time.

Yet again stupid production almost let down a performance worth remembering. A new and symbolistic way of producing Wagner may be a good idea. But an old fashioned realism which makes nonsense is strongly to be condemned. The corpse of Siegfried was carried away, like furniture, while Birgit Nilsson approached the ascent of the "Immolation". Consequently she found herself alone on the stage at the culmination. The stage was as though changed to a concert platform. I almost expected to see a bouquet handed up. Why are the sensible points of Wagner's instructions often ignored by producers of the "Ring" nowadays? Would they dare flaunt them in Wagner's presence?

The "Ring" at Covent Garden

KONWITSCHNY'S "DAS RHEINGOLD"

21 September 1959

The productions of the "Ring" at Covent Garden have for four years been conducted by Rudolf Kempe, who presented the cycle as a succession of musically-moulded frescos, reversing Wagner's theory that music should serve as a means to an end, the fertilization of drama. But Wagner, being first a musician, himself often contradicted his own aesthetic; and we can be sure that he would have revelled in Kempe's tributes to him as a consummate and independent composer.

It was time, though, that Covent Garden heard again a large-scaled large-toned Wagner. The conductor this year, Franz Konwitschny, set to work from Kempe's extreme. His handling of the score and orchestra on Friday was energetic and comprehensive; his climaxes were powerful with accurately calculated peak to each. The emphasis in this performance of "Das Rheingold" was on the subterranean depths, on the fundamental and evil germinations, on Alberich, Nibelheim, on the giants' granitic trustfulness of Wotan, and the corruption of elemental simplicity into hate. The smoke of Nibelheim got into the orchestra.

Harmony was brutally cleft asunder as Wotan and Loge descended to the underworld. Alberich's curse was terrific – we shall hear it echoing throughout the present cycle. In fact, when we came away from the performance it was Alberich who filled the imagination –Alberich and all that pervades "Das Rheingold" with primeval rapacity. So vividly did Otakar Kraus personify Alberich that he actually won our sympathies momentarily, when he was duped by Loge and the ring was filched from him. By adding to subhuman power-lust a quiet human sense of shameful deceit, Kraus eloquently stressed the pitiful Wotan dilemma – godhead fettered by its own moral decrees even while these same decrees are being outgrown by evolving consciousness and wisdom . . . . Herr Konwitschny's deeply hewn conducting naturally missed something of the music's contrasts of light and ascent, depth and descent; he remained very much in Nibelheim; but we cannot have everything. The opening scene lacked wave-like motion. The rhythms were deliberate; and too soon the shadow of Alberich loomed over the sportive aquarium . . . . A rare virtue in conducting as drastic as Konwitschny's was that he allowed the singers time and opportunity for clear articulation; few important words were lost.

Alberich and Loge dominated the action, with Peter Klein sketching the outlines of his wonderful Mime in "Siegfried". Richard Holm's Loge was superbly pointed; maybe a little too sophisticated in its conscious shafts of quite Mephistophelian irony. Loge's cunning is instinctive; he is flickering flame, not intellect. Richard Holm's Loge is not distantly related to Goethe's denying Spirit; but I do not complain at a rewarding enlargement of the part. The pungency of Holm's gibe to Wotan, after Fafner has slain Fasolt, was a masterstroke of sardonic relish: "Was gleicht, Wotan, wohl deinem Glucke?" – "What luck, Wotan, could you beat it?" (my own free irreverent translation).

Wotan, in "Das Rheingold", is more or less an onlooker, as the coils begin to bind him. But Hans Hotter, majestic as ever even while standing around doing nothing, hinted plainly of the grandeur and downfall to follow soon enough. The endearing Freia of Una Hale made a pathetic foil in the presence of Fafner and Fasolt, both credible and not unsympathetic. The Fricka of Ursula Böse was often vocally splendid; here is a mezzo-soprano in a hundred. She is rudimentary so far as an actress with nothing of Fricka's regality . . . .

In one or two ways the production could be improved. If realism is to be trusted at all in the "Ring" nowadays, it should at least be consistent in its correspondence to the orchestra's suggestions. If the orchestra tells us – which it does – that Alberich is climbing the Rhine rocks and finding them slippery, we should not see him firmly rooted to the river bed, immobile as any ordinary professional batsman these days. The orchestra, after one or two mis-hits, responded skilfully and sensitively to Herr Konwitschny's promptings. Whether we shall get the necessary plastic harmony in the later music-dramas time will tell.

At Home in the World of Wagner

REGINALD GOODALL

4th October 1959

For the performance of "Die Walküre" in the second cycle of the "Ring" at Covent Garden the conductor was Reginald Goodall, and a magnificent job he made of it. If he had been an unknown German from Chemnitz he would have been hailed by most of the critics here, achieving fame in a night. He was as sensitive to the lyric loveliness of the Sieglinde-Siegmund scenes as he was strong, broad, and imperious in the Wotan climaxes. The long colloquy in Act 2 between Wotan and Fricka could not have had a more logical and more musically dialectical handling by any of the most experienced Wagner conductors. The accentuation was admirably timed in the quasi-recitative passages without hurt or hiatus in the wonderful onward movement of the orchestra. Maybe the exquisite chamber music at the beginning of Act 1 was a shade deliberate, but as the drama developed Mr Goodall more and more entered into the great heart and world of the work.

The orchestra responded to a man. It is a long time since I heard instrumental playing at Covent Garden so rich and sure and as refined in tone and texture as this. We could now realize the price we have recently been paying for the drastic larger-than-Wagner-size cataclysms of Konwitschny, not that they were unwelcome for a change. In Mr Goodall's interpretation I found most of Kempe's fine musical characteristics combined with a power of climax and a continuous surging rhythm not always present in Kempe's interpretations. Mr Goodall should be the first in command at all future productions of the "Ring" at Covent Garden – failing the presence of an acknowledged German master and authority. Amy Shuard, as Sieglinde, also added to the laurels of English music and singing. I could not hear her performance in the "Walküre" in the first cycle. It was rather mildly received, praised only up to a discreet point. It is in fact the most satisfying and rounded performance of Sieglinde heard at Covent Garden since Sylvia Fisher sang the part with Flagstad – and wasn't sung off the stage by any means. It is a much more memorable and touching Sieglinde than any German artists heard in the last few years at Covent Garden.

We can say much the same of Miss Shuard as Sieglinde as we have said of Mr Goodall. Had she arrived here fresh from Darmstadt, all the fashionable places in town would now be raving about her. I have heard most Sieglindes of the past thirty or forty years, and not many have had a more poetic distinction than Miss Shuard's, after only one or two efforts at the most endearing of all Wagner parts.

The Wotan of Hans Hotter is the greatest of our period, as far as penetration into and suggestions of mind and godhead are concerned. Nobody has given us a Wotan of greater vocal stature and of a more majestic physical presence. None has softened more touchingly as he has kissed away the godhead of Brünnhilde. Vocally, in this memorable performance, he was matched by the Fricka of Ursula Böse. The consort's case was superbly declaimed. Martha Mödl I found disappointing as Brünnhilde, short of radiance, just a good German dramatic soprano of no large power of evocation. Why, after Wotan has commanded Brünnhilde to do his bidding and connive at Siegmund's death, is she not given armour sadly to pick up as she sings or sighs, "Schwer wiegt mir der Waffen Wucht"? (My weapons' weight weighs heavy on me.) Why don't producers do as Wagner plainly ordered – that is if realism is to be practised at all? The Hunding of Kurt Boehme was impressively hairy chested, a tough guy unmistakably; and though Ramón Vinay's singing has often to be listened to with histrionic rather than musical attention, he conveys, in the main, a very sympathetic impression of Siegmund.

The production, of course, needs thorough revision. All in all, though, this was an evening to remember, with Goodall and Shuard scoring heavily for English talents.

The Winds of Musical Taste

March 1967

Years ago, a decade at least, I heard at Covent Garden a performance of "Die Walküre" . . . . The conductor, then more or less unknown to the public or the critics, gave so splendid an account of the score that I at once described him in these columns as a born Wagner conductor, adding that his handling of the music of "Die Walküre", orchestrally and vocally, was as sure and comprehensive as any I had heard, here and abroad, for years. This conductor, English, has remained, since that distant performance, fairly lost in obscurity until now. He was none other than Reginald Goodall, at present conducting "Die Meistersinger" in a revival at Sadler's Wells. Had he been born in Prague, or Sandershausen, he would to-day rank high in the esteem of the public and the publicity men. Perhaps at last he will be encouraged to come into his own . . . .

The Latest Love-Hates

9th October 1965

The case of Wagner goes on. It has gone on over the years since Nietzsche opened it ("Der Fall Wagner"). Counsels for and against have included Bernard Shaw, Ernest Newman, and more recently, Bernard Levin, Sir Victor Gollancz and, last but not least Lord Boothby. In the "Ring" Shaw discerned propaganda for socialism. The Nibelungs were symbols of exploited industrial slaves. The Tarnhelm was the capitalist's tall hat, lending unnecessary show of respectability. And now, today, men of ripe sage years have found the odours, the anticipations even, of Nazism in the "Ring" – men who before the advent of Hitler had known and given themselves to the "Ring" without dreaming that it contained anything at all socially, ethically, or psychologically reprehensible. Thus, from the grave, Hitler is still having influence, even on aesthetic susceptibilities.

The latest reaction to Wagner is to his power to pervade us by the suggestions, the very atmosphere of evil. Naturally enough, the present age is abnormally interested in the psychology of mortal sin, lust, the sense of man's guilt. We have been conditioned to an awareness of evil; we have in fact come to revel in such an awareness. Nobility is out of fashion. Nietzsche's Superman (and Wagner's) is "old hat", like Carlyle's Hero. Mime and Alberich are "real" in the consciousness of today; Siegfried is "out", a boring lay figure. With an ironic parallelism, the spirit of the age (as far as it involves Wagner) is magnetically attracted to Wagner's presentation of evil destructive forces. "The truth is that the grotesque little genius, for such he was, saw deeper into human nature as it is than any psychiatrist, including Freud and Jung." Thus has spoken Lord Boothby.

It is a compliment to Wagner that he has become, in 1965, a source and inspiration of the latest love-hates. Nobody, in the discussions now under notice, has put much stress on the characteristics in Wagner most admired half a century and more ago. The climate of opinion was then not allergic to emblems of devotion (Brünnhilde and Sieglinde), to the melting tenderness of Wotan's "Denn so kehrt der Gott sich dir ab" – as he kisses godhood from Brünnhilde, or to the thousand other great humane embraces of Wagner in the "Ring", his breadth of understanding and sympathy for and with all his creations, from the "Wurm" to the All-Highest in (and out of) Valhalla. Of course there is evil expressed and pervasive in the "Ring"; it is dramatically necessary. Wagner's creative energy, like the sun from heaven, gives life to the just and the unjust, to good and evil alike. Wagner is as generous with his creative seeds and juices to Alberich as to Sieglinde or Wotan. He was the first to realize in art a convincing embodiment of evil. Milton's Lucifer is anything but satanic. Pizarro in "Fidelio" is a conventional operatic villain. Even Iago, at bottom, is related to the villain in melodrama. We are not obsessed by these representations of evil. Mr Levin has never, I fancy, been kept awake at night haunted by visions of Lucifer, Pizarro and Iago.

But Wagner was never for a moment thinking of the human situation at large, subconsciously prophetic of Freud or Jung. He was obsessed by his own theories about opera and drama. For some six years he composed not a note of music, stubbornly declining to cash in on any success or prospect of success of "Lohengrin", completed in 1848. "The Art Work of the Future" was written in November and December 1849. Not until he had found the right musical language for the "Ring" did he compose again. And what was one of the aims of his proposed "Art Work of the Future"; what was one of his aspirations as a maker of the new music-drama? Simply to produce a "great united artwork that must embrace all the genres and in some degree undo each of them, in order to use it as means to an end – namely the unconditioned immediate representation of perfected human nature . . . ."

"Perfected human nature", Freud, Nazism? Well, in the "Ring", Alberich, Hagen, Mime, and everybody else coveting power, perishes. In the "Ring" power corrupts, absolute power corrupts absolutely. Really, it is the most comprehensive of moralities.

I have tried to account for the current emphasis on the expression of evil in the "Ring". There is probably another reason – the old story. Listeners and spectators attending performances have missed the art of it – momentarily, let us charitably say – and gone behind the art to the raw material out of which music and drama have been forged. Catharsis has failed in its effect on thousands. As I say, the "evil" forces in the "Ring" are identified with our latest everyday "images". Once on a time Siegfried was symbol of the Superman, of man's rising stature, evolutionary man, Darwinian, Nietzschean, and all the latest nineteenth-century labels. Then, for folk old enough to have lived under the menace of Hitler, Nazism is thought of as the generating stuff which spawned Alberich, Mime, and Hagen. I wonder if any young newcomer to the "Ring", uninstructed and not warned in advance, has ever sniffed a sniff of the dread presence, the hidden Freudian sewer.

Oh, for a return to the music and genuine musical criticism of the "Ring" in particular and of Wagner in general! – to something like Newman's "One of his longest motives is that of the 'Volsung'. Its length is justified by the duty it has to perform: to concentrate the nobility and suffering of that race into a chord or two would be beyond the powers of any musician . . . ." Or something like Samuel Langford's, "Music is an art of cadence, and however broad, as in the overture to 'Die Meistersinger', the banner of tone may be opened out, the cadence and the fall of the music must come, and the most humane and loving tones at last must fall upon the air. But that they may die as the sheer ripeness of a reconciled humour, from which every essence of sourness has been strained, and of which nothing but the purest love of one's humankind remains, is a lesson more thoroughly to be learned by hearing an ideal performance of 'Die Meistersinger' than by anything else that the arts have given us." Yes, while we are talking of Alberich, Hagen, Nazism, and Freud, it is as well to remember Hans Sachs.

TRISTAN AND ISOLDE

"In tragedy the imaginative energy concentrates, not spreads; it draws all things into its circle of obsession; for tragedy means obsession."

Frustrated Young Love and Poetic Pain

5th December 1932

"Tristan" has been called "erotic" and an "orgy of sexual ecstasy" by folk who did not know what they were talking about. Passion in its physically indulgent sense is never present in either the music or the text of "Tristan". Wagner touches human love with a no less poetic frailty and sadness than Shakespeare's in "Romeo and Juliet". He shows us Tristan and Isolde caught in the great snare of the world, their love is "death-devoted", and as they live their brief hour in the magical garden we can always feel how pathetically thin-spun it is. Brangäne, Isolde's maid, keeps guard in the watch-tower, and we hear her bodeful lonely voice singing "Lonely I do watch the night". The music is marvellously coloured with the glory of the summer night and with the lovers' immortal longings and their tragically encompassed mortality. The heart that is not melted to pity in this scene is made of stone. And yet it is this scene which has been called "erotic".

The music-drama treats of love not only in the ordinary sexual aspect. Nobody apparently had noticed this fact before amongst Wagner's critics; yet there it is for anybody with sensibilities to find out for themselves. In Act 1 we have the awakening of love between the ill-

103

starred princess and her knight. Then in Act 2 we look upon love glorified, content to count the world well lost. And in Act 3, when Tristan lies on his deathbed, we see maternal love as poignantly expressed as ever it has been in all art; Isolde nurses the broken Tristan and as she leans over him and tenderly ejaculates "Die Wunde!" she is not only the beloved but all womanhood and healing pity.

So much for the "illicit passion" of Tristan and Isolde. There is also the generous love of Brangäne for Isolde, a symbol of sister-love. And there is, greatest of all, the love of Kurwenal for Tristan, the devotion of man to master; Kurwenal follows and serves Tristan through a tragedy he cannot comprehend, but he knows he must give him his care, and he is like a great gruff watchdog, loving because that is his job. The music-drama, so far from exhibiting just one aspect of physical passion, ennobles all manner of love. And everything is rendered poetic because it is set against the background of the inimical world – the world that cannot afford to lend itself entirely to obsessions, since it can continue its work only by not giving itself entirely to any one thing and by a certain ruthlessness.

Among the great themes of the score is the "Day" motif; it stands for the enemy of all things beautiful; for beauty lives by excess; and the world will have none of it. One of the overwhelming moments of the score is in Act 2, when Isolde gives the sign to Tristan, who waits outside the garden. She tells Brangäne to put out the torch: "Quench thou its warning glare; let my beloved come." And Brangäne says, "O leave the warning beacon; let it now show thee thy danger." (Brängane knows that peril is afoot for the two lovers.) But Isolde herself seizes the torch and, singing out her soul in the most gorgeously proud and reckless music ever composed (we have to go to the Shakespeare of "Antony and Cleopatra" to get the equal of it), she declares: "The torch! – though light of my life it were, laughing I quench it." And she casts the burning brand to the earth, where it dies out, and as she does so the orchestra announces the sinister "Day" motif, and then the whole of the music incredibly sizzles and smoulders to extinction.

Wagner was painter, poet, and musician, all one and indivisible in his aesthetic psychology and perception. He does not attempt literal musical description; he is not, like Strauss, an externalist. When he creates a scene it is in this world and yet also in the deeper world of the heart of his men and women. "Tristan" begins with the sea surging through the score; the waves of it are also the waves of Isolde's torment as the ship carries her to King Marke. In Act 2, when we are in Isolde's garden at night and we hear the hunting horns in the distance and the whispering leaves and the mysterious murmurings everywhere, and the acute sense of things tense and expectant – all these external traits of expression, true though they are as tone painting, also tell us of the suspense and turmoil and hope and fear in the hearts of the lovers as they wait for the sign to come together. So in Act 3; the scene once again is changed utterly; but at a single stroke in the orchestra Wagner tells us where we are: the waves beat at the base of the cliffs; the sea is vacant; the orchestra *shows* us Kurwenal looking over the sea, sadly finding no trace of the ship that brings Isolde to the dying Tristan. Rising thirds in the violins tell us all; the music conveys simultaneously a gesture and a psychological interpretation.

Of the score as sheer music, living in its own organization, independent of words (which merely served as Wagner's scaffolding), it is not possible to write in detail. The score grows out of basic themes, like a universe unfolding by the inevitable law of growth. And the end crowns all; Isolde's death-song burns away like the funeral pyre of the whole world. Heart-wounding is the close of Act 3. Tristan is dead and King Marke sings his wonderful song of forgiveness. But when he is finished we can see that Isolde has not heard a word. Her life is with Tristan's. The orchestra sounds the "Union in Death" motif, and Isolde sings "Mild und leise wie er lächelt"; "Look, my friends," she says, "how gleams his glory." And on the word "friends" Wagner makes a tender little grace-note that pierces compassion through and through. Then the music seems to fill all space with its flamelike adoration; and the end comes with Isolde's ascent to a sustained F-sharp, as she sings of the vast wave of the world which envelops all – to sink and find eternal engulfment. As the curtain falls we hear the same motif which begins the work; the wheel has come full circle; it is like dust to dust.

After Wagner finished the tragedy of "Tristan and Isolde" he wrote "The Mastersingers". The one work glorifies night and death and frustrated young love and poetic pain; the other glorifies life and the simple tasks of the day, and the pride of youth and the dignity of resigned old age. If no other works of art existed save these two, we should be able to show to the gods a fair justification of man's lot and strivings on the face of the earth.

Furtwängler at Covent Garden

"TRISTAN AND ISOLDE"

22nd May 1935

In a way we have to thank Sir Thomas Beecham for an experience of rare poetic beauty at Covent Garden last night, for it is not every conductor who is at any time prepared to vacate the desk and allow an opportunity to a distinguished colleague in opera in which he himself has been heard only an evening or two before. There is no call for comparisons between the two artists' interpretations of the greatest of all music-dramas. There is one glory of the sun and another of the moon. Beecham gives us lyrical splendour and an excitement of rhythm that brings the tragedy actively in front of us. Furtwängler feels the sadness of it all reflectively; he strikes a graver note; he touches everything with the "pathos of distance". His "Tristan and Isolde" belongs to romance and the night. He approaches Wagner through the text and the poetry; and that is the way Wagner composed the music. Sir Thomas is interested mainly in the score as a gorgeous medium for so much sumptuous instrumental playing and fascinating conducting; in Furtwängler's conception the orchestra is an eloquent commentary, or Greek chorus, a miraculous and beautiful part in a larger whole. He never permits the singing to be overwhelmed by instrumental tone; the stage action and the orchestral playing are in his control sensitively and subtly related. He has a genius for mingled quietness, roundness, and intensity. With Furtwängler tragedy is an internal idea, a spiritual experience, not a disturbance or upheaval of physical forces. Pulsation and not emphasis is the mark of his art; I have never heard the scene of the meeting of the lovers in Act 2 done with Furtwängler's proportionate power; we could hear every note and cry of the singers, yet the urge of the orchestral crescendo was grand and reckless, giving us a glorious sense of the primrose path to the everlasting bonfire. The effect was achieved by passionate rhythmical stress and concentration – not by noise.

Furtwängler presents a comprehensive "Tristan and Isolde". He reveals not only the fate-ridden ecstasy of the lovers; he does grave and dignified justice to King Marke; the treatment of his music was moving indeed because of the unforced pathos, the noble tempo with its suggestions of manliness controlling the broken heart. Also Furtwängler draws the humanity out of Kurwenal's devotion; it is no accident that at this performance Kipnis as Marke was magnificent, and that Janssen actually struck a deeper note than in his other presentations of the part of Kurwenal. All the singers, indeed, seemed to enjoy an ease which seldom is to be felt in their work at Covent Garden; the unity of the performance was most satisfying, broken only by some scenery in Act 2 which vividly made me think that we were in Kensington Gardens not far from the Albert Memorial.

If we must stress the point of difference between Sir Thomas Beecham's and Herr Furtwängler's conceptions – and no matter how we seek to avoid comparisons the imp of sport will steal capriciously in – we might leave it at this: Sir Thomas loves the score of "Tristan" as a conductor's and a born lyrical musician's happy hunting ground, but does not love the music of Wagner itself, has no interest in the poetry behind it and might indeed deny that it is poetry at all; but Furtwängler loves "Tristan" for its own sake as a music-drama and finds in it something that calls to his own emotional nature and poetic idea of life. Not for Furtwängler the common notion of Wagner the rhetorician. I am ready to read the criticism of Furtwängler's performance that it was emasculate or over-refined in tone, that he dallied too long over a phrase and thinned out the texture in consequence. Admittedly the texture did lack richness in places; but the climax from "Die im Busen mir die Glutenmacht" to "Meines Lebens Licht" will not be forgotten by some of us for years to come. The proud, reckless catch in the voice of Leider as she uttered the words "Lebens Licht" was beauty mocking life and death, kings and brothers, at the same time.

We could realize that we were about to go through a "Tristan" of uncommon romance and pathos as soon as Furtwängler began the prelude to the work at a daringly slow tempo and with some equally daring pauses. The inevitable arch of the performance did not reveal itself all at once, and, of course, it would have been no great arch had it done so. Furtwängler seemed to be able to attend to the fine art in

Wagner without endangering the imaginative conception in its vast bulk. He revealed to us lovely inner parts of the score, parts which often get scant attention in performances that are dynamic rather than thoughtful. But at the evening's end the noble stature of the work had emerged with an impressive inevitability. The astonishing fact is that Furtwängler was able to get his conception expressed by a strange orchestra after inadequate time for rehearsal – with an orchestra, too, that has played "Tristan" under no conductor but Sir Thomas, who is by training and temperament at the extreme from Furtwängler. No wonder there were moments of hesitation now and again; but these moments were few. The orchestra's adaptability was wonderful and it deserves the highest praise. Furtwängler warmly congratulated the players at the close of a memorable night. The orchestra voted him a master and applauded him with pride and enthusiasm.

Of Tristan and Isolde

31st January 1953

The current performances in this country of "Tristan and Isolde" can give little idea of the impact made by the music-drama on those of us who were young many years ago. "Tristan and Isolde" is now taken for granted as part of a repertory: conductors, singers, and orchestral players tackle it in their day-by-day stride. Even the skill and intensity of Sir John Barbirolli will not produce the right tone, especially the right fundamental tone in an orchestra at all fastidious and routined. And without fundamental tone "Tristan" is as the sea without surge or the night without darkness. So unaware is the contemporary generation of the significance of "Tristan" that a distinguished representative of it expressed to me at Covent Garden the other night his satisfaction at hearing the score sounding like extended chamber music. At all times this marvellous music must be stylishly and beautifully played and sung, but the texture and colour should not suggest satin and Des Grieux and Manon. "In the folds of the dark banner that casts its shadow over 'Tristan'," wrote Wagner to Liszt, "I shall enshroud myself." Wagner could never have understood the persistence in these present times of the notion of music as part of social service and amenity, or as a background or accompaniment to everyday "culture" and leisured enjoyment: least of all as an acoustical phenomenon to be contemplated as "pattern", much as Mr Micawber contemplated the nail on the wall. Music for Wagner was a means of subjective expression in symbols; in fact the stuff of music was for him the stuff of his consciousness. Music shaped his experience. His genius did not follow the ploughed field of his life as man of "sensual supersensual desire"; it was not entirely out of passion for Mathilde Wesendonck that "Tristan" came into being. The metabolism of the artist needing to create "Tristan" urged the man Wagner to seek the living symbol and shape of romantic and renounced love. His luck was always with him in the end; Mathilde was the perfect notional catharsis in the "Tristan" tragedy of his imagination. Cosima provided the bridge-passage to the autumnal surrender of "Parsifal". After he had been through the fire of "Tristan" Wagner became born afresh, purged of human – all-too-human – ecstasy and sense of life-and-love's death and transfiguration. He could now get back to the abstractions and bourgeois mythology and ethic of the "Ring"; he could modulate from the restless unfulfilled chromaticism of "Tristan" to the assured diatonic geniality of "Meistersinger". Those of us who first heard "Tristan" with young ears also shed skins in other ways and emerged from the immolation with different experiencing senses. We had been acquainted, some say for better, some say for worse, with a work which gave us knowledge musically of good and evil. I say that it was inspired by each of these and transcended both.

When Wagner interrupted work on "The Ring" for seven years, it was not only because he was disheartened by the practical obstacles between him and realization in the theatre of his vast conceptions and reforms. So far his music had fed on gods and giants and dwarfs and other strange wild-fowl, had plumbed the waters of earth and under the earth had given a tongue to the elements, all put before us dramatically, representative themes leading imagination's vision outward. The erotic impulse in Wagner needed liberation before he could achieve consummation as man and artist. With the advent of Mathilde Wesendonck and the crashing-in of the "Day" (or Minna) motif, the influence of Schopenhauer stole into Wagner's consciousness like the stain of chromaticism which was falling over all his music for the first time. It is easy and dangerous for criticism to relate effect to cause in the processes of a genius as mixed in his elements as Wagner; but there is a protest recorded by Wagner himself against autobiographical interpretation.

"How deeply in love he must have been when he wrote 'Tristan'," so Wagner quotes a saying he has heard, adding: "People do not understand how apart from all experience, all actuality, these things occur. I felt a longing beyond bounds to revel in music, to pour myself out in music as if I were writing a symphony."

Music, as much as experience external and physical, led him to the "Tristan" theme, a drama beyond time and place, beyond phenomenal appearance, a drama of no or little visible action. Music for him needed no longer to seek connections by compromise with a world outside itself; and the music of "Tristan" unfolds from the erotic coil subtly and as though endlessly. In the cauldron of the orchestra a chemistry of tone distils all to essence; all except a few traces of sediment here and there. It is, in Wagner's own phrase, "art of transition". It is more than that: it is transfiguration. The ecstasies of the lovers are but as gleams thrown for a moment over the purple night of a will-less, selfless music. The stage pictures in "Tristan", the visible protagonists, the words, words, words, should accompany the music.

We are forgetting the secret of the interpretation of "Tristan", in this country at any rate. We are obliging the music to wait on the singers and subduing its powers to a visual transitoriness. Sight and sound are one and indivisible in the dimension where dwells this music. Kurwenal looks over the vacant sea for a sign of Isolde's ship; the rising string harmonies wander farther than mortal weary eyesight can go, and they imaginatively find the horizon and mingle with it. When Melot exposes the lovers in the garden the "Day" motif, transformed on the horn, comes through the dawning sky like a bodeful light. The motifs in "Tristan" are not pictorially static, and they do not refer to things or characters. The "Death" motif for example, is not as the "Contract" motif of Wotan: it does not identify, does not denote a relationship correspondence. It is itself a presence; we are indeed by the poetic context made to feel death's presence itself entering the imagination symbolically and hauntingly. The music in "Tristan" has time to expand and work spells of orchestral hypnotism. But too much is made of the sorcerer's gestures; the fundamental brainwork behind it all is stupendous. The musical spectrum is dissolved. Chromaticism liquefies harmony, defying resolution until suspense is felt as a manifestation of the music-drama's innermost ache. And through all the fever and ebb and flow of passion and conception the calm mind of the artist craftsman and artificer of the orchestra works with the most calculating touch, so that every semiquaver is a stitch in time in the gorgeous texture. To present "Tristan" without a great orchestra is almost as though "Antony and Cleopatra" were put on the stage in dumb-show.

Wieland Wagner

30th July 1964

With a mixture of curiosity and embarrassment I met Wieland Wagner on Sunday for the first time. His grandfather had not suffered music critics gladly, and I had no reason to think that Wieland would have more charitable feelings towards a representative of Hanslick's tribe. The fact is that Wieland received me with a quite disarming courtesy.

He resembles Richard in features, distantly maybe, but there is no mistaking the nose and the mouth, although there is no hint of obstinacy or truculence in mouth or chin. For this meeting I had recollected George Moore's description of Siegfried Wagner, son of Richard, as seen walking the streets of Bayreuth years ago – "How like the Meister, yet how unlike. The same head, nose, chin. Alike, yet not like – a sort of deserted shrine."

Siegfried was unwise enough to compose a music-drama, thus tempting invidious comparisons. Wieland, working in another direction running parallel, has won renown, not to say notoriety, in his own right as a producer and visual interpreter of Wagner. There is nothing negative about Wieland, for all his quietness of manner. I resisted an impulse to begin our conversation by asking him if he could remember the exact date when he became an anti-Wagnerian. I compromised, content with: "How did you first get the general idea or starting point of your productions? Did you react against traditional picture-frame tableaux?" His reply, simple and unhesitating, was this: "I didn't react at all against tradition. I ignored it. I found all my ideas in the scores of Wagner. There is nothing in my productions which is not suggested and justified by the music." I hadn't the heart to ask why, then, had Wagner himself not discovered these ideas, or in his precise stage-directions hadn't indicated that he didn't want any suggestion of a ship at all on the stage of Act I of "Tristan"; and had he not in his music alone vividly told us that Hans Sachs did not begin the Flieder-monolog staring at the audience – and so on.

Such questions stuck in my throat, so courteous was he, so sympathetic. He readily admitted that he has never yet been satisfied by any of his own stage settings for Wagner. He disdains the uncritical approval of audiences. He was more critical than myself of Wagner's music-dramas. "'Die Meistersinger'," he maintained, "really ends with the Quintet. The rest, nearly the whole Act 3 is pantomime, merely a pretty picture." He smiled tolerantly when I asked him what would have happened to a music critic had he said as much as that in the hearing of Villa Wahnfried in the period of Richard or Cosima. Only "Tristan" of all his grandfather's output did he think was unified as music-drama, adding: "There are many imperfections in the 'Ring'."

Many of us would go a long way with Wieland Wagner, or anybody else, in an effort to recreate the Wagner *mise-en-scène* imaginatively and in terms of the latest techniques of stage production. Most of us have long since tired of the old cardboard rocks and canvas woods older than the prima donna who sits among them or the tenor who goes bird-watching in them. As far back as October 1889, Bernard Shaw made fun of the Bayreuth Wagner productions, adding that "every fresh representation should be an original artistic creation, not an imitation of the last one." But originality isn't achieved simply by turning existing or long-established order and ideas upside down. One of the great strengths of dramatic irony in all Wagner occurs towards the end of Act I of "Tristan und Isolde". The lovers are in thrall, the love potion has been drunk. The ship is about to touch port; King Marke is about to come on board. We hear the sudden, marvellous, quickening of the orchestra's tempo; we hear the sailors singing hail as they are at work getting the ship ashore, oblivious of the tragic happenings on Isolde's deck.

In Wieland Wagner's production the love potion is drunk with sailors more or less visibly present. A small, male voice choir, presumably of the Able Bodied Seamen's Union, actually stand stock-still singing the hail with Tristan, Isolde, and Brangäne wringing their hands under their very noses. There is of course no evidence that the tragedy is taking place on a ship. None of the Wieland Wagner settings is geographically or topographically relevant.

The scene and atmosphere of the first act of "Tristan und Isolde" could serve equally well for the first act of "Parsifal"; the setting for the second act of "Parsifal" (Klingsor's garden) and the one for the second

act of "Tristan und Isolde" (Isolde's garden) could be swapped about
and none of us a penny the wiser. A more serious frustration of our
imaginative responses is the static attitudes which Wieland forces the
characters to take, usually a distance apart. In fact, none of the people in
Wieland Wagner's worlds of "Tristan und Isolde", "Parsifal", even
"Die Meistersinger" seem really to be on speaking terms. Kundry
hardly ever comes into personal contact with Parsifal. She is enclosed,
the upper part of her spotlighted, on a middle height. Parsifal stands
below not facing her but facing us – the audience. And Kundry sings
the "Herzeleide" as though giving a vocal recital. I could continue this
catalogue of incongruities ad nauseam. No known logic could be used
convincingly to justify them. Maybe the production of "Parsifal" is the
best of all. In a more or less metaphysical or shadowy universe, scenic
abstractions needn't be particular about relevance to time or space. The
Grail scene was truly impressive, the knights seated at a wide circling
table in semi-darkness, and Amfortas above, framed in a sort of
sacrificial light and colour, the Grail cup theatrically red and glowing.
The sad fact is that the more intensely symbolic this scene is made the
more distasteful it seems, the music also!

An alarming consequence of Wieland's undramatic attitudinizing of
the characters is that as we are starved of interesting action on the stage
we are obliged, more than ever before in Wagner, to concentrate on the
music. Frankly – and I have never thought I would live to say it – the
music doesn't continuously survive, as music, this absolute test.
Wagner believed he was fertilizing drama with music.

As frequently the music is fertilized by what imaginatively we see on
the stage of his works. I am not a "square", insisting on the traditional
obvious correspondence between stage gesture and music in Wagner.
But there is a loss, visually, musically and imaginatively all round, if we
don't see Isolde's scarf waving at the orchestra's wonderful prompting.
It is possible that Wieland will in time himself come to see where in his
often talented conceptions he has too much allowed the "modern
producer" in him to take the rein. He should remember that for all his
grandfather's metaphysical and symbolistic tendencies, he was essentially a man of the theatre, vividly and potently so.

For the performance of "Parsifal" old Knappertsbusch took up the
conductor's baton without asking for a fee, just for the honour of
making yet another of his contributions to Bayreuth. He is still, all in
all, the most authoritative of living Wagner conductors. The singing in
general was only so-so; but Jon Vickers as Parsifal reminded us of what

a Wagner tenor should sound like. He is not perhaps in command of the naïve vocal inflections called for by the part; but surely he is the great Siegfried of tomorrow or the day after.

Hans Hotter was Gurnemanz giving to his spate of words a quite noble garrulity. But the orchestra is really the thing at Bayreuth – and the theatre's unique acoustic. Here are we, in an age of ubiquitous science, spending fortunes on concert halls in which music is made to sound as though produced from deep-freezes. Wagner, without the guidance of our modern notions, contrived an opera house possessing the power to change all sound to music, even at times persuading us that the Bayreuth bark is musical.

After my labours in Bayreuth I have come to Munich. Sorely in need of relaxation I went to a Beethoven recital announced by billposters everywhere in this beautiful city, billposters pasted on new buildings, on buildings a hundred years old, and on buildings now in the processes of construction. Every time I have visited Munich posters have advertised ubiquitously a piano recital by the same local professor. I decided to sample his playing in a hall crowded mainly by students. The professor came to the platform attired in a white evening coat and bow tie. The posters had told us he would play the four best-loved Beethoven sonatas, and he began with the "Pathetique". Only in Germany has such a way of playing the piano been preserved. The manner was apocalyptic, hands held aloft to begin with, then left hand went its way regally independent of the doings of the right, a left hand endowed so much with free-will that it could, at the right moment, disengage itself from the keyboard and Beethoven, to remove perspiration from the professor's brow and straighten his hair. The audience listened in solemn rapt silence – which was significant of much in the educational part of Munich's musical culture.

Nothing in my busman's holiday these last days has given me a more memorable musico-dramatic experience than Inge Borkh singing and acting as the Frau in Strauss's "Die Frau ohne Schatten", heard in the new and fabulously handsome Munich State Opera. She was truly superb, actually making the difficult parts sympathetic and young enough. At yet another hearing of this opera, still to be produced in London, I am more than ever convinced that for all its recurrent post-Wagner excesses, it contains some of the most original and imaginatively moving music in all the Strauss output.

DIE MEISTERSINGER

> "In a great comedy the creative energy must send out its rays left
> and right, giving or liberating life everywhere. Everything must
> happen to everyone taking part, not only in the protagonists of
> the main theme.
>
> In every nook and cranny of Wagner's Nürnberg vitality
> shines like the sun, enduing everyone with life, pride of
> movement, contagious humanity."

The British National Opera Company

"THE MASTERSINGERS" IN MANCHESTER

6th March 1928

Tonight we are to hear the only performance during the British
National Opera Company's season of "The Mastersingers" and if we are
wise the theatre will be crowded. A great audience is essential to a
presentation of the work for it is the most democratic of operas in its
embracing humanity, its kindliness towards all sorts and conditions of
men. Such a work as this is very welcome at the present time, when art
tends more and more to grow dry and inhumane because of a critical
exclusiveness. The performances (as Dr Johnson would call them) of
our Sitwells, our Schoenbergs, even our Wellses and Dreisers, may be
chock-full of high skill and inspiration, but even the admirers of a
certain school of modern literature, poetry, and music do not claim that
it is exactly juicy and so comprehensive in fellow feeling that one touch
of it will make the whole world kin. "The Mastersingers" lives in a

humour so broad that it may be called as sublime as the sublimest note of tragedy struck by a "King Lear" or an "Oedipus".

How spacious is the world of "The Mastersingers"; how godlike is Wagner's understanding of the meanest of his creatures! Hans Sachs is the dominant character of the work, of course, but he dominates only as the sun dominates on a summer day – giving life and sweetness to all that comes under the warm light of his nature. The artist's selectiveness never, in "The Mastersingers", leads Wagner into the exclusive attitude; his humour has in all the arts no equal outside the pages of Shakespeare and Cervantes; it is a humour that does not depend on the chastening of fools or on the pointing out of incongruities. Rather does it enter genially into the mind like a benign solvent, melting the hardest animosities there. Beckmesser is not maliciously treated in the music, and the commentary of Sachs on the midsummer madness that comes over the world from time to time – it is a wise sad commentary which ultimately reconciles man to man.

Like every great work of art "The Mastersingers" is a world in itself. The energy that gives life to it blesses the biggest and smallest of its people. It has been said of Balzac that even his scullions possessed genius; we may say the same of the scullions, the small fry, of "The Mastersingers". Wagner's art, like Nature, dignifies with independent vitality all that it calls into being. Nature does not take more pride in the making of her kings than in the making of her clowns. And in "The Mastersingers" the night watchman who comes before us only for a few moments is given by Wagner, out of a vast store of immortal substance, an immortal blood and humour. The universe of the opera is alive in every hole and corner; David does not less proudly announce the sweetness of life than Walther; the apprentices are as triumphant in the eyes of God as the mastersingers. Jack is indeed as good as his master, when Wagner's reconciling art has finished with them.

The opera is the most superb glorification of song that we can find in all music. Who is the hero in this immense world of divinely humorous beings? Is it Sachs or Walther? Let us say rather that the Preislied is the hero! If so multitudinous a work as "The Mastersingers" may be narrowed down at all to any one pivotal spot, then we must agree that it lives, moves, and has its being around the Preislied. Consider the audacity of Wagner. In effect he says to us: "See! I will make for you a masterpiece the main point of which rests upon the creation of a melody so beautiful, so unlike any other melody in its freedom, that I will be able to use it as a deus ex machina, and by its means make sport of the folly that lies in pedantry and all the hardened schools of art." Wagner must have known, when the conception of "The Mastersingers" first stole into his mind, that it involved the writing of a *mastersong*; unless he could rise to a tune which filled the heart at once and, because of its free improvisatory beauty, seemed born of the woods and meadows – without this tune the opera would not have been written. Wagner never did doubt his genius! In one of his letters he writes to a friend that he has almost finished the "Ring" – the libretto is completed he says – only the music remains to be composed now! *Only* the music! The man's faith in himself takes the breath away. So with this Preislied; when the time arrives for its introduction in the work, at the crisis of the narrative – well, Wagner is ready, and the melody comes forth as easefully as a bird's. We do not forget, in writing down all this, that people here and there have been known to find the Preislied commonplace. But that merely shows the inability even of genius to please everybody. Our present discussion of the tune is simply to lay stress on Wagner's sublime audacity; he tackled a theme which could not have led anywhere unless a magnificent glorification of song was achieved in the end, if not to the satisfaction of everybody, at any rate to that of most folk, Beckmesser included.

Of the more familiar marvels of "The Mastersingers" score one need say nothing at this time of day. Where in all music will you discover a more effortless and yet a more manifold and *golden* polyphony? Where else is there a score with the twofold aesthetic value of "The Mastersingers"? – it is at one and the same time, beautiful music and sheer human nature. Music today is in some quarters supposed to have escaped from the "bondage" of nineteenth-century romanticism and from the idioms and forms invented to contain the romanticism. Well, for "free" music, where is to be found anything less burdened by law or tradition than (for example) the first monologue of Hans Sachs? This music is as free as Sachs's own thought; it moves according to no sequence of music known in the art before or since Wagner. It paints for us the scene, lets us feel the quietness of the summer night in old Nuremberg. Yet, also, the music simultaneously gives us Sachs's meditations; Walther's song steals into his mind again and again and will not be dismissed. Nobly and tenderly this music turns upon itself and goes into solitude. Then at the end, by means of transitions of key each of which is a stroke of genius and nothing less, the monologue comes back to earth and attains a happy faith in man's daily and common labour. Again, at the opera's climax, how sweet is the note of sadness that comes suddenly, at the end of the paean of praise to Sachs, when the grave renunciation theme sounds in the orchestra, reminding us of Sachs's lonely lot and yet, as the theme closes in a new cadence, tells of a ripe, manly philosophy. For the like of this healing "Mastersingers" music we must go to Shakespeare. Here is "a chronicle of day by day"; with Prospero, Wagner has given us "a third of his own life". If Manchester is sensible there will not be many empty seats in the Opera House tonight.

The British National Opera Company

"THE MASTERSINGERS"

7th March 1928

Like the River Pegnitz, which flows through Nuremberg, Wagner's great orchestra flows through "The Mastersingers", giving refreshment to the dry places of the text, which in the English translation used last evening is not always a source of sweetness and light. Not for the mere sake of size does Wagner here ask for a multitudinous orchestra; there is not a particle of tone wasted as he marshals his instrumental forces. Even the hurly-burly of the street fight can be made musical, granted the right conductor and band – as anybody will admit who has heard "The Mastersingers" played by (for example) the State Opera Orchestra of Vienna. Because the canvas of "The Mastersingers" is immense, so had Wagner's orchestra to be immense – it provokes the sense of a natural amplitude, of a laughter broad as ten thousand beeves at pasture. You cannot very well – if you happen to be a Wagner – sing to the glory of song, and to man's simple love of his kind, on a penny whistle. Wagner's orchestra is never larger than the man himself and how tenderly he relaxes at times from his strength and bigness, and creates for us beauty in miniature. The apprentice scene, the episodes between David and Magdalene, the exquisite night piece where the Watchman ambles through Nuremberg's old alleys, the tender scene where David sings his song to Sachs, and is overwhelmed when he realizes that the Day of St John is also his master's name-day – and offers him a sausage; all these are touches of the miniature done by

Wagner in the vast stride of the work; for a while he turns his back on the opera's main burden, fondles a conceit, a gentle sentiment, and then with all the ease in the world, strides up to the heights of the sun again.

For the want of a full orchestra last night's performance was unable to do more than suggest the greatness of the work. And for so long as we put up with the precarious conditions of present-day opera we must not hope to hear anything like the orchestra of Wagner in the theatre – which is its proper place. The orchestra worked nobly last night, and in the end actually achieved the illusion of the superb girth of the music. Mr Barbirolli dominated his band; he was not content to be a merely helpful conductor. Sometimes he drove hard, especially in the first act, where the tangled argumentation is better treated with a yielding rhythm. Mr Barbirolli is perhaps too particular in his control of musical energy for the mellow humours of "The Mastersingers". He made the work dramatic in an occasional way, and, of course, it is epic, with an untroubled gait and the largest magnanimity. The playing lacked the deeper, richer colours, but, all in all, the orchestral side of the performance was as good as it had the chance to be.

"Die Meistersinger" at Salzburg

TOSCANINI IN CONTROL

28th August 1936

Salzburg remains Salzburg, in spite of the strange doings of wealthy visitors from England and the United States, who buy the "native costume" and climb the mountains in handsome, expensive cars. There is no truth in the published reports that the festival has suffered a decline. Probably Toscanini brings a discipline that is not in character with the genial and comfortable spirit of the place, but it is nonsense to suggest Salzburg has deteriorated as a festival of music and opera. I have been present during the last few evenings at performances which for beauty of conception and finish of technique could not easily be excelled in the world, performances which for the moment seem to put most efforts in England at opera on the plane of the hopefully amateur.

The ideals set up by Toscanini are so high that only a genius such as his own could reach out to them – with rich resources of execution at his disposal. Under Toscanini the Vienna Philharmonic Orchestra has recaptured the old assured touch, without loss of bloom and brilliance. A few years ago the playing was capricious, superb one day and lazy the next. And the ability to obtain a pianissimo was temporarily lost. Toscanini has made the Orchestra afresh; it needed his ruthlessness, his simple passion for thoroughness, his simple faith in hard conscientious work. The chances are that Toscanini would listen with some impatience to the critic who spoke to him in terms of subtle personal musical insight, psychological penetration, and all the rest of it. "I study the score" is Toscanini's unspoken credo, "and try to get the players to reproduce it as written." What Toscanini brings to a work is the rarest of gifts – pure musical understanding and feeling. These attributes – and his long experience – are enough to account for him, as far as genius can be accounted for at all.

His performance of "Meistersinger" will remain in the mind for a lifetime, because of its beauty and dignity of proportion. The curve of the work was vast, yet none of the contained and varied energy, the multitudinous detail, was missed. The whole opera came to abounding life, until we forgot the illusion of art and entered the comprehensive and golden world of the work. Not all at once did we find this world easeful and sunny; Toscanini gave to the first act a certain rigidity; the mastersingers were made to toe a strict line, and David in his explanations to Walther was allowed no time for a boyish appreciation of his own momentary authority over the knight and the scene. For a while I chafed under Toscanini's Latin clarity; I wanted the humour that expands and releases, not the wit that contracts and braces up. Probably the interpretation never did find the girth of a Richter's humour, that large mildness of laughter which has no use for the crack of the whip of an epigram.

But before Toscanini had finished with Act II the miracle of re-creation was complete. It would be impossible in words to convey the summer magic which fell over the Nürnberg scene; the tenderness of Sachs's first monologue; the steady burgeoning of beauty in the Sachs and Eva scene, "Gut'n Abend, Meister"; the vividness of the orchestra in the cobbling song; the unbelievable control of the crescendo of the fight in the street, with the dominant musical motif in charge of all, the whole texture indeed clear and musical for the first time in living memory. Then the decrescendo, the watchman's horn and call, and the lovely modulation to the lyrical, the peaceful, and the miniature. The performance's shape and life-giving forms were never forced before us after Act I. To the end – where the banner of song was opened with a width and nobility that caused happiness and sadness, laughter and tears, to express one and the same pride in life – Toscanini held us like children listening to a tale told in the chimney-corner, lit by the glow of olden times.

On Salzburg's small stage clever ingenuities of grouping and production are done. The scene in Act II showed us Nürnberg's straggling alleys and streets, and the gabled houses talking to one another; the characters came down the steps from a height which created perspective. In the mêlée the action seemed to have a more varied life than usually is seen in the same climax on stages much bigger; the details were vivid – a sort of medieval Rowlandson was suggested. Then the prelude to Act III: it moved slowly, laden with a sadness which ennobled but did not weigh down. The performances made foolishness of the current chatter about Wagner, the theatre charlatan; the man who wrote this prelude was one of the three gods of music. And after the prelude, the running waves of song to the finale – Eva's heart-wounding cry of adoration to Sachs; the reconciliation of all things gay and sad in the quintet; the colour and Shakespearean love of all sorts and conditions of humanity in the beginning of the meadow scene; the swelling heart of the music in the homage to Sachs – all was brought to a high noon of love of life.

We left the Festspielhaus profoundly grateful to have been present. Old-stagers who for a lifetime have visited Bayreuth were glad to say they had never before heard a "Meistersinger" so beautiful in the whole. A man might be born many times, and in his journey through the world miss Toscanini's interpretation of the wisest and biggest of comedies in music; it was a privilege to hear it. Individual parts could probably have been better done here and there. Toscanini it was who achieved the ensemble. Lehmann's voice and appearance are too much related now to the Marschallin; she sang with much tenderness as Eva, but we needed some innocence in the voice, not experience. Nissen's Sachs was admirable, and the Walther of Kullmann was vocally the best I have heard: he looked young too. It was good to hear the Trial Songs sung, not as though Walther were afraid of Beckmesser, but challenging in his pride and ardour all the Beckmessers and mastersingers of the world. This was one of the evening's towering moments.

Karl Boehm and the Dresden Opera

8th May 1939

From HMV comes a set of records giving Act 3 of "Die Meistersinger". They come at a time which lends to the music a new, sad, and ironical significance. Nuremberg under Sachs, or not under but *with* Sachs – and the Guilds; Hitler might surely have chosen another place for his circuses. Then, when the curtain rises on Act 3 and after the enchanting scene between Sachs and David, we hear Sachs's monologue, "Wahn! Uberall Wahn!" – "Madness and craze everywhere!" His perplexed query: "God knows how it all befell!" – To hear these accents today is to feel more than ever the wise beauty of the music, and to feel more than ever the tangled mess of life. If *all* our statesmen in all countries would listen to the voice of Hans Sachs, listen to it with faith, understanding, and tolerance, a way could be found out, surely, from our present blindnesses. I commend the idea especially to Herr Hitler, who regards Wagner as his favourite composer.

It is good also to have these "Meistersinger" records at the present time, done by artists from the Dresden Opera, because there is a tendency in this country to make too much of the "superman" strain in Wagner and to forget that he could condescend and melt into poignant enough humanity. The patriotism in "Meistersinger" is broad-chested, no doubt, and can easily be superficially associated with the worst sort, the most swollen sort. But the note of philosophy is constantly sounded; even at the height of the tribute to Sachs we hear the lonely cadence of the resignation motif. There is unfortunately one moment in the performance of these records when we are allowed to suspect that Wagner's love of Germany has been confused with the contemporary phobia. Sachs, at the beginning of the closing scene, ignores Wagner's instructions to sing in a voice "tremulous with emotion" and lets out an aggressive blast, as though into the propagandist microphones. On the whole, though, Hermann Nissen sings the music of Sachs with manliness and insight and lacks only a little of geniality. An occasional rasping accent may have been caused by the reproduction machines.

The records are vivid and full of colour especially in the orchestral and choral sections, under Karl Boehm. Recurrent infelicities of detail do not matter here – as they would matter in a Mozart opera. The great thing is that we are granted the superb surge of the score. I can never hear without emotion the entry of the chorus into the singing of the "Prize Song" at the glowing sequential climax and then the cry of Eva, with the fluttering appoggiatura which tells of her heart's state. The Eva in this performance is Margarete Teschemacher, and, though she sings beautifully, at times she becomes something of a shrew in loud passages. She fails to hit every note with the ease that is essential to the lyrical nature of the part. Walther is more the knight than the poet; Torsten Ralf, the singer, scarcely learned his art from nature. Still, he does nothing that is upsetting, and certainly does not let down the performance as a whole. The finest vocal actor of the cast is Eugen Fuchs. His Beckmesser is authentic. He does not make a caricature of the part. After all, Becknesser was the Marker and could not have achieved so responsible a distinction had he been a fool. Wagner set out to lampoon Hanslick in the part; but the artist in him stifled malice. Beckmesser emerges in the music as a tragi-comedian, and Fuchs brings to his interpretation his own queer pathos and a rather moving kind of defensive dignity. We are enabled to see Beckmesser's point of view in the scene where he enters Sachs's workshop; here Fuchs magnificently expresses the struggle going on in the man's mind; the physical and mental stabs and bruises; the skein of his fears, suspicions, hatred of Walther, craving for Eva's love and the Master's goodwill; his self-pity and consciousness that he is not without pride – all these elements are balanced in a finely conceived piece of histrionic vocalism – song-speech perfectly realized. After this admirable album of Act 3, appetite is whetted for a completion of this recording of "Meistersinger". HMV must go forward and finish a job begun so handsomely.

PARSIFAL

"All his life Wagner had echoed the cry of Faust – 'Entsagung' – renouncement; renouncement, that is, on the part of others, for the benefit of Wagner. But now, for the purposes of "Parsifal", he throws over Siegfried, image of the Superman, and thus sickens Nietzsche. And in Siegfried's place he puts Parsifal, symbol of pity. Siegfried forges 'Nothung'. Parsifal breaks his bow because his arrow has shot a swan. Yet Nietzsche became hypnotized by Wagner's music. Its slow-moving monotony fixes like the eye of the Ancient Mariner."

"Parsifal" in Manchester

22nd February 1927

Though "Parsifal" did not attract its customary big audience last night, a fine performance was attended to in a silence which seemed to prove that the charm of the work is still potent. There was much beautiful playing in the orchestra, and Mr Buesst contrived to give the melodies their marvellous sense of lean asceticism and at the same time maintain an impressive monotony of rhythm – and to what hypnotic uses Wagner does turn the art of thematic and rhythmical reiteration!

The music has a luminous austerity; it gives us the very odour and white light of mysticism. We were conscious of only one considerable defect in the performance; the stage action in the Grail scenes are surely too real, too tangible. We should always seem to be looking at "Parsifal" from a remote place; here are not men and women of the familiar world, but types of human aspiration, passion, love, despair, pain, and affliction. The Grail scenes in particular ask for a slow, monotonous stage action; simple pose, which suggests impersonal thought and emotion, are wanted – not the gesture which has in its movement a point and emphasis relating it to familiar speech. The action in "Parsifal", we take it, should aim at an illusion of arrested motion. The posing and grouping should not even possess the rounded tangibility of sculpture, but rather should remind us of the flat, conventional surface and attitudes of decorative tapestry. This illusion, no doubt, is not for human beings to create on any but an almost dark stage, and then, possibly, the very tangibility of the singers' voices would sound incongruous. The problem is as old as the hills – how may mortal man embody on the substantial earth his insubstantial and immortal visions? Music is the art, before any other, in which we may escape from our material habitation, and there are times when we think "Parsifal" could be enjoyed best with closed eyes.

As an argument, the world saved by "a pure fool", may not appeal to the rationalist's cognizance of the iron chain of cause and effect. But we need attend no further to the quasi-religious significance of "Parsifal" than we need attend to the curious compound of Schopenhauer which Wagner put into "Tristan" before he purged his libretto by the fire of his music. "Parsifal" is an allegory, and, as Hazlitt once said of the "Faerie Queene", we need not be afraid of it – it will not bite. Faced with the problem of existence, the dualism of flesh and spirit, man has sought to ease his perplexity in many symbols, some beautiful and some crude. The symbolism of "Parsifal" may or may not move us; behind it is a wise man's experience of life, his world-weary acceptance, after much walking about in the places of the earth, of one or two articles of faith that now sweeten his dish of disillusion. "Parsifal" does not lean on dogma; the music transmutes it all into the world of intense art. And, superb though the work is in itself, we shall feel its beauty most if we see it in its place at the close of Wagner's stormy artistic life. Think of "Siegfried" and its announcement of the joy of the visible world; its pagan worship and love of wind, rain, storm, fire, and flame. Wagner gave a tongue to the elements, and young Siegfried was an eagle flying unabashed into the sun. Then came the embracing faith in humanity of "The Mastersingers", and "Tristan's" deathless glorification of passion. And at the end – "Parsifal". The fires are burning out; storm and stress, pride in the brazen, abundant earth are gone, and the old master's vision is turned inwards, content now to look on simple things, not of this world. "Parsifal" is an old man's work, true, but how nobly it brings the great wheel full circle!

"Parsifal" at Covent Garden

1st May 1936

Last evening at Covent Garden at a quarter to six a vast audience sat in the theatre's darkness and the prelude to "Parsifal" began; we all knew we were imprisoned there for hours, with only short moments of respite. At the first interval the multitude came out of the anaesthetic and escaped to the streets to get another and reassuring glimpse of the normal universe. We uttered our protests against the unreasonable tyranny of Wagner, his inordinate length and prolixity. "It is preposterous," we told ourselves, "and heavily German, utterly lacking in poise and taste."

But we all went back to our seats well in time for the other acts; we had no choice; our resentment grew as the music's monotony, its timeless ebb and flow, numbed personal sense and identity in us. "Never again," said a noble old lord, at the fall of the last curtain; "It is too much." He has been saying the same thing for many years and will probably die saying it. You must avoid "Parsifal" like the plague if you do not wish to fall under the sway. Wagner's power outrages reason and decency; he draws men and women out of the tangible world of pleasure at the beginning of a London season; he unfolds his austere scroll, shows the rites of renunciation, reveals to us the agony of Amfortas, half-revolts us with a vision of a sacrament that is Mithraic; and he sweetens disgust by pity's own cadences when the voices in the Hall of the Grail come down from the heights singing "Made wise through pity, the blameless fool" – (there is no translation for the phrase). Wagner did not intend "Parsifal" to serve the uses of the fashionable opera-house; this was his spiritual crucifixion and resurrection: to some of the disciples of the master who wrote "Siegfried" it is his act of apostasy and decadence. The fact is that "Parsifal", whether we admire it or not

126

(once we are free of it), is the most uncompromising presentation in all art of a great genius's and great sinner's effort in his life's falling day to find some way of reconciling experience and faith, the needs of the soul and the appetites of the senses. As music "Parsifal" shows Wagner failing in strength and inspiration; he is burdened by his own system, drowsed by a repetitive melody and harmony. But for the purposes of "Parsifal" the old energy and rhetoric would never have done; there is a special providence that gives to genius in the autumnal period as much as is taken away. The eternal recurrences in the "Parsifal" score convey to us the inner universe of Wagner's last testament.

A musician new to Covent Garden conducted on this occasion – Fritz Reiner, who gave a devout and thoroughly German reading. He skilfully attended to the demands of the text and the music; like most continental conductors, he approached the score through the words, and saw to it that the singers were not distracted from a faithful treatment of the verbal accents by a purely symphonic performance from the orchestra. English conductors seldom take the trouble to learn by heart the text of the Wagner music-dramas – that is why their readings are usually faulty in the important matter of balance between voice, stage, action, and instrumental emphasis and illustration. Reiner was not afraid of the pauses in the prelude to the work; he allowed the unison melodies to uncoil themselves and die of their own weary supplications. He blended the instruments beautifully, and even in the crescendo of the Amfortas agony there was no danger that Janssen's voice would be overwhelmed. There was nothing strongly personal in Reiner's interpretation – it was all the better for that; the devotion and knowledge of a fine musician and conductor were to be felt always. The most beautiful singing of the evening was by Ludwig Weber, whose effortless resonance and simple dignity of movement made Gurnemanz almost a pleasure to hear and see through his longest homilies. Janssen's Amfortas was, like everything this great artist attempts, poetically conceived; but his voice is naturally kindly and humane; it cannot easily pierce us with the spear of Amfortas's pain. As Parsifal Torsten Ralf was only adequate; he seemed to remain outside the circle, not only of the Grail scene but of the work itself as a whole. Leider's Kundry is imaginative acting as well as splendid singing. Habich lent to Klingsor's music the proper accent of evil; we should always feel that Klingsor has traffic with the base elements – though no stagecraft seems able to discover a convincing means of presenting the daemonic and the evil. The singing of Robert Easton, as Titurel, was most moving in its remoteness and tenderness. The choral singing in the Temple scene could not easily have been better, especially that of the choir in the dome. But what a terrible tune Wagner wrote for the knights to sing after the ceremony of the Grail!

The setting was old-fashioned in lump, despite some "dissolving views" which take the place of the old peripatetic scenery of the Transformation. The Flower Maidens and the Magic Garden were thoroughly up-to-date in decorations by Mr Volkoff; they suggested that Klingsor ran his own private Lido. We were well on the verge of midnight before we found ourselves out of Wagner's grip – exhausted in mind, sense, and body. Many years ago I attended a performance of "Parsifal" in company with Samuel Langford. He grew restive during the Grail scene and whispered to me, "Amfortas is the wisest man here tonight; he's brought his bed with him."

The Message of the Rattlesnake

7th March 1966

From six o'clock in the evening, rush-hour not yet exhausted, the Opera House in Covent Garden is packed with an audience partially made up of hungry folk fresh from offices and shops: now they are sitting in the dark, and will sit there until after eleven o'clock, with brief intervals in which to scramble for expensive sandwiches. And what have they come there to see and hear, and paid high prices to do so? Why, "Parsifal", a music-drama so-called, not an opera – no solo arias, not even an aria as skilfully and as dramatically disguised as the "Liebestod", sung by Isolde, or the Immolation scene which ends "Götterdämmerung"; no Rhine journeys or forest murmurs, nothing at all to catch the impressionable ear, except, maybe, the coy Flower Maidens' warblings, and the march music on the way to the temple of Montsalvat . . . .

What is the fascination of "Parsifal"? Conventional religious links – Kundry washing the feet of Parsifal? A *tableau vivant* of the Last Supper? The wound of Amfortas inflicted by the spear which pierced the body of Christ? Wagner repudiated the notion that "Parsifal was in any way symbolical of Christ." "Christ a tenor?" he asked. For hours "Parsifal" goes its ways in a slow tempo; there are hardly twenty quick bars in the entire score. There is no dramatic stir to expectation. As soon as Parsifal comes on the scene, we know he is the awaited redeemer. None of the characters in "Parsifal" has a human identity with which we, the audience, can identify ourselves. These are abstractions, concepts of Wagner's own way of responding in his mature age to ideas half-religious, half-philosophical, all deeply felt no doubt in his mind's German red-hot crucible.

Here in "Parsifal" are no soprano heroines, tragic or triumphant, no Brünnhilde, no Sieglinde, no gloriously resolute Wotan. Even Parsifal has nothing that a tenor is aching to sing. Moreover, Wagner throughout the score denies the singers those very notes which the general public expect to hear in opera. The upper and lower register of the men's voices are seldom used. Kundry, the only part for a woman, sings mainly speech-song. The "Herzeleide" music is an orchestral conception, really, with the vocal part grafted on. It is in the orchestra, more than in the voice, that Kundry lives and is depicted. So with nearly all the vocal music in "Parsifal", which really is the abnegation of opera. It is ritualistic and symbolical. It is, indeed, an abnegation of all that Wagner had consummated of his theories and experience of music-drama.

A curious paradox, which I have not so far noted in Wagner commentaries, is that in "Parsifal" Wagner denies his evil genius – his genius to evoke and embody in music the sense and presence of evil, of corruption, of erotic allurements. In "Götterdammerung", finished only three years before Wagner began to compose "Parsifal", Hagen breathes and exudes evil. As far back as "Tannhauser", Wagner called-up the seductresses of Venusberg in drowsy tones of inimical enchantment. In "Parsifal" the music sung by Klingsor's Flower Maidens is almost chaste by comparison. Kundry herself is as much the penitent as the sinner, ready for the Salvation Army of Montsalvat. Compare the music of Hagen, Alberich, or Mime with Klingsor's, and I think you will admit that Klingsor's music is more or less composed to an operatic formula dating back, in the evolution of Wagner's mind and art, decades.

Wagner in "Parsifal" marvellously metamorphosed himself "for the Cause". A truly powerful Klingsor oozing evil, contaminating the whole score and scene, and a truly potent Kundry, ravaging the score, would have gone counter to the static timeless tempi needed to present the essential ritualistic pageant, stylized in fresco-musical attitudes. Hence the slow motion, bar to bar. Another important point – in "Parsifal" two lifelong contending elements in Wagner's make-up, as composer, are resolved, reconciled, synthesized: the chromatic and diatonic. At the last the feverish chromaticism derived from Tristan's agony, is resisted. Dissonance and passion are exorcized, and perfect harmony provides the catharsis.

The orchestra for "Parsifal" is different in its spatial-time constitution from the orchestra as used in any other Wagner work, though "Lohengrin" provides the tone-dimensional embryo. In "Parsifal", the style and *sound* are fundamentally harmonic-choral. There is a fourfold division of woodwind, combined with threefold brass, a terrace of vocal and tonal groups. Here, as Gurnemanz says to Parsifal, time is one with space. It is a wonderful transition of voice, texture, and tone that Wagner achieved in "Parsifal" at the dictate of compulsion of spirit and imagination.

It is silly to say that Wagner, in "Parsifal", seemed to think that sacred music should of necessity never be quick of tempo. As I have suggested a steady fundamental tone and movement were essential for the conceptual purpose of "Parsifal". From the swing and bell-tones of the bass to the high voices, the score takes gradually the shape and altitude of a dome, architectural and outside time. Moreover, as Wagner was concentrating in "Parsifal" as never before on harmonic expansion and change, he naturally could not attend also to swift alterations of rhythm . . . .

So there it is. We still sit in the dark for hours seeing and listening, as Wagner works his spell – Wagner, the arch-egoist, most defiled of composers as a man, Jew-hater, Nazi before his time, and all the rest of it. We sit there, while this same Wagner teaches us, in our own day of advancing nuclear science and technology, that the ever-opening wound of Amfortas, and the wound of the world, will be healed only by somebody entirely unsophisticated and unscientific – made wise through compassion.

Indestructible Wagner

22nd May 1963

One hundred and fifty years ago, Wagner was born in Leipzig. For a third of this time I have known his music, lived with it, been under the spell of it, reacted, not to say rebelled, against it, have been drawn back again to it, have submitted and gloried in its sensuous allurements and tried to follow the wonderful thought processes by which the music is organized. Time is the critic that discovers the masterpieces. Before their lasting powers are proven to us, we must *experience* them with mind and imagination. We must go through disillusionment with them, even hate them periodically. When we have been thrust away from them we are in a better position to appreciate why they have drawn us back.

There are anti-Wagnerians with us, like the poor, always. Wagner was, as composer and man, a test of moderation. People aren't tepidly warm about him; either they hate his music at first hearing and never afterwards feel comfortable with it, or they are at once dominated by it, never again entirely to be free of it. The winds of changing taste, the snows of "reaction", have fallen and gathered around him as the snow on Mont Blanc, merely emphasizing his place in the world and geography of music.

There is today as strong a movement of antagonism against Wagner as at any time. All the old denunciations are heard. "Excess. Erotic. Long-winded. Tasteless. Abnormal. No poise. German – all-too-German." And so on. I often suspect that the anti-Wagnerians (the fanatical ones, who could be just as fanatical as the early Houston Stewart Chamberlain Wagnerians) must lament that "Die Meistersinger" was ever written. You cannot sensibly call Sachs, Ev'chen or David and the apprentices erotic or Wagnerian in the pejorative sense.

There is "sweetness and light" in the music of Sachs and Ev'chen in the shoe-testing scene. In all opera there is no music that falls with such gentle balm on our senses and soul as the orchestral postlude to Act 2 of "Die Meistersinger". Nürnberg in the summer moonlight.

The anti-Wagnerians (those who are "anti" on principle, so to say) concentrate on the "Ring". Here, surely, is monstrosity and assault on what is possibly defined here and there nowadays as vulgarly masculine susceptibilities. Music more than life-size. The raging and nagging of Wotan and Fricka. The absurd galumphings of Siegfried. The nausea that is distilled by "Parsifal". For every accusation of this order I will bring one or two which obviously escape their notice. Listen to the music in "Die Walküre", where Wotan tells Brünnhilde that she did what he himself would have done – "So tatest du, was so gern zu tun ich begehrt." Let the "antis" listen to the "Good Friday" music, to Isolde's "So bange Tage." Let them listen to a single phrase at the beginning of Act 2 of "Tristan und Isolde" – "Nicht Hörnerschall tönt so hold." Anybody who is not touched to the heart, melted to it, or thrilled beautifully and mysteriously in his imagination by such music is not necessarily lost to all music, not beyond the pale. He has only missed some of music's – and of all art's – revelatory and unique moments.

Wagner's mind worked on two planes. He saw with his ears and heard with his eyes . . . He looks backward and forward at the same time, a binding strand here, another there, a gathering of the skein, a great unravelling of it. The needles flash endlessly. The Wagner theory of music-drama has come to little or nothing, apart from what he made of it himself, often while instinctively going against it. The idea of "endless melody" is to-day momentarily obsolete. Obsolete also the Wagner theory that there is a particular "stuff of music", that music cannot cope with quick moving circumstantial drama, that it is happy and free only when it feeds on broad types of character and emotion. Music for Wagner was an art of emotional expression. The librettist had to make his text musical in shape and contrast of mood, especially in the rise and fall of emotional tempo and tension. Opera to-day ignores this method. The irony of Wagner is that he, who insisted in theory that in opera music should be the potent means but drama the end, achieved the greatest glorification of music the theatre has ever known.

Those composers of the nineteenth century who emulated him were engulfed in Wagner's full flowing sea. Another irony of the "Case of Wagner" is that even the music-makers who shied away from him, "reacting" most violently against him, on grounds not of musical reasoning but of "taste" and temperament, really owe it to him that they found, as they were repelled from Wagner, their own quieter plots of land to till, their own secure islands. Had Wagner not closed a path, inviting enough until he blazed his trail, heaven alone can say what might have happened to – What's-his-name and Never-mind! As Ernest Newman used to say: "Genius ends, not begins, epochs."

7

BRUCKNER
(1824–1896)

He opened no new paths and was not aware of them if his genius led him to a fresh direction. In Vienna today musical opinion ranks Bruckner with Beethoven. But Bruckner had neither Beethoven's range of imagination nor his tremendous smithy. There is no anvil in Bruckner, no hammer, no white-heat. Bruckner's music is sturdy, without protest, sure of itself even if it stumbles now and then. Every symphony of Bruckner is a mountain moved very much by faith. It is music which, for its unaffected idealism, faith and embracing humanity and kindliness, we need today as much as we can possibly come upon and hear, and take into our hearts, minds and consciousness

J B Neville Cardus

The Fourth

6th November 1929

Bruckner needs a conductor who can vivify his ideas. He was a naïve writer; the symphony for him apparently possessed in its dignity of structure, and the mighty tradition hanging upon it, the significance of ritual, divine and immortal. It would appear that he believed that by faith alone in the symphony could a great one be created. His themes need therefore to be played with fervour; and nothing much of account is left in his music. The playing last night, with all its technical excellences, lacked conviction. Bruckner's themes are not often remarkable in the Fourth Symphony; his development sections are tedious. He piles up his perorations in good German fashion, solemn and industrious. This naïve seriousness – naïve because it goes so often with trivial ideas – cannot perhaps ever be appreciated by English instrumentalists; Bruckner is for German-speaking folk, and nobody else. He has no use for the succinct phrase; he takes his time over every sentence, and then says it all over again.

The prolixity of the German language, its clauses within clauses, paragraphs and sub-paragraphs, can be felt in all of his movements, even in his treatment of a scherzo. He tries to unify his diffuseness by linking together his movements; by giving them portions of his thematic material to share in common. The call of the horn in the first movement of the Fourth Symphony is heard or echoed in the second and the closing movements; and there are other instances of an exploitation of the cyclic method of unifying the symphonic form. The trouble with these repetitions or transformations is that, if we happen to fall asleep at a period of prolixity, when we wake up and hear a theme to whose prosaic cadence we began to slumber, we then are liable to suffer a momentary fear that the music is never going to finish, but is about to begin all over again. Bruckner's transitions and modifications are merely musicianly; they seldom quicken the imagination by taking an entirely unexpected turn. His developments often proceed by sequels to the point of making us wriggle in our seats; his use of the pause ought to move us poetically, but somehow it doesn't. He is, indeed, constantly promising us beautiful music; now and again a warmth comes into his violins, a rich songfulness begins – only to be dispelled by the pious symphonist, conscious of his mission of another "Immortal Nine".

The time for introducing Bruckner to this country seems to have passed, though the later symphonies ought to be given a hearing. His piety and his naïve romanticism will strike a modern ear as ancient, and, worse still, as hopelessly handicapped by the symphonic cliché of his period. There is a better chance for Mahler to-day than for Bruckner, as far as this country is concerned. Mahler's naïvety of outlook was combined with a subtler, a more dexterous art than Bruckner's.

The Fourth: A Wind of Change

BRUNO WALTER AT THE EDINBURGH FESTIVAL

28th August 1951

It was an event on a wet Sabbath in Edinburgh to listen to Bruno Walter and the New York Philharmonic Orchestra in the Fourth Symphony of Bruckner. The interpretation was really imposing; masculine and robust in the great and sudden accumulations of tone and quietly expressive during Bruckner's long inward-looking meditations. I do not agree that the New York Orchestra is concerned mainly with streamlining its technique. Whenever an orchestra visits these islands and plays all the notes as truly written down in the composer's lifetime the cry invariably goes up: "No soul, no wings – cold-blooded efficiency", and so on. It was the same years ago when the Berlin Philharmonic first came to London, under Furtwängler. Our attitude in music is rather amateur, using the word in a modern way, to suggest technical casualness, without necessarily implying that what is being done should be done with love. The New York Philharmonic Symphony Orchestra makes music; the tone is opulent but not wasteful; it is spent with the true economy of the rich of the earth.

Attack and balance are quick, sure, and instinctive, not mechanical. The playing has natural character; not excluding the roughness. There is nothing here of the chromium plate of the superb Philadelphia Orchestra, which, even if it fell into mortal error or insecurity, might easily find reason for not playing at all.

Bruckner is not understood in Britain, and it is not likely that the music public as a whole will ever come to a grasp of his greatness. Our critics certainly live too briskly to lend him patient ears. I like to think, as they listen to Bruckner whenever duty calls, their writhings are a foretaste of the boredom awaiting them in heaven and through eternity. Bruckner asks for patience, love, and faith. He needed these virtues himself for the composing of his mountain range of symphonies. Bruno Walter easefully spanned the summits in the golden (and brazen) sunrises. Better still, he led us down into the valleys and along the winding, not so say meandering, rivulets. The astonishing point about the interpretation was that all the apparent discursiveness of Bruckner was given connection and romance. Bruckner is not formally logical. But he was given connection and relevance. Meditation is not obliged to avoid laws which exclude riddles and non-sequiturs. A priest at his devotions, as he praises God, need not be afraid of repeating himself. Raptness is all. Herr Walter saw to it that though the Andante of the Fourth Symphony might seem long, not a bar of it would lag or sound superfluous.

It was an interpretation, too, which was likely to throw a new light on Bruckner's mind and thinking processes to those of us who regard him as among the masters, though not yet do we know him inside out, as we know Beethoven and Schubert. The general idea is that Bruckner was a sort of inspired schoolmaster, with the brains of a peasant. On the contrary, he was complex and subtle in his ways of symphonic conception; the ordinary logic of the symphony, the point-to-point procedure, and synthesis of, say, Brahms was of no use to Bruckner, whose mind was free and spacious and open to the visitations of spontaneous creation. A study of symphonic form in Bruckner will reveal a plastic power and flexibility not perhaps suspected even by many of his devoted followers. But the steering-wheel, not to say the radar, of a Bruno Walter is necessary for a thoroughly charted excursion or pilgrimage in the land of Bruckner – which really is tone incarnation of the Austria of his period; nature changed to music and religion by love and genial gusto, by one who was a great soul before he was an accomplished artist.

Neville Cardus's first notice for the "Manchester Guardian" on being appointed its principal critic in London.

The Eighth

23rd October 1951

Last night in the Royal Festival Hall the London Symphony Orchestra played the Eighth Symphony of Bruckner, magnificently conducted by Josef Krips . . . The audience listened intently during the vast extent of the four movements. It is not the easiest of the symphonies to approach: it has no long-phrased, singing melodies like those, say, in the Seventh. Bruckner here builds from short, almost platitudinous figures which he repeats on rising levels; sequences suddenly interrupted either by descending brass passages or by a change of key or by total silence. We can, if we are attending to all this for the first time, easily understand and sympathize with Hanslick's tirade: "Bruckner begins with a short chromatic motive, repeats it over and over again, higher and higher in the scale and on into infinity, augments and diminishes it, offers it in contrary motion, and so on, until the listener is crushed under the sheer weight and monotony of this interminable lamentation."

Only by a comprehensive musical art could Bruckner's material in this work have been shaped to ends and heights so suggestive of bigness of style. The old notion of Bruckner as a naïve composer won't entirely do; the paradox about him is that he is simple in emotional and psychological texture and responses but intricate in his ways of musical thinking, as we may easily understand from the subtlety of his key relations; the expected resolution is avoided as naturally as the change of tone of a man's voice. The critics, of course, will come out again with the old charges against Bruckner: "too long", "diffuse", "no form". Meditation allows the mind a freedom not permitted by formal logic. No sensible admirer of Bruckner will deny his faults: the tediousness and redundancy which are the consequence of his nature, defects of his qualities – we know the catalogue by heart. The Eighth Symphony is no favourite of mine; but he would be a rash man to deny that a power of genius generates the mass and spaciousness and the waste places of it all.

The work is recognizable at once, the accent, the flavour, the attitude, the tremendous sincerity, the aspiration, courage, and patience. These are moral rather than aesthetic matters, no doubt. But they are bound to intrude into any discussion of Bruckner who composed out of a contrite heart for the glory of God and from love of his Heimat. He is a sort of Austrian Elgar, with a different catholicism and the baroque thrown in – and also his love of country and nature was that of the peasant, "der Deutsche Michl", with no concern about bounds of empire being flung wider still and wider.

It is not likely that Bruckner will at the present time find any large acceptance in this country. He has not even the obvious instrumental allurements of Mahler, that culture of orchestration to which one or two of our contemporary composers help themselves, much to their profit. There is no tone in a Bruckner symphony which is not as true to the man as any physical part of him during his mortal existence. It is, in the deepest sense, art and not artifice. And from the point of view of mastery defined as unself-conscious instinctive control of means to an end, free of the spectacular and the over-sophisticated, the score of the Eighth Symphony is so consummate that it will repay years of study. Even after an experience of Bruckner that rather bored me – for I have not yet found a way to the heart and centre of the Eighth – I am more than ever aware of the genius of the music and the greatness of the man.

Naïve Genius?

20th March 1954

We must bear in mind that Bruckner was not of the German but Austrian habit of symphonic composition, not at all kindled to the "thoroughly composed" or durchkomponiert method. He has the length, heavenly or other, of Schubert, with deep religious inwardness, and an equally religious enjoyment of the landscape of his countryside, not perceived or felt as scenery or atmosphere, though there is plenty of both in a Bruckner scherzo, but as a way of worshipping God in nature:

God, in fact, as peasant. Moreover, he has nothing to do with the heroic-ethical "humanity" or "brotherhood" symphony which the Ninth of Beethoven threatened for a while to perpetuate. In Bruckner there is no struggle against fate or doubt; man is safe with God in Bruckner. But though the sound of the Bruckner orchestra, with its rich string melodies, deep-toned brass, and the organ registrations of wood wind, tell of a man sure of soul and faith, there is no smugness, nothing suggestive of a comfortable bourgeois pew. It is risky even to call Bruckner a romantic; his symphonies stem from the nature romance of Schubert; but he is never the full-throated lyrist, never consciously in search of sensuous beauty. His diction is rather that of musical prose than of musical poetry. It is, of course, stupid to link him to Wagner, merely on the strength of his use of the tuba. Almighty God Himself could not create two minds, two natures, as opposed as those of Bruckner and Wagner – Bruckner who never wore a mask, never the Tarnhelm, but was always himself.

The duration of a Bruckner symphony is not for clocks to measure. Bruckner in his music grows on big and not small matters; and the shaping of his structures was controlled in the main by his conception. Like any other composer, excepting Beethoven, he is sometimes put into chains by obligations to form as a thing in itself; but on the whole he fills his capacious surfaces pertinently enough. His redundancies, his sudden fullstops, his fallings back on the familiar devices, inversions and imitations, are part of his make-up as a man and artist. I know no other composer in whose style it is as difficult as in Bruckner to suggest how the "faults" might have been remedied without concealing the Bruckner some of us have come to love . . . . In the best, indeed the only, essay in English that understands Bruckner, Mr Richard Capell truly and eloquently writes: "His uniqueness is this: that in the century par excellence of individualism, he achieved a major work – major and original by the century's own standards – by applying himself, with no deliberate aim at originality, no conscious exploiting of his personality, to a job of work, the writing of symphonies to the glory of God, in the frame of mind of any honest craftsman." But we should not emphasize Bruckner's austerity. He can sing a broad-chested song; the length and extent of his adagio movements are a consequence of the span of his melody. His scoring for strings is frequently rich and ornamental. (Why, by the way, are conductors nowadays ruining the ineffable second melodic subject of the adagio of the Seventh Symphony by taking it too quickly, without leisure for cadences and the lovely woodwind echoes?) His scherzi are vigorous and genial. No composer has written music of happier heart than Bruckner's . . . . He is not witty, clever, or agile; he cannot run faster than Wagner, which is the only characteristic the two composers share; and on a first hearing there is a certain sameness about all his symphonies. He was not protean. But use him well, and he can be vastly satisfying.

Composers in different periods feel or react to the material of music in different ways. Bruckner was concerned mainly with tone, blending orchestral and organ textures; for he was a master of both instruments. Rhythm in Bruckner is secondary to song and to contrasts of sound values. Tone, rather than rhythm, is the musical symbol for the Brucknerian moods of meditation and of thanksgiving. He made the adagio a crisis or centre of interest of a symphony. That is why more than once a Bruckner finale comes to us as an anti-climax. Only the adagio of the Ninth Symphony of Beethoven will survive comparison with a Bruckner adagio for sustained raptness of song; but Bruckner was denied Beethoven's genius for transition. He is constantly coming to a fullstop, then beginning again. A man at his devotions, communing and praying and contemplating, is not particular about logic, the clause of the excluded middle, and what not. The impression sometimes from Bruckner's music is of an unawareness on the composer's part of the fact that anybody is listening. Bruckner is aloof from the little battles of the hour; he stood apart from the romantic wallowings and the nineteenth-century crowings of the Uebermensch or his prophets. He was a great composer, nonetheless great for being a good man; which at the present time seems a curious saying.

The Third

HORENSTEIN

10th February 1965

Jascha Horenstein conducted the Third Symphony of Anton Bruckner in the Royal Festival Hall last night, with the London Philharmonic Orchestra. Horenstein is a learned and authoritative Brucknerian, so we can safely infer that the edition of the score he used for a very impressive performance was the 1878 edition, which is regarded by scholars as the closest approximation of Bruckner's definitive intentions. He was engaged on the score from around about 1873 until his death in 1890, revising and reconsidering.

Mahler made a two-handed arrangement of it, and Wagner heard an embryonic version and admired the opening trumpet call. The symphony, like all the Bruckner symphonies, curiously symbolizes Bruckner's creative processes. It emerges from a tonal abyss, throbbing and germinal, and out of it comes a signal call, usually having the intervals on the fourth and fifth within the range of an octave. Horenstein very skilfully obtained from the orchestra the necessary urgency from the first bars; he was also skilful in defining the initial outer-movement rhythm, as characteristic a feature of the Bruckner style and physiognomy as anything else in his music – quintuple with a triplet accent.

Frankly the Third Symphony, which goes on for an hour, is not one of Bruckner's most memorable, despite passages of choral grandeur in the slow movement. Nonetheless, it is prophetic of the more fully realized symphonies to follow. It is, as each of them sometimes appears to be, a blueprint for the planning and erection of the next. To the end, to the great consummatory Ninth, the technical formulae, the conceptual and expressive processes, remain much the same – the introductory amoeba, the proliferating secondary themes or periods, the pauses, the sequences, the beginnings-again, the ranging unisons, the summing up in the fourth movement of basic material – no great composer has gone as far as Bruckner on germ-cells so circumscribed.

Particularly satisfying was Horenstein's control of the Bruckner pause, the intake of breath, the meditative silences when Bruckner seems to have for a moment lost thread. The pulse should seem to be heard beating in these general pauses. They must be perfectly timed. Few conductors, since Furtwängler, have kept a grip of Bruckner's silences more musically vital than Horenstein's. Yet not even his long-viewed direction could convince me that this Third Symphony is truly organic. I was here and there reminded of Sir Thomas Beecham's experience with a Bruckner symphony. "In the first movement alone I took note of six pregnancies and four miscarriages." Naughty, with a grain of truth in it. The LPO and Horenstein made the best out of the Bruckner imposing sonorities, already noble enough in the Third Symphony. While walking in the Upper Styrian landscape with Mahler, a friend admired the distant mountains. "I have set them to music already," said Mahler. He was mistaken; it was Bruckner who made the mountains into music.

Horenstein and the LPO also were very musical in the Dvořák 'cello concerto, with the gifted Jacqueline du Pré the soloist. She is really a lovely player; she has not only command over a considerable range of tone but, also, an apparently inborn sense of phrase, the singing phrase that runs naturally into the next, blending easily – a rare gift.

The Ninth

BARENBOIM

9th June 1971

Over last weekend Daniel Barenboim was heard playing one of the late piano sonatas of Beethoven. Last night in the Royal Festival Hall he conducted the Ninth Symphony of Bruckner.

This young Barenboim is really a remarkable event in our recent musical life, probably the most gifted musician of his years since Busoni . . . . True, so far, he has given us no compositions of his own, but he easily could, I imagine. Myself, I could, after a year or two's study of the technical know-how, compose sounds like those of Stockhausen and Berio; but I could never make a sound like late Beethoven on the piano, or get out of an orchestra a sound and diction like Bruckner's. I hesitate to describe Barenboim as a young genius because of an old-fashioned reluctance to apply the word to any musician not specifically creative. But, said Mahler, music is not alive or real till it is heard; the performer becomes part of the creative process.

Barenboim certainly seemed absorbed in the Bruckner tonal forge; and the New Philharmonia Orchestra was his plastic and sensitive collaborator. The Ninth Symphony, never finished and born in much travail, is a severe test of a conductor's long-viewed grasp of the whole and his power to concentrate on passing details and parts. The first movement – "Solenne Misterioso" – with its three groups of themes, can easily run to discursiveness . . . . I much admired Barenboim's judgment of the contrasts of a quite complex use of related and non- related tonality with the true Bruckner singleness of onward, if sometimes apparently static, motion. The broad lyric phrases were beautifully songful. And the sense of a movement, at first earthbound, intent on a final aspiration, was another of Barenboim's rare points.

The scherzo was perhaps here and there a little too precisely fingered. In the best of books about Bruckner, Dr Robert Simpson writes of the "infernal gates" flung open in this scherzo; but I can find no hint of diabolism in Bruckner. This original scherzo dances on the toe or hoof fantastic; sometimes it, for me, anticipates even Sibelius.

The crown of the Ninth Symphony is the Adagio, again diverse yet curiously unchanging. Barenboim and the New Philharmonia came close to the heart of the matter. The coda was as a benediction and release. But the problem for the conductor of Bruckner is that he must be technically masterful yet anonymous. He must be content to serve Bruckner as a sort of possessed unseen medium of spiritual communication.

Only two living conductors are able to conduct Bruckner with, let us say, invisible omnipresence – Klemperer and Horenstein. The impression we sometimes get from Bruckner's music is an unawareness on the composer's part that anybody is listening at all. We cannot expect complete self-abnegation from a young musical interpreter. But Barenboim is on the way towards freedom from the personal equation. Bruckner would surely have embraced him last night, calling him a "Wunderkind", maybe giving him a Trinkgeld, a tip, as once he tipped Richter.

Ad Lib . . .

1st April 1970

Once on a time, not long ago, a Bruckner symphony was seldom to be heard in London; the Bruckner "pioneers" (myself one of them) prayed for a Bruckner performance.

I am now reminded of the Scottish parson who, in a season of drought, offered up prayers for rain. There followed a week of deluge overwhelming the Kirk. So next Sunday the parson addressed Omnipotence, "O Lord, last Sunday we supplicated Thee for rain – but dear Lord, don't be ridiculous."

8

MAHLER
(1860–1911)

"Legend, undoubted genius, daemon-driven seeker, and ultra-sensitive barometer of mankind's vicissitudes"

The Fourth Symphony

25th November 1927

The Fourth Symphony of Gustav Mahler, composed twenty-seven years ago, was given a first performance here by the Hallé Orchestra last night, and though a fairly large audience found much to please them in its amiable and bucolic tuniness, the applause at the end of the work was rather a case of heralding a dawn that rose in the long, long ago. The attempt to place Mahler amongst the immortals of music has ended in failure on the Continent – save in Vienna, whose devotion to Mahler can easily be understood; it knew Mahler in person, and to know him was to love all that he did, for a nobler spirit never worked himself to death in the service of the arts. His Fourth Symphony is perhaps the least tedious of all the nine symphonies he published, because it is the least pretentious. In this work Mahler's naïve melodic invention goes well enough with a naïve theme; in the later interminable symphonies this naïveté is positively banal and ridiculous. The older Mahler grew the less did he seem to be content to keep within the limitations of his mild and prosaic imagination. He ought to make a universal music, and to range, like Goethe, through the great and the little world. (In Mahler's country symphonic music is no laughing matter!) It is a pity that Mahler, who was an earnest student of Goethe, did not obey his wise teacher's constant warning to all artists: "Only by working within limits does the master reveal himself." Mahler's finest music is in his songs. The smaller the form he worked in the more convincing was his touch.

The Fourth Symphony, like some of the others – though not in so aggravating a degree – is long-winded; it is supposed to describe the "Heavenly Life". And the great point about the heavens we have ever been told about is that they go on for ever. The slow movement last

151

night gave us a most penetrating glimpse into eternity. Mahler's trouble seems to have been that even though he did hit upon a good musical idea he had not the skill or wit to develop it. Unless a composer is master of the art of transition, he cannot hope to build a symphony. The form is kept going by themes which breed themes, by sudden modulations which show us some fresh aspect of beauty already before us. Mahler was a discursive composer; the present writer is unable to recall in all the music of Mahler known to him a single really poetic transition – one of those transitions whereby music is inevitably born out of music, one of those swift surprises that make you catch breath, and set your imagination aflame. Mahler tries to sustain our interest in his symphonies by changing his ground. Perhaps he himself half guessed at his weakness as a symphonic writer. For he once said that whenever a musical conception flooded his mind he felt the need of words to make his conception articulate and logical. Romain Rolland writes somewhere that Mahler hardly ever composed melody or a theme that does not cry out for the support of some definitely poetic idea.

Ought Mahler to have written symphonic poems? But even here a genius for transformation of theme is demanded; moreover the symphonic poem insists on a vivid dramatic imagination. Mahler's imagination, musical and poetic, was mild and not plastic. Take, for example, the scherzo in last night's symphony. We are told on the authority of Richard Specht – Mahler's best critic – that the movement is intended to suggest the mediaeval Dance of Death. "Friend Death," Specht tells us, "strokes the fiddle and calls for a dance." But the music has none of the half-lights or twisted energy of the grotesque style; if this scherzo was intended as a Dance of Death, then its strains are as though heard by a soul very much at ease "beyond these voices". Even Saint-Saëns's merely ingenious "Danse Macabre" has more of the grotesque style than Mahler's easy-going movement. Most of us would be content to accept Mahler's scherzo as a rustic dance, with the village fiddler more than usually out of tune and in his cups.

Mahler's finest attribute was devotion to the masters of music. Ah, that by touching the garment of the immortals, a Mahler could become immortal too! The sincerity of Mahler's emulations of the great composers cannot be questioned. He borrows from them, not for his own glorification, but that he may himself make some worthy tribute to their genius. His nine symphonies must be thought of as a vast shell in which may be heard the far-off murmur of the mighty seas of the German romantic movement in music.

Twenty-seven years ago Mahler's instinct for an instrument's quality must have been remarkable in his own land. For German orchestral music was at that time bowed under a dead weight of harmonic mass. Bruckner himself was heavy enough to fell the symphony to earth for all time. Like Mahler, Bruckner was naïve, but his simplicity led him to heaviness of harmony and rhythm. Mahler's music is usually free of harmonic congestion; indeed, so eager was Mahler to give to his instruments sharpness of outline that seldom do they blend for long into colour or make a texture. There is "air" in the Mahler orchestra, space for free instrumentation. Sir Hamilton Harty conducted with splendid judgment on the whole, though now and again he appeared to over-accentuate. Perhaps he thought Mahler's ideas could not in charity be sent into the world to fare for themselves.

The Ninth Symphony

"ELOQUENT APPLAUSE"

28th February 1930

The first performance in this country of Mahler's Ninth Symphony made a deep impression on last night's Hallé audience; at the close of the fourth movement – one of the great slow movements of music – the applause was not noisy merely, but eloquent. With not more than three rehearsals behind them the orchestra could not hope to exhaust every detail in a score which has no equal for significance of subsidiary figuration; yet the symphony as a whole came to us with a constant bigness of style, a constant vitality of movement in most of the parts. Seldom indeed have the Hallé players so clinchingly proved their technical resource and their quick responsiveness to a strange musical aesthetic as on this occasion. The city has indeed cause for pride in the country's finest orchestra. Admirable too was Sir Hamilton Harty's control of the work, a control which combined sensibility to the inflected phrase – and Mahler insists that even the least important of his manifold instrumental parts shall be given nuance of its own – with a large-minded grasp of the structure's main lines. Not many more performances would be needed to ripen the music from beginning to end. Passages which may at the moment seem unplayable would in time justify the composer's demands; no composer has ever had a more imaginative grasp of orchestral potentialities. Mahler's requirements, of course, involve artists even in the back desks; this symphony is a symphony for soloists. There is no concealing texture in his writing; he is fond of thinning with abruptness the tone of the orchestra – a trait of style which leaves this or that instrumentalist suddenly exposed.

As a conductor Mahler strove after clarity of melodic line with a fanatical zeal; in the Ninth Symphony he challenges the arts of intonation as they have never before been challenged. He asks his violins to hold daring high notes of many bars at a stretch; his spacing of parts is frequently so wide that unless they are given the utmost warmth of tone the effect is bound to seem bare; his exploitation of trilled notes calls for not only a flexible melodic touch but also for the nimblest rhythmical adjustment. The wind instruments are asked to mingle in one another's being – horn and flute, for example – in a way that suggests that Mahler found in their unusual combinations of sound the marriage which admits of no impediments. To read a score by Mahler, to take notice only of the marks of expression, is a task calling for more than two ordinary mortal eyes . . . .

All these fastidious preoccupations of Mahler were the outcome of his experience and genius as a conductor. Music for him had to be rendered articulate by pointed expression. Mahler himself once confessed that, whenever he composed, his inspiring force was "The Word". Yet at a time when Strauss was making illustrative music the only wear, Mahler kept to the symphony, though in only three of his nine did he trust entirely to instrumental values. The paradox is more apparent than real; Mahler turned to "The Word" not for support for music, but to give to music an unambiguous meaning. He felt that "pure" music could be even more precisely used than programme music as a means of expressing the spirit of man. Because his art meant stark things to him, he identified his significance many times with "The Word". And in the Ninth Symphony, which is wholly instrumental, he does duty to his naïve literal psychology by directions and cautionary tales which, if any conductor nowadays attempted to observe half of them, would bring the music to the sort of disaster which befell the chameleon which one day found itself on a Scotch plaid and tried to do its duty faithfully and all round.

Last night's performance, by its directness, did Mahler a valuable service. The first movement was not altogether blended either in its rhythmical or tonal elements; a larger string team was required here. But the second movement was happier; here the music had a precision of touch which let us understand how absurd it is to write of Mahler (as somebody has recently written) as a romantic decadent. If labels are to be used at all, there is nothing twilightish about Mahler's romanticism; he in fact gave lightness and poise to German music at a time when its harmonic movement was heavy and sluggish, like stuff out of a churn. In the Rondo Burleske we could realize how, twenty years ago, Mahler was abreast with the contemporary problems of music. We have from the cultural point of view been in this country too late in the day finding Mahler; in his context amongst the great composers he provides a bridge which, had we crossed it at the right time, might have landed us long before now in a position to look intelligently at modern music. If Mahler is no longer played persistently on the Continent, it is because music has passed him by; last night's audience was mistaken if they thought they were listening to a "modern" work. But they couldn't very well have thought that! – This Mahler was too clearly a nest of singing birds.

The First Symphony:
A Little Known Work of Genius

20th January 1939

Tonight at the concert of the Royal Philharmonic Society a blow has been struck in the cause of Mahler. Magnificent conducting by Bruno Walter achieved a performance of Mahler's First Symphony which came closer to the composer's mind and style than any other I have heard in this country. Only the richness of the Vienna Philharmonic strings was needed to make the interpretation thoroughly convincing. But in general the playing had all the necessary virtuosity, and it even captured the curious Mahler secret of mingled naïveté of idiom and dexterity of instrumentation. The conducting was really remarkable for control and imagination, rhapsodic freedom, and steady vision.

The First Symphony is probably the most original and comprehensive in technique ever composed by a young man of 28 years of age. All the devices which later Mahler polished to the subtlest fancifulness are already in action – spiccato effects in the strings, daring portamentos, muted brass, flutter-tonguing, individual clashes of woodwind timbre, macabre use of the usually celestial harp. Also there are hints of Mahler's extraordinary orchestral transparency – he puts the instruments under an X-ray.

Nothing else quite like this work exists in music. It makes poetry and naïve drama out of a landscape in which Mahler spent his boyhood. Cuckoo calls are answered by horns of elfland, the Ländler dance is touched with the Dance of Death atmosphere. Mahler indeed obtains one of his greatest strengths in the third movement by emulating a mediaeval grimness of expression in a burlesque marche funèbre. Then in the finale the conception leaps forward to the Faustian conception of heroic struggle with forces of nature. This was a fashion of the period and was observed by all the nineteenth-century symphonic writers.

It is a pity Mahler did not remain outside the main stream of his period's music, for once he became the greatest conductor of his day he often not only conducted but composed from memory. Not until he found in "Das Lied von der Erde" a theme that drew out his lonely tired heart did he recapture entirely the personal vision of his earlier works. He lived for too long in other men's music, unselfishly serving it. Even after he had composed the original "Das Lied" he took farewell of music in the closing movement of the Ninth Symphony, his last act of composition, by a slow movement in Bruckner's manner of devoted melody with the characteristic flattened interval.

The cause of Mahler in this country is not likely to be helped by the extravagant claims that are being made on the composer's behalf by writers who apparently have only just discovered him. A few years ago I was severely admonished in Vienna by members of the Vienna Philharmoniker because I extolled Mahler above the perfect second class. Vienna knows Mahler's music backwards, of course, or at least knew it well until the new regime caused a failure of memory. Vienna also admired Mahler – in reason.

The wisest criticisms ever written on Mahler were by Samuel Langford, who examined him twenty years ago, and almost before any other writer in this country had heard of Mahler set down the following judgment – which long study has satisfied me as a generous and final judgment: "In his early songs both the melodies and the instruments were imagined in the terms of the country life he had left. This life remained the light of all his seeing. When he came to write his truest music he took again the snatches, instrumental or vocal, of these orchestral songs and made them, in more or less obvious allusion, the key to all his poetic and musical feeling. He never separated the instrumental from the vocal imagination in music."

Of "Das Lied," which is Mahler's masterpiece, Langford wrote: "It is a 'Tristan' only in miniature, for if 'The Song of the Earth' is supreme in beauty among Mahler's works, it is because its touch is of the lightest and it ravishes the heart by the sheer wonder of its certainty and its magical technical brilliance."

These questions from a critic whose insight and prose style reduced most of his contemporaries (and successors) to so many first-rate musical journalists, pierce to the core of Mahler's artistic psychology and define his methods of expression with an inspired grasp of essentials. All that is lasting in Mahler answers to the "miniature" description. His failures occurred when he tried to conform marvels of orchestral rhetoric (in, one suspects, some jealous strivings against Strauss) and when he forgot the association values which the songs of nature and the country had for him. There is in all his perfectly fused music the cadence of his loveliest song, "Ich bin der Welt abhanden gekommen".

His orchestration, which is so highly praised by his "modern" adherents, gains its special distinction from the fact that it is a singing instrumental counterpoint which is impatient of harmonic let or hindrance. Mahler will not allow melody to become locked in any system of conventional chording, and here is the reason why he seems to show us the instruments of the orchestra stripped naked, so to say. I see no sense in the contemporary attempt to connect Mahler with systems or movements; he has even been called a fore-runner of Schönberg. When he wrote out of his heart, and in the silence of the mountains forgot his cosmopolitan culture, he was the true "primitif" with the primitive's subtlety and purity of speech.

The germ of the authentic Mahler we have heard tonight in the First Symphony; he can never be enlarged to a world figure, and he himself ran in the face of his proper bent when he attempted the Goethean gesture in his Eighth Symphony. There is no need to inflate the real and genuine Mahler. Supposing he were no "greater" than Dvořák in his own way; would that not be good enough reason for listening to him and cherishing him? Our concert halls are the poorer for knowing as little as they do of the remarkable and vastly interesting work we have heard this evening – obviously a work of genius.

The Second ("Resurrection") Symphony

"IS THE NEGLECT OF MAHLER HERE A RESPONSIBILITY TO BE SHARED BY THE CRITICS?"

12th April 1952

On Wednesday night in the Royal Festival Hall a magnificent interpretation was heard of Mahler's Second Symphony. Josef Krips is the finest musician of all conductors at present resident in this country, and he brings to his work a Central European seriousness and love which are not generally shared by contemporary English musicians. He transformed the London Symphony Orchestra out of recognition, also the Goldsmiths' Choral Union.

The reception at the end of this long turbulent masterpiece was tremendous . . . . But it was not a crowded audience. In Sydney the town hall has been packed on three consecutive nights by the Second Symphony, but here in London Mahler is still not appreciated at his best and most comprehensive and not known as a full man; not only a passionate explorer of life temporal and spiritual but a composer of fascinating and varying music, ranging from the simplest melodies to the subtlest thought processes of music-making.

Mahler himself said that he only really lived when he was composing, and only composed when he was living . . . . The C minor Symphony called "Resurrection" is Faustian in conception; for it experiences by imagination the little world of man's earthly duration and the great world of his spiritual aspiration. The vast orchestra is a welter of sensations, feelings, strivings, and grapplings with tone, to turn it to conception, thence to the realized idea as music. No symphony since Beethoven's Ninth takes us so close to the creative forge, and here in Mahler the heat is more intense, because energy is not as masterfully fused all the time as in Beethoven.

The fire of the first movement consumes Mahler and licks us. Then follows the lovely calm of the second movement. A glance back to youth, to the "Vergangenheit", with its Ländler graciousness and the nostalgia of the Wienerischer Lokaltöne, the ache for the homeland, the Heimat. There is little in symphonic music that is more beautifully scored than this second movement, which tells us where fancy is bred – in the heart and in the head . . . .

After the third movement Mahler needs the human voice to attain catharsis. The fresco of the Last Day is revealed in a dawn of trumpets sounding through a void, no other flicker of noise left on earth but a nightingale singing; then the apotheosis of soaring choir, orchestra, and bells. But though Mahler began from words and a "programme" they are not more than a sort of scaffolding for the musical matter, much as plots and Holinshed are accessory to the poetry and prose in Shakespeare.

Mahler draws all through his mind, which was, even more than the mind of Berlioz, avid to change any poetic or verbal impression into tone. There are comparisons to be made between the Mahler of the Second Symphony and Berlioz, but only external and stylistic; the natures of the two men, their psychological texture, were poles apart. The Second Symphony of Mahler contains enough material, pregnant musical ideas, to set up the average composer for a lifetime. To this day it is borrowed from; the instrumentation is prophetic and fertile; it breeds like pond-life.

But this Second Symphony represents Mahler still in the throes of parturition; not until after the discipline he subjected himself to in the three wholly instrumental symphonies, the Fifth, Sixth, and Seventh, and after the poetic resignation of "Das Lied von der Erde", did he achieve the clarification that enabled him to compose the wonderfully blessed and consummating closing Adagio of his Ninth Symphony.

The soloists of this memorable performance were Kathleen Joyce and Margaret Ritchie. Once again Mr Krips and the LSO deserve our thanks for removing us temporarily from the routine of music in London by giving us an experience, not just another concert. Only a warmer violin tone was needed to take us to the heart of Mahler. I imagine that another performance of the symphony, given at once on the heels of this one, would attract a much larger audience than last night's. The work never fails to move and inspire, excite and brace up. Why then is it not generally well known? It calls for immense executive resources, true. Why then is the less elaborate Fourth Symphony of

Mahler not a favourite in this country? For none is more entrancing, more melodious, warmer in song or happier in rhythm. Is the neglect of Mahler here a responsibility to be shared by the critics?

Mahler's Growing Influence

4th October 1952

The BBC this week have served the cause of Mahler well by the performances in the Third Programme of the Adagio of the unfinished Tenth Symphony and the whole of the Ninth Symphony, conducted by Hermann Scherchen. Seldom, if ever, have I heard an English orchestra, in this instance that of the BBC, come so closely to the Mahlerisch tone and flavour. The string tension was absolutely right; and very few English violinists play Mahler with enough vibrato.

The cause of Mahler, apparently a lost one twenty years ago, gathers in influence. It is no longer permissible or civilized to refer to him as a decadent romantic, or as a composer of pastiche, derivative, and eclectic . . . . We can perhaps understand the impatience of a French mind and musical aesthetic with Mahler – to this present day. He has no reserves, no poise . . . he wallows at times in his Sehnsucht, in his ache for what he is seeking. It is not at all surprising that Debussy and one or two others of his school walked out of a concert during a pause between the movements of a Mahler symphony. His intensity, typical of the Central European who has the Jew in him, easily invites satire. By force of his orchestral culture and the subtlety of his thinking processes the modern age is ready to collaborate with Mahler's romantic quests for unattainable things. After all any "age" can be scratched into a simple enough emotional reaction; we are all islands essentially . . . the loneliness of Mahler, and his strenuous reachings after some certainty of beauty to be passionately, even aesthetically but certainly not ethically, seized and lived with, provides a wave-length on which most of us may find his music in increasing numbers, as the contemporary scientists go out of fashion, with their insistence on music for the sake of its patterns and little else.

The best brains in actual music-making nowadays are attending diligently to Mahler. In this country, though in large numbers we still fight shy of original Mahler, we readily take to him if and when he is diluted by – well, So-and-So and Never-Mind. Those who listened to the broadcast of the Adagio of the Tenth Symphony must have realized how prophetic it was when Mahler composed it more than forty years ago, and also must have understood why the name of Mahler has for several decades been pronounced with devotion and respect by such as Schönberg and Alban Berg of the Elders and by the most original and agile of our contemporaries, Britten, Shostakovitch, and Copland.

Apart from what Mahler says in this Adagio of the Tenth Symphony, there is much for the strict musician to consider. Mahler was heading for new paths when he died in May 1911, at the age of 51. It is a sentimental conceit to imagine that in "Das Lied von der Erde" he consciously made his farewell to the world. The Ninth Symphony gives us the consummation of an exclusively orchestral and symphonic technique, the full fruits of the discipline Mahler put on himself when in the Fifth, Sixth, and Seventh symphonies he denied himself the aid of the voice and words. He needed poetry and song for the expression of all that was personal in him; then gradually even Mahler reached forward to an impersonal vision, or rather a more introvert one, where words and suggestions relating to anything outside his innermost being could not be heard or have relevance.

Mahler expressed the wish that the manuscript sketching for his Tenth Symphony should be destroyed, though he changed his mind on the point more than once. Two movements were "reconstructed" by Berg, Krenek, and Franz Schalk, and with so much insight and sympathy was their work done that the most experienced student of Mahler was not likely to detect a false note during the broadcast of the Adagio. All the familiar characteristics were to be heard: the high strings at great tension, a tendency of melody to vacillate around the tonal centre, the vague movement of isolated woodwind wandering up and down in short intervals, sudden crescendi with the orchestra full and harmonious, the old restlessness, pauses and upward violin leaps alternating – here we can still recognize the habitual dress and physiognomy of the composer. But there is also a subtler logic, a more elliptical syntax. The development is more onward-moving than in the past, more polyphonic, the parts weaving a tissue only as a consequence of juxtaposition or contiguity; this is a counterpoint born of freedom and range of thought and feeling; it is not imposed on the conception academically. So freely, indeed, do the melodies go their ways that if atonalism is not actually achieved it is suggested. The Adagio is entirely original, compact of keen musical thought and deep emotion. To hear it but once is to deplore the waste of Mahler's genius at its prime, for though he was romantic enough always to ache as he glanced back, he was a progressivist too, the "Fortschrittmann" and searcher.

We cannot expect to hear public performances of Mahler's "Unfinished" Symphony, but why is the Ninth so seldom played in this country? Harty gave a splendid performance of this masterpiece at a Hallé concert in the 1930s, after only one or two rehearsals at that. Harty introduced "Das Lied von der Erde" to Manchester, also Mahler's Fourth Symphony . . . . The Ninth Symphony is the ideal work for Sir John Barbirolli to conduct. Why hasn't he been drawn to it these several years?

Approaching Mahler

21st November 1953

Early next year Sir John Barbirolli will conduct the Ninth Symphony of Gustav Mahler at a Hallé concert . . . .

Mahler is still not really liked or understood in this country at large. There is a big and growing appreciation of him in America; because the conductors there are mainly of Continental origin and training, they learn to approach Mahler very early in life. Few English conductors seem to have the faintest clue to Mahler . . . their programmes, especially those given in London, rouse irony and irreverent mirth from any student of music coming from Brisbane, Kansas City, or Bulawayo. I have often wondered if these conductors of ours are born lazy or acquire laziness by practice. Neglect of Mahler here is most times excused by reference to the expense involved by the large orchestra he needs, and to the number of rehearsals required, and so on. Mahler certainly does, in nearly all his works, call for lavish instrumental forces; also he expects as much imagination and passion as technique. But Henry Wood conducted the First Symphony at a promenade concert in 1903 . . . and the Seventh in 1913. I doubt if the Seventh has been heard in England since . . . . No, we needn't carry our investigation too far as we seek the cause of the average English conductor's shyness in the presence of Mahler.

The bulk of the writing about Mahler in English reveals much the same innocence or ignorance. Some of it strikes me as having been written about another composer altogether. Mahler is to this day described in English as though in a Teutonic tradition ("long-winded and metaphysical"). A composer less Teutonic than Mahler, in mental tissue or orchestral method, has never lived. He is supposed to have written perpetual "swan-songs" of nineteenth-century Viennese and Central European culture; yet he opened up "new paths", and you will hear his influence at work, assimilated by nothing less than genius in, for instance, the orchestral preludes of "Peter Grimes". He is persistently linked to Bruckner, even as Bruckner is linked by the half-educated to Wagner. Mahler and Bruckner are both marked off from Wagner by the basic fact that neither is erotic in the least. And Mahler is marked off from Bruckner by Bruckner's absolute sure faith and patience. Bruckner is integrated – by God, as he himself would surely say. Mahler, in spite of his colossal Catholic *mise-en-scène* and "properties", displayed on the canvas of the Eighth Symphony, subsided into the autumnal pessimism of "Das Lied" and the slow movements of the Ninth and Tenth symphonies.

More than any other composer, not excepting Wolf, Mahler lived on his nerves, his music is, so to say, very frequently so many exposed nerves. Even in the Adagio of the Ninth Symphony, where at last he achieves a full, broad, simple, contained and close harmony, he is soon impelled into the familiar intensity. Thirty-three years ago the first of discerning English writers on Mahler nearly touched the spot: "To be naïve and to be direct are not quite the same thing, though Mahler did all that was possible to make them so, and a writer may be both and yet come short of the sincerity of emotion without which nothing is true or enduring in the arts. There are some grounds for suspicion of Mahler's emotional sincerity in his art, in spite of his naïveté and ruthless directness of style. He is a Jew and a Catholic, and while there is every reason why a Jew should show some sympathy with Christianity from its origin and make it prominent in his art, the Jewish-Catholic standpoint is complex to the normal sensibilities." Thus wrote Samuel Langford in 1920; nobody since has got closer to the core of the matter in Mahler.

I don't agree, nonetheless, that Mahler was ever insincere. Only in the Eighth Symphony are we likely to be worried about the Catholic-Jew complex. His trouble was not insincerity but a frustration. This receives so powerful an expression in the finale of the First Symphony, for example, or the "Sturmisch bewegt" movement of the Fifth, that we may even think of this frustration as a source of inspired greatness. The fury is terrific, and takes the shape of bare, steely harmony. "Pitched battles against the world and the demons of life", wrote Langford of these movements. Inspiration seldom fell on Mahler by grace; he had to "hammer it out". But the ring on the anvil, though many times jarring and discordant, is desperately honest. Sometimes the true and right idea eluded him, so he resorted to gestures. He was by nature unable to wait patiently during a dry creative period, wait like Bruckner, strong in the faith that, as Goethe told Eckerman, ideas come when they will, and you'll find them one morning sitting on your shoulder, like children from God, saying: "Here we are."

But I am making the common mistake of talking of Mahler as though he were mainly a pathological case, and not a composer of immense range, worth endless study as musician and music-maker. There is in him occasionally an invention so sharp that it almost stings, and a reckless profusion of energy properly to be called daemonic; the Rondo-Finale of the Fifth Symphony, with its triple fugue, is an example of the Dionysiac (but I had better say "Walpurgisnacht") aspect of Mahler. The Rondo Burleske of the Ninth is as though all that we associate with the style of the grotesque scherzo had been let loose in a gigantic scornful flagellation of notes. Mahler was imprisoned in the shackled rhythmical periods of his times; he tries hard to break the bars. As early as in his Second Symphony, he changes his time-signature twenty-three times in thirty-six rehearsal "measures" in the fourth movement. Flexibility of rhythm is not one of Mahler's strongest points: he was temperamentally taut. And nothing appears in Mahler's music that is not true to the man himself. His influence on orchestral technique has been greater already than any other composer since Berlioz . . . .

The Cause of Mahler Victorious

JASCHA HORENSTEIN AND A GREAT NINTH SYMPHONY

15th January 1957

An emphatic victory was won for the cause of Mahler, in the Festival Hall on Wednesday, by great conducting from Jascha Horenstein and by great playing on the part of the Royal Philharmonic Orchestra. I have heard many performances of the Ninth Symphony, some under the direction of the renowned Mahler interpreters. This one went deeper into the score than any of my recollection; and the playing was absolutely right in tone, attack, in its vehement string tension, its snap and also pathos of woodwind; and the brass and horns ranged from romantic evocation to sounds which seemed to come from a charnel house.

By what marvels of hypnotism does a conductor conjure from an orchestra a tone the like of which it has seldom produced before? This was the voice of Mahler; it was more than that – it was the Mahler ectoplasm. At the end of the performance there was a scene of enthusiasm and tumult seldom equalled at concerts in this country. Young people in the audience shouted, waved hands, and stamped feet. The sight of it all warmed the cockles of the heart. The battle for Mahler in London has been long and hard, and now that he is coming into his own we might think gratefully for the moment of the name of the first critic pioneer, Samuel Langford. This performance has surely established Horenstein's position among the very great humane orchestral interpreters of our time.

His conducting was clear-sighted and yet intense enough of brain work and emotional voltage to endow the work with unaccustomed constant and vital connection. It has seldom sounded less diffuse. And what a work! – for all its prolixities and obsessive assertions. It is at one and the same time a poignant human document and a synthesis of the romantic symphony's technique and psychology, with prophetic glimpses towards the next twist or turn of evolution. It moves the heart, excites the nerves; also it arrests and engages the acutest musical intelligence. The audience must indeed have fallen entirely under Horenstein's spell; for they listened absorbedly throughout the symphony's exorbitant length – and it demands very close attention.

Mahler's observance of the classic symphony's formulae goes only as far as the broad outlines; within them, he uses his own intricate and sometimes elliptical logic. The themes are not compact and not contrasted in easily recognized sequence. The development from long episodes is variational, phrase by phrase, each division germinal. The episodes obey in their courses the symphony's content. Music for Mahler was a means of rendering his life as man and artist articulate. All that he suffers, all that he strives after and clutches; all his struggles and all his moods, change naturally to orchestral music. He is never merely "descriptive", never going more beyond the bounds of music than Beethoven himself in, say, the "Eroica". But there is scarcely an heroic gesture in the whole of Mahler; his daemon allowed him no self-mastery! And constant self-mastery is the sign of the hero. Mahler was always reaching beyond his grasp. His marvellous technique is usually strained to the limits – sometimes the string tension positively aches. In the inner movements of the Ninth Symphony the rhythms and the stark contention of congestive melodic parts makes a tremendous contrast to the more familiar Mahler nostalgic indulgences.

Horenstein very finely brought out the ambivalence. The "Rondo Burleske" was given the proper bitter sharpness of stress and tone. And, without the usual obviousness, Horenstein pointed the ironic relationship of the flippant mocking tune of the middle section of this movement to the great pathetic melody of the closing adagio, with his characteristic Mahlerish appoggiatura. Even the weakest section of the symphony, the Ländler scherzo, was unusually convincing under Horenstein: the pace and the alternating phrases of heartache – forestalling the "blues" of a later day – were controlled so that the whirl of notes and the modulation to relaxed rhythms had relevance and not as much waste as in most performances. The terrific crisis of the first movement, with the crack of doom and the spectral procession, was as potently and proportionately done as the deep-toned adagio, where at the end, and for the first time in his stormy, Heaven-aspiring, and often

Hell-skimming life Mahler achieved the warm, full, close harmony that tells of some sort of peace, if only the peace of submission.

In the critic's routine, an experience happens occasionally when from the many sounds made by instrumentalists, many of them also frequently and inevitably routined, music comes that incarnates genius and extends our sense of life and its splendours, miseries, and mysteries. This concert provided such an experience.

A Dedicated Performance of Mahler's "Eighth"

23rd March 1959

Mahler wrote of his cosmically-planned Eighth Symphony that in it the universe begins to vibrate and to sound. On Friday the Albert Hall was made more or less to vibrate with sound by 750 voices and instrumentalists engaged in a presentation of the work to an assembly which filled the enormous place from floor to topmost gallery. In the chorus were humans of all ages, children choiring like cherubim, more or less; venerable basses, and young girls at the spring of life. Eight soloists sustained the revolving world of Mahler's aspirations standing there like supporting pillars. Jascha Horenstein controlled the apocalyptic structure firmly and purposefully, avoiding the occasional chasms and glimpses into vacancy, and scaling the heights without haste or waste of breath.

At the end, the audience broke into tumultuous acclamation. Seldom, if ever, have I known in an English concert hall so tremendous a demonstration as this. No doubt Mahler's apotheosis of heaven-storming brass and bells, heaven-arching sopranos and infant warblings, was partly responsible for the outbreak, but throughout the performance attention had been riveted and breathless, so we can assume that the roars of "Bravo" signified more than excitement due to an assault on the senses.

Horenstein encompassed the work with simple, impressive technical mastery. He indulged in no histrionic gestures. He did not attempt to persuade us that he was sharing with Mahler the labour pains of creation. He put himself devotedly at Mahler's service, had faith in the music, and he had patience. It was a dedicated piece of conducting; indeed, the performance itself was dedicated and a great credit to all taking part. The young folk singing Mahler to Goethe's German from the closing scene of "Faust" will surely remember this concert all their lives.

It is difficult in the Albert Hall for any conductor accurately to calculate nuance, subtle, change of tone. The wonderful finale, after a spellbound intoning of the Chorus Mysticus – "Alles Vergängliches – All that is past of us" – failed to revoke the sense of floating rising melody when the "Mater Gloriosa" theme is wafted on the higher voices. The tempo was too deliberate. The dome of heaven was not revealed. There were no echoing reverberations. But Horenstein had no choice but to insist on the strictest rhythmical precision, no opportunity for the finest shading. He was conducting the symphony for the first time, with forces not familiar with words or music, which, in the Goethe section, might well have come to them as alien from contemporary English modes of thought, symbolism, and feeling. There was, perhaps, a lack of string tension in the wonderful anchoritic orchestral introduction to Part 2; the familiar Mahler fingerprint of the appoggiatura and tremolo needed a more abandoned and passionate bowing.

Also, for want of the right understanding tenor, the beautiful if operatic invocation of Doctor Marianus short-circuited into sentimental prose. The only other important miscarriage in a remarkable performance was during the superb setting of Goethe's terrific and elemental declamation by the Pater Profundus, from the depths, "Wie felsenabgrund mir zu Fussen – "At my feet a craggy chasm". The fault was not so much the solo vocalist's as one of orchestral playing a little over-careful.

But I make these critical points in no carping spirit. I wish only to be fair to Mahler, for magnificent though this interpretation was in bulk, it did not entirely give us the right voltage, the feeling of almost excruciating search for the right tone-symbols.

A remarkable point of Horenstein's conducting is that he succeeded in holding together the first part, based on the medieval hymn "Veni, Creator Spiritus", composed mainly in the starkest and most intricate polyphony, with challenges to high voices even more cruel than Beethoven's in his choral apotheosis. Only by sweat of brow does Mahler evoke the Creator Spirit to dwell in our minds and strengthen our weak bodies. The aspiration is terrific, also the desperation.

The Latin text and the neo-classic vocal polyphony employed was not really instinctive in Mahler. We feel the release of strain as soon as Goethe enters, and the atmosphere of a German poetry and metaphysic is breathed. The work, in fact, is dichotomous; the two parts do not mingle, in spite of a closer thematic connection than is apparent even after much study of the score. For example, in three bars of the simple chorus of angels – the major themes of "Ascende" and "Mater Gloriosa" are both sounded in some dozen notes.

The score is an amazing torrent of ideas, supplication, doubt, spiritual effort and exaltation wrestling like beasts with relaxations to quiet even miniature islands of escape, in which Mahler composes with a delicate touch prophetic of "Das Lied von der Erde". At times, for instance, in the advent of the "Mater Gloriosa", soaring on high, the violins and harp play a melody perilously saccharine and reminiscent of Gounod rather than of Goethe.

But, all in all, Mahler in this work subdued his ego and by the will-to-believe, and out of his momentary ideal of universal brotherhood, composed his most objective music. A thousand pities that another performance could not follow at once on Friday's, so closely did it get to the heart of the matter . . . .

Langford should have been living to witness Mahler's victory over thousands; he was the first to write of Mahler in this country nearly forty years ago. He was then alone in his advocacy.

Mahler's Centenary

7th July 1960

Mahler needed *time and space* for the development of his material. He did not present an easily defined theme, then a second – and proceed to develop them in a separate compartment before repeating everything all over again. A symphonic movement in Mahler, especially an outer movement, consists of *many* themes which he first of all groups in one period. Then the themes are separated; a single phrase in a melody gives birth to another. This is why he needs room to develop them and bring them to a unity and solution at the end.

He once said, "In a symphony I build my world." Music was for him his only way of life, his only way of expressing himself, finding himself *in the* world. In music, Mahler tries not only to relate himself to God but also to himself. He did not compose pattern-music. He could never have shared the present-day notion that music is a thing in itself, and cannot express any human emotion. I tremble to think what he would have said about Stravinsky's theory that music has no meaning apart from the sounds and patterns made from and by it. Mahler maintained that not all the music is in the notes. He also said that he could not compose at all, except with a definite human experience as the first urge to inspiration. But he did not compose "programme-music", merely descriptive music – though often in his symphonies he uses echoes of sounds heard in the everyday world . . . . If Mahler makes a noise like a cuckoo, or a trumpet-call announcing the Day of Judgement, he does not imitate actual sounds heard in life itself; he *symbolizes*, he does not reproduce. Unlike Richard Strauss, he does not tell a particular story in music; he does not characterize an individual – a "Don Juan" or a "Till Eulenspiegel". His music is no more descriptive than Beethoven's Eroica or Ninth Symphony. When he was once asked what was his religion, he answered: "I am a Musician."

There is a fallacy hard to kill: that Mahler was a pessimist. Of his ten completed symphonies, six end on a triumphant, hopeful or heroically battling note. The Fourth is one of the happiest and most melodious symphonies in existence. The Fifth finishes with an exuberant rondo-finale, a marvel of gusto and happy invention. In the Seventh Symphony, the "Night-music" is as fanciful, as swooning in melody, as gorgeous in orchestration, as anything composed by Tchaikowsky. The Eighth glorifies the eternal life. The Third sings the praises of the summer, the flowers, the animals in the forests, the grandeur of night and the beauty of the world. "The Song of the Earth" praises good wine, the autumn mists, the everlasting greenness of spring and nature. Mahler was no doubt a highly strung man, intensely sensitive to the mystery of existence and creation. Must we call him a poor artist because of that?

Between the years 1897 and 1907 Mahler was the director of the Vienna Opera and he made it famous throughout the world. As a conductor and director his influence and activity were equal to those of Toscanini. The range and intensity of Mahler's genius might forcibly be brought home if we imagine that Toscanini, besides bestriding the world as the greatest conductor, also in his spare time composed nine symphonies and left a tenth unfinished. Moreover, let us bear in mind Mahler's life time, a little more than half the length of Toscanini's. Mahler called himself a "summer composer" – only in his holidays could he find the leisure to compose his own music. It is one of the miracles of artistic creation that Mahler in a pathetically brief life-span could spend so much of his genius. He was a living dynamo; and he wore himself out for music. Like Toscanini he was small in inches, and like Toscanini, he was daemonic. Even in the photographs of him we can see the pulse throbbing in the veins of his great forehead.

His life was terrific from the beginning. He was a Jew born in the Bohemia of the old Austrian Empire of Franz Josef, in a shack of a house which had no glass windows. His father was first a coachman, who had social ambitions of a middle-class order, but he got no higher than proprietor of a rather dubious wine shop. Mahler's mother, daughter of a soap manufacturer, was frail, with a limp. Mahler inherited her weak heart – and he walked with a twitch or jerk of the legs. The parents did not love one another; but none the less produced twelve children. Five died of diphtheria at an early age; another succumbed to heart failure when he was thirteen. Leopoldine, a sister, perished at twenty-six of a tumour on the brain. Brother Otto committed suicide. Brother Alois fled to America to escape his creditors. In such a home Mahler the child grew up. A coffin in his infancy must have seemed to him part of the domestic furniture. But though his father was no better than a man should be, he had the sense to realize that Gustav was a potential musician. Sacrifices were made so that the boy could study at the Vienna Conservatorium where, like most born geniuses, he was brilliant and not always industrious, except in his own way. His tremendous energies when he created the Vienna Opera were triumphant in spite of constant intrigue and rampant anti-Semitism. He was broken on the wheel. He himself said, "I am thrice homeless: as a native of Bohemia in Austria, as an Austrian among Germans, and as a Jew throughout the world."

It is natural enough that a legend has arisen around Mahler, making him out to have been perpetually self-pitying and abnormally neurotic . . . . But tragedy and unhappiness are not the same in an artist as they are with ordinary people; the artist uses his happiness and unhappiness alike to produce his masterpieces. In Goethe's play "Torquato Tasso", the poet says:

"Nature has given us tears and the cry from the heart when a man can no longer bear his pain; and to me and for my grief she gave melody . . . .

and if others are speechless in their suffering, a God gave me the gift to speak my sorrow."

One of the reasons why Mahler is now coming into his own is that his music is never smug or bourgeois in a nineteenth-century way. There is no middle-class complacency in Mahler. Young people to-day are listening to Mahler because they hear in his music an urgent creative voice not content with the old rewards and profits. In his technique and orchestration, he appeals to fresh young ears that cannot quite "take" the rich, plush, sonorities of the romantic Teuton school . . . . There is hardly a note in Mahler that is not entirely suffused with his own personality – not a note that isn't steeped in his blood or intense with his great brain and supersensitive nervous system. If Mahler had taken "God save the Queen" and scored it for orchestra, the anthem would have sounded absolutely strange – un-English and Mahlerisch. Probably it would have lasted longer – I mean taken ten times as long to play . . . .

It is true that his music is often egocentric. He was honest about it. "Whoever listens to my music intelligently will see my life transparently revealed." In "The Song of the Earth", he is perhaps less subjective than anywhere else. He found inspiration for this unique work in old Chinese poetry telling of the brevity of life, but also of its beauty and everlasting freshness of creation . . . . Remember, when you hear the orchestration, so original and evocative, so finely spun in parts, coloured with exquisite tints in the "Autumn" movement, silver grey and murmurous, or in the "Youth" movement, music enchanted out of the distant Chinese landscape – remember as you listen that Mahler never heard this work; he died before its first performance. This subtle tone chemistry he heard only in his brain and imagination. The recitative of the voice in the "Farewell" is silence made audible; the orchestration at the end is gossamer, with star dust on it. The end sings of the green earth that will blossom for ever.

We take our geniuses very much for granted. We make fashions of them. We put them in their places. "No," says somebody, "I don't like Mahler – don't like Schoenberg, don't like Elgar" . . . and so on. The mystery of genius is not honoured or kept in mind. Of course, one needs to have some intuitions out of the ordinary to be able to recognize genius. After all, it is we who lose if we miss the good things given to the world by great artists. There are no difficulties about listening to Mahler. He only asks for patience. I myself did not find Mahler in a hurry. But now after living with his music half a lifetime, I know that if he does not always give us a full rounded musical satisfaction, he was none the less a genius. As we celebrate we can be sure he has a long future before him.

Faust's Man

18th August 1972

Mahler to the right of us, Mahler to the left of us, volleying and thundering, but not always thundering. He is to-day all the fashion in this country; he is every conductor's bandwagon. Bernstein is conducting Mahler on television tomorrow, and also twice next month. The other week the Proms were packed. Whirligig of time and changes of taste.

In 1927 I persuaded Hamilton Harty to conduct Mahler's Fourth Symphony at a Hallé concert; and, bless me, if I didn't describe the symphony as "the least tedious of all the nine." In 1947, when I returned to London after years in Sydney, Eric Blom, esteemed music critic, told me that I was wasting my time in my advocacy of Mahler. "Turn to Carl Nielsen; he's the symphonist of tomorrow." Tomorrow and tomorrow! Nielsen is a very appealing regional composer; Mahler, with all his short-circuitings of conception and communication, is wide-reaching in his appeal.

Twenty years earlier, and more, we were approaching Mahler, from the wrong point. He was generally played and conducted as a neurotic, self-pitying post-romantic, with a Jewish wail of the wall. As recently as 12 years ago, during Mahler centenary celebrations, a distinguished colleague said to me: "I cannot stand a composer who wears his heart unashamedly on his sleeve." To which I could not resist replying: "And I cannot stand a critic who wears his middle class intelligence unashamedly on his forehead."

Young people here were quick to find the Mahler wavelength. They responded to his so-called "banal" rhythms. In the first movement of the Third Symphony, following the introduction convulsive and primeval, there was a march which is prophetic of to-day's "pop".

Mahler was the first composer to remove German pomposity from symphonic procedure. Also he lightened the movement and the gait of the symphony. Two souls dwelt within him – to translate his beloved Goethe. He *could* wallow in self-pity, as in the great slow finale of the Third Symphony; but also he could dance, as in the beginning of the Fourth Symphony, and enchant the ear with the second movement of the so-called "Resurrection" Symphony.

A typical early twentieth-century opinion of Mahler was this, a quotation from Gabriel Engel: "From beginning to end, Mahler's music is a deeply personal expression, the vivid reflection of his intense spiritual experiences. It is in no respect, save in its unprecedentedly abundant employment of solo passages, of a radical or revolutionary nature."

Goethe said that it made all the difference, even to a genius, if he were born ten years earlier or ten years later than his actual birthday. Mahler was caught in a transition period of music's vocabulary evaluation. He glances back – and forward. The dichotomy is not always musically annulled. After the gigantic energies of the first movement of the Third Symphony, we are taken to the mincing artificialities of the Second, "What the Flowers and Meadows tell Me", café-music marvellously orchestrated.

He was indeed mixed in the elements – that is why he has been, still is, a constant source of fascination to me as a critic. I am engrossed in his enigma, his compound of close austere thinking and uninhibited indulgence of emotion, personally presented. What is still not generally appreciated about Mahler is his protean power of conception and way of communication, the man and his style.

Think of the Mahler transitions – from the light-fingered "Wunderhorn" Fourth Symphony to the immense scale heights and depths of the Fifth and Sixth. But the most miraculous of all Mahler's protean manifestations is from the Eighth Symphony – "Symphony of a Thousand", Latin hymn and Goethe in rhetorical symphonic apotheosis – to the entirely different tone-world and dimension and musical diction of "Das Lied von der Erde". None the less, for all the ranging variations of symphonic and aural changes, the essence of Mahler is there all the time, his keen brain, palpitating nervous system, his physical and psychological inner self, bloodstream, tissue of intellect of the hypnotic man who, with a baton, could put orchestras, and audiences, under a spell almost tyrannical.

"My time will come in fifty years," so it is reported he said. He was right almost to the moment, at any rate to the period. He has been fortunate in his disciples, first Bruno Walter and Klemperer . . . . later and more to the point of the swing in his favour since Hitler, there have been Horenstein, Barbirolli, Kathleen Ferrier, and Bernstein.

A section of the London critics have, until yesterday, shied at Mahler. Round about 1950 I wrote in this newspaper of my amusement that these critics could happily accept Mahler, second-hand, via Shostakovich and Britten, but not original Mahler. Without knowing it, apparently, they were absorbing and digesting Mahler all the time . . . . Were he alive today, nothing would give Mahler so much pleasure as the fact that young music-lovers are all for him, a pretty good assurance that he has a considerable future, not to say posterity. He would certainly have something caustic to say of the tendency of critics, and of certain composers, to seek in his music for fingerprints pointing to an "abstract" way of composition.

Mahler himself never wrote a note *qua* music. "Not *all* the music is in the notes," he said. He composed to give an account of himself to God, to the fates, and to Mahler. To use his own words again, "I do not compose; I am constantly being composed." The failure of a portion of his output came from his inability to subdue Mahler, the Faustian, exploring man, to Mahler the artist. It is, perhaps, the Mahler dissonance, the tensions and contradictions, expressed in his music, that brings him home to our own period. Anyhow, he has definitely arrived.

9

ELGAR
(1857–1934)

Sir Edward Elgar

2nd June 1927

Sir Edward Elgar will to-day receive congratulations on his 70th birthday not only from this country but from other lands. Only a few years ago England was regarded by Germany as "the land without music". Sir Edward Elgar was the first of our latter-day composers to make an end of that legend, and it was Richard Strauss himself who welcomed the writer of "Gerontius" into the great European company. Strauss's tribute to Elgar at the Lower Rhine Festival of 1902 was generous and at that time unexpected even in England. To-day one is not going too far in describing Elgar as a true and inspired follower in the great orchestral and choral tradition. In the late years of the ninteenth century English music was technically and aesthetically outside the great European stream. It is no disparagement of Elgar, but indeed a compliment, to write that his superb orchestra has often shown the influences of Strauss and Wagner. It was not permissible twenty years ago for any composer to make orchestral music and not use all the instrumental resources then at hand waiting for imaginative exploitation. The sum total of the technical equipment available in any period provides for an artist a sort of atmosphere.

Only after years of experiment in a given musical form and idiom is a potent engine of expression evolved, and until it is ready there must be a limit beyond which a certain order of imagination may not go. Schubert, for example, could not well achieve Hugo Wolf's subtleties of dramatic characterization in song, for the simple reason that Wolf, coming to work after Wagner, was able to use a more elaborate means of psychological delineation than was available in the *Lieder* writing of Schubert's day. Likewise Elgar found in the orchestral technique of his

179

period a source of dramatic suggestiveness that enabled him to put new life into oratorio – a form which seemed pretty obsolete before he wrote "Gerontius". When Elgar brought to oratorio a quasi-dramatic orchestra by borrowing the leitmotiv device of Wagner there were critics here who saw in this usage a departure from what they called the proper course of "national" music in England. George Moore even called "Gerontius" "holy water in a German beer barrel". But in art there are no frontiers. Elgar saved English music from parochialism; he assimilated the finest technical machinery at hand and turned it into his own, as every other great composer before him had done.

Mr George Bernard Shaw has said that Elgar makes music like a "perfect gentleman"; properly understood this is not a gibe. Elgar's music tells of a way of living and thinking which is indigenous to the part of our land that nurtured him. Fully to appreciate his greater works you must hear them in a setting of one of our cathedral towns, say, at Worcester, where his music gives a tongue to the place's very stones. Goethe once called architecture frozen music; we may, when we hear "Gerontius" in Worcester Cathedral, say that Elgar's music is thawed architecture – the old immemorial sacred stone made molten and warm.

His music is not that of a full man living dangerously in what Mephisto in "Faust" calls "the greater world". In Elgar's psychology there is nothing of the *dämonisch* (his evil spirits in "Gerontius" are mild and quickly cast out). But if he has turned his back on much that is warp and weft of modern existence . . . there is no getting away from the Elgar touch; his accent, his idiom, his flavour is as unmistakable as Wagner's, Strauss's, and Brahms's. And always does the music of Elgar speak of a big, if not an expansive attitude to life . . . .

Elgar has never wholly spanned the symphonic form with the authentic German mastery over structure and development; his music is more often than not episodic; his themes lend themselves to vivid statement rather than to fruitful development. None the less, he has not shirked the severest challenge music can put before a composer – he has come masterfully through the test of writing a slow movement. Not since Beethoven have slow movements of bigger heart and richer consolation been written than those of the symphonies and the "Enigma" Variations. But the peacefulness of Elgar's slow movements is not, as the peacefulness of Beethoven's slow movements certainly is, a calm that follows storm, a refuge gained after only great wrestling with demons of doubt and despair. Elgar's faith has always sounded in his art deep, firm, untroubled. These slow movements speak of a faith that might well move mountains; whatever our creed, we must all give ear to their strong onward-moving song. For they tell, surely, of some essential holiness in life. And in any age of the world some such faith must be sustained if life is to be deemed worth the living.

"Falstaff"

CONSUMMATE CRAFTSMANSHIP

26th October 1928

It would be a pleasure to write at length about all the music that was played by the Hallé Orchestra last night. But we wish to discuss the "Falstaff" of Elgar and, as far as we are able, bring into some prominence a neglected masterpiece which has not been heard at a Hallé Concert since 1914. "Falstaff" is not likely ever to become "popular". The average listener is bound to miss something of the closely knit argument. Moreover the composer's attitude to Falstaff is not a little austere. For our part, we call it an "apologia for a misspent life". Here is a Falstaff actually set in a minor key. Elgar has called his symphonic poem a "study"; he intends us to listen to it as a personal commentary on Falstaff, not as a picture of the man as the world knows and loves him. To attempt a "study" of Falstaff was in itself an un-Falstaffian act, surely; Elgar goes so far as to hold up Falstaff for our moral compassion. One of the most poignant passages in the work is an interlude of Sir Edward's own imagining – a dream-picture showing us Falstaff as he was when he was page boy to the Duke of Norfolk; the interlude seems to ask us to dwell sadly upon "what might have been" had Falstaff's life in the after-years fallen amongst different companions in different places.

Most of us decline to accept even Shakespeare's effort to cast Falstaff out; we feel the untruthfulness in comic art of King Hal's "Fall to thy prayers; how ill white hairs become a fool and jester!" We know that Falstaff was not to be put down in this world by any but a wit more comprehensive and forgetive than his own. Elgar seeks to stress the fate of Falstaff, and as he does so he seems so eager to reveal to us the royal stature of Henry that he belittles Falstaff. The work's most triumphant note is sounded at the end, where the royal procession moves along. Here Falstaff is undoubtedly swept aside by – let us say – pomp and circumstance. The music's colour has not been exactly proud until now; as Falstaff is banished from the royal presence the orchestra swells visibly – and we cannot help thinking that the grandeur of tone achieved is a moral as well as a spectacular grandeur. But what lover of Falstaff is going to believe in the man's fall, or that he had in him, or could have possibly had, greater potentialities than those which carried him to that vastness of humour which, because it is as wide as the world, cannot suffer banishment? Elgar, of course, has a right to his own view of Falstaff, and his symphonic study, according to its lights, is a masterpiece. But it lacks the humane view; to most of us the lesson of Falstaff is to take life lightly and put into all of life's pleasure and follies and weaknesses the gusto of imagination. It is hard to believe that Elgar's Falstaff ever slept for long on the benches after noon. This Falstaff has energy, but scarcely wit or spaciousness of spirit. The principal Falstaff motif is not genial, though it is broad. Elgar draws on a Straussian tautness of rhythm for the purposes of much of his portraiture. As a consequence, the familiar Elgarian abruptness of energy is often to be heard when we ought to be listening to a more easeful and tolerant music. There is not much point in the exploit at Gadshill if we are not allowed to share Sir John's account of it. We are shown the discomfiture of Falstaff in a marvellous stretch of music which throbs with wild deeds and scamperings by night. But Falstaff is not given the chance to turn all to laughter . . . . This Falstaff can snore gigantically; he cannot laugh as the Falstaff of Verdi can.

Elgar finishes the work with the most moving death scene in music; compared with it Don Quixote's end, in Strauss's poem, is merely sentimental. The music is spun here with pathetic thinness; wisps of bygone tune float through the old man's mind; he babbles of his green fields. Elgar's Falstaff, if he cannot make us laugh, can land us very near to tears. There is another poignant episode in the work, the interlude which depicts Shallow's orchard. The music breathes the soft air of Gloucestershire countryside under the moon; now comes in the sweet o' the night. ("You shall see mine orchard, where in an arbour we will eat last year's pippin.") Elgar loves his England – "I could not love thee, Jack, so much, loved I not England more". Grant the point of view, and this "study" is one of the really valuable things in our music. The craftsmanship is consummate; Strauss himself never put together a score so closely woven. Every theme is graphic, yet, in the mass they make a texture of astonishing homogeneity. Sir Hamilton Harty's performance last night was the best the present writer has ever heard of the work.

The Violin Concerto

MENUHIN

19th November 1932

HMV have produced records of Menuhin in the Elgar Violin Concerto, conducted by the Composer. There is something which appeals to the imagination in the conjunction of a wonderful boy fiddler, aged 16, and our greatest composer, now 75. And Menuhin is perhaps the most remarkable prodigy we have known in recent years, for he is not only gifted with a natural technique of astounding range and ease; also he plays like an experienced and sensitive musician, as you will soon discover from these magnificent records. The texture is lifelike; the orchestra is obviously the LSO – they know the Elgar secret; they respond to his presence . . . . Menuhin's fiddle has a glorious tone, vital and broad; his combination of range, singing melody and lithe, effortless figuration, swift yet diamond clear, takes the breath delightfully away . . . .

The point about Menuhin's interpretation of the Elgar Concerto is, of course, whether it really is Elgar's when he has finished with it. Frankly, I don't think so. For one thing, he makes the work too much a solo affair, though this fault may be one of focus when recording . . . . But his interpretation, I fancy, misses the Elgar secret because of some essential quality of his art, not at all the consequence of his youth but of the very make-up of his temperament or psychology. The rhythm is much too volatile for Elgar; the phrasing is too assertive in the lyrical periods; we miss the composer's recurrent austerity, his curious way of suddenly retiring from the garish highway of the world and of withdrawing to some cloister in his heart. Elgar's duality of mind must always keep him at a distance from the comprehension of foreign musicians, because it heightens and exaggerates (according to the nature of art) the English contradiction between a physical bluffness, even aggressiveness, and a private weakness or sentiment or romantic indulgence. Church and State find complete expression and realization in Elgar's music; we could scarcely expect Menuhin to know all that is concentrated in those two natural ways of looking at man's journey through life to the grave . . . .

The effect of Menuhin's interpretation might be described if I say it is as though Rudyard Kipling had been done into the prose of George Meredith.

Kreisler's Tribute to Elgar

AN UNFORGETTABLE CONCERT

4th June 1934

This afternoon in the Albert Hall a vast audience listened to Kreisler's tribute to the memory of Elgar. He played the concerto which Elgar years ago dedicated to him, and the performance was one to dream about for the rest of our lives. The interpretation, indeed, was itself a dream – Kreisler's ripe musings on those distant days when he and Elgar were friends in art, and when they came together and gave form and spirit to the work. Many years ago, on a mellow autumn afternoon, a lover of music wandered about the Close at Gloucester, during the week of the Three Choirs Festival. Suddenly there came through an open window strains strange and unfamiliar played on a violin as only one man could play a violin. It was Kreisler trying over the new concerto for the first time. This afternoon we have felt throughout Kreisler's performance the sense of a loving glance backwards: the music told us of the West Country fields, of sunsets falling on them, of September quietness in the cathedrals, of strong and hearty walks through the lanes where Elgar found his happiness. The astonishing fact about Kreisler's tribute was its "Englishness". Never before have I heard the music sound so born of the part of England that nurtured Elgar.

Kreisler is still the incomparable violinist; sometimes, as we listen to him, we feel he is the only violinist, that he has himself absorbed into his own being the soul of the instrument, and left only wood and catgut for the other fiddlers to get on with as best they may. With Kreisler a violin is not a material object which he carries in his hand and puts under his chin. We do not notice any point of separation between Kreisler and his instrument: it is a part of him, a sensitive limb of him. The tone, always the most beautiful that ever came out of a violin, is to-day rich with the man's deepened experience of life. Into the glorious song of it has come a sad, quiet wisdom. And Kreisler's physical aspect is but another mode of his playing. He is his own art made visible – in his face, with its kindly eyes and tender mouth, his grace and pride of bearing, his adoring listenings to his violin, his princely releases of his bow from the strings. There will never again be his like; even bountiful nature cannot repeat a Kreisler.

He made the Concerto vital everywhere, even in the many passages of figuration which with other violinists can easily sound so much conventional passage-work, marking time between one episode and another. It is Kreisler's own secret how he can give tone, full and unusual, to every note in the quickest bravura phrase. He, the perfect Viennese singer, was able to give to the second subject of the first movement the proper Elgarian reticence. It was here that Kreisler surprised, by the sureness of his understanding of the work, even his closest admirers. He could easily, being Viennese, have sweetened overmuch a theme that is in itself sentimental, but sentimental in Elgar's own fanciful and shy way. None of us would have complained if Kreisler's touch here had gone slightly astray. But the theme was exactly right in phrasing and quality of tone. It was unselfconscious, intimate, meditative. Yet it was in the last movement, the most difficult of all to bind together, that Kreisler's playing asserted its unparalleled genius. He sent the living current of his violin running through the whirling ornamentation. There was none of the looseness or "scrappiness" which the movement usually seems to have in other performances. And Kreisler's superb chording, which is as resonant as trumpets, was strong enough to match the Elgarian explosiveness in the orchestra. The cadenza was not as exciting as it is in the youthful hands of Menuhin. Kreisler played it as a reverie, as though the music were turning upon itself before coming to its full close, which it did in this unforgettable concert, like a great ship finding harbour.

Sir Landon Ronald conducted the London Philharmonic Orchestra in perfect accord with the master's most sensitive inflection.

"The Dream of Gerontius"

10th February 1939

The people who go to the Hallé Concerts only to hear fashionable soloists stayed at home last night, so that the rest of us were able to listen in peace to one of the most beautiful performances of Elgar's masterpiece which a long memory can recall . . . . Every artist who contributed to this deeply moving experience may well be proud of his share in it. Dr Malcolm Sargent has done nothing more compelling than this. There were small errors . . . . Now and again there was a want of distance; of disembodied rapture, in the sighing of the semi-chorus, the Angelicals; and the violins failed to give purity to the high E's during the ecstasy of "O gen'rous love". But, taking all in all, the choir sang with affecting eloquence and always musically; each part was expressive as though the vocalists had gone well beyond the ordinary procedure of the concert platform and were perfectly "translated" . . . . Dr Sargent achieved an ideal balance between choir and soloists; there was no hint of strain, little forcing of effects beyond the ends intended by Elgar. It was a performance which went far to make the work Dr Sargent's own amongst contemporary conductors . . . .

The work itself sounded as great as ever it did, in spite of occasional flaws which, as Brahms might say, any fool could see. The air "Go forth" is possibly vulgar – at any rate it seems so when blared out by the brass in the prelude. But it is not more vulgar than the notorious chorus of the Knights of the Grail in "Parsifal"; and we do not think the less of "Parsifal" because of that. The debt which Elgar owed to "Parsifal" has been commented upon often enough by the enthusiastic hunters-down of the obvious. The echo of the agonized cry of Amfortas may be heard by all as early in the work as in the prelude. At one point only does Elgar fail completely and that is in the Demons' Chorus. Strauss in a letter to

Hofmannsthal confesses that he cannot find the right music for Joseph (in the "Joseph Legend") because there is no strain of piety in his family. Elgar could be pious or devout with the best of them; but he did not understand Satanism. His devils are even more gentlemanly than Milton's Lucifer is noble. The Hallé Chorus were not to blame if the demonic laughter had less of irony in it than any laughter (ironic) heard night by night in the House of Commons. Satanic music is rare; the art scarcely lends itself to the expression of irony, which is an intellectual matter. Only Liszt has come close to putting into music the sinister colour and accent of Satanism. "Gerontius" is great exactly where it *had* to be great; the demonic elements in the argument are episodic and not essential. Elgar in "Gerontius" is not less vivid than Strauss is in "Tod und Verklärung" in suggesting the dreadful sense of man's dissolution, "this emptying out of each constituent". But also, in the Chorus of the Angelicals, he lets us feel the white paradisal light – Strauss failed here and gave us only a Teuton Christmas-card view of heaven. The contrasted drama and "transfiguration" in "Gerontius," the almost macabre portrayal of the "faltering breath", the "chill of heart", of the opening of part one; and the quiet, timeless, radiant intensity of the opening of part two – here, surely, are some of the most vividly and individually "seen" pages in the whole world of imaginative music. The lovely swaying figures of the muted violins create in a flash the changed scene, the changed state and plane; I know nothing in music more moving in its simple beauty of statement than Elgar's use of the reiterated notes at the words "I went to sleep", followed by the inspired rise to the F natural on the word "strange" at the phrase "a strange refreshment".

Not half enough has been written of Elgar's style of recitative in "Gerontius"; it seems to me to solve instinctively the old problem – how to find the proper element that divides a full lyricism or song from the prosaic levels of declamation. Could a lovelier 'via media' be discovered than the speech-song of Elgar's when Gerontius says: "I hear no more the busy beat of time"? If this is not genius, original and final, then I do not know what genius in music means. Why have Germany and France neglected "Gerontius", Germany especially? The work was given in Düsseldorf in 1902; the performance made history. If a German or an Austrian, a Czech or a Bashi-bazouk, had composed "Gerontius", the whole world by now would have admitted its qualities. On the point of current discussion of "freeing melody from harmony", what of Elgar's recitative writing in "Gerontius" – has Mahler surpassed it? As I say, it is easy to point to the defects in "Gerontius" – to the occasional hints of a too familiar melody, and what not. The flaws in "Gerontius" are those of greatness; the power of beauty is, to use the old language, inspired.

The First English Symphony

"THE AIR IS FULL OF MUSIC AND A COMPOSER
NEED ONLY TAKE AS MUCH AS HE WANTS." (Elgar)

5th February 1955

The other day I heard a recording of the A flat symphony conducted by Sir Adrian Boult and played by the London Philharmonic Orchestra, and once again I was reminded that a critic is constantly under a necessity to overhaul his catechism and to avoid living on fixed ideas. Less than a year ago I decided that the A flat Symphony was a work which I had lived through and exhausted or it had exhausted me, during a long experience of it; for I was present at its first performance by the Hallé Orchestra more than forty years ago. My reaction against it was natural enough at the present time; the fashions of style and the ways and modes of life, emotion, and thinking are at the extreme to those in force when Elgar composed his masterpiece. Opulence and the gesture of greatness, conscious or unselfconscious, are to-day considered, perhaps rightly, insincere and histrionic; and none of our composers uses the technical formula or set-up which was at Elgar's hand and disposal. This symphony is in its technical rationale really a German symphony, with something of the cyclic method of César Franck added. I am of course referring only to Elgar's means of expression as I discussed derived elements in the symphony; the originality of what the music says, the individual force of Elgar's genius, is not in question.

"The work still sounds peculiarly composite," wrote Samuel Langford of this symphony in 1924; "almost everything that was in the air at the time the work was written seems called into service." The recurrent motto theme is put through Franckian changes. There is a Beecham story which throws a searching light into the style and facture of the A flat Symphony. In its first year no fewer than a hundred performances were given. Even Beecham, not a devoted Elgarian, included it in his repertory. But he considerably reduced the duration of it by drastic cutting. The composer protested against Beecham's editing, so at the rehearsal of the next performance Beecham addressed his orchestra in these words: "Gentlemen, the composer of this immortal masterpiece in A flat has objected to our well-intentioned efforts to improve it; he wishes the work to be given in full, as written. So this time, gentlemen, we shall play it with all the 'repeats'".

There is certainly a hint of mechanical recurrence in Elgar's treatment of sections of the great theme, with the strong, nobly treading bass notes, which begins the first movement. And in the working out of the finale the military rhythms and the calculating and fussy sequences of echoes or imitations of phrases of the "motto" seemed to get Elgar into a terrible cul-de-sac; yet how grandly he emerges from his thicket of tricks of the trade and unfolds the controlling melody to a bannered glory of tone, with the bell-like syncopated crashes of harmony! There is a truly imaginative sweep and range in the introduction to the finale, as the symphony's basic material is reviewed and transformed by Elgar's own mind and chemistry. The slow movement remains one of the most beautifully contemplative of all, and as much inspired and enervated in its arched mounting curves of prayerful song by the architecture in the West of England cathedrals as the slow movements of Bruckner were inspired by the influence of the Baroque. In a way, Elgar is an English Bruckner; both composers devoted themselves mainly to two aspects of existence: love of God and love of land and country.

But while there was in Elgar a pride in pomp and circumstance and in the crown imperial, nothing of this kind of patriotism visited Bruckner, whose love of the Heimat was that of a peasant, naïve and incapable of conceptions of earthly grandeur. Bruckner was God-intoxicated; in Elgar there is as much of ritual as of religion.

He was as much a man of the world as a Catholic; he feels "Gerontius" as much a drama as a spiritual experience. "Gerontius", in fact, is Elgar's "Parsifal"; the prelude is obviously derived from the "Parsifal" prelude. "Falstaff" is technically born of Strauss's "Till Eulenspiegel" and "Don Quixote".

Once upon a time a genius in any of the arts was not regarded suspiciously if he conformed to a type or school. Elgar absorbed everything in the musical atmosphere of his time into his own being: the exultant brass of Elgar recalls Strauss, so does the upward urge of his strings; compare the beginning of the Violin Concerto with the beginning of "Ein Heldenleben". The opening of the Introduction and Allegro for Strings and much of the writing of this lovely work in general brings to mind the gorgeous Serenade for Strings of Tchaikovsky. The beautiful leaping figuration of the solo part of the Violin Concerto obviously echoes the slow movement of the Brahms Violin Concerto.

Nonetheless, for all his continental accents and gestures, Elgar is English and Edwardian, unmistakably English of his period, but – and here is the subtle point – with a curious and contradictory side to him. At times he turns his vision inward to a fugitive realm of fancy, reflective, poetic, and sometimes of a sinister or inimical order or taint; in the slow movement of the Second Symphony for instance.

We tend to write and talk about the obvious characteristics of Elgar, of the way he achieves the English synthesis and compromise, making the most of the visible and the invisible worlds. We should honour him by a more intensive study of the thinking processes governing his major works. For an example of large-span symphonic conception, sustained by original musical logic and syntax, I quote the first movement of the A flat Symphony as one of the finest extant, surpassing any exercise in musical cerebration done by Bruckner or Mahler, or by any other English composer.

Twenty Years on . . .

17th September 1955

After one has lived a lifetime with Elgar's music, and after having written thousands and thousands of words about it, the task of saying new things or casting fresh light is not made any the easier if the occasion of a centenary is prompting an article on this subject. I am certainly not inspired to fresh views by writings by the young critics who first heard Elgar's music after he had died in 1934, and after the reaction had set in against deliberate expression in music of subjective or personal emotion. The objections they bring against Elgar are like so many fences and ditches that I leaped over years ago. I have had revulsions against Elgar; it is not possible to listen forty years or so to any man's music and not periodically get tired of it and for a while feel that its defects cancel out the qualities. Let the present-day detractors of Elgar wait until they have lived a life-time with Britten; they will then be in a position to assess comparative staying-power. It is Time that has the last word in the discovery of masterpieces.

The aesthetic of music, the attitude of mind to it, is different now from that of Elgar's day, so much so that music, with the rest of the world, might well seem to have entered a new dimension. The main and inspiring themes of music for centuries had been belief in God and belief in the richness and pride of human life. These beliefs urged composers to the production of works on the one hand such as the B minor Mass, the Missa Solemnis, "Zauberflöte", the Brahms Clarinet Quintet, "The Dream of Gerontius", "Falstaff", the A Flat Symphony; and on the other to "Figaro", Verdi's "Falstaff", "Die Meistersinger", and the Gilbert and Sullivan operas. These two beliefs are not generally shared at the present time, hence the need of another language, another means of expression. A composer today is under the compulsion to look round cautiously and suspiciously before beginning to write: "I must beware romanticism, beware romantic orchestration, vulgar scorn, thick resonances. I must not double the parts. I must think vertically on the whole. Most important of all, I simply must not in any bar remind listeners of the nineteenth century or show signs of any emotion." Elgar had no need to make experiments. He knew what he wanted to say and by hard work he had learned the language then spoken by civilized musicians . . . .

The astonishing fact is that no other composer has needed to fight as strenuously as Elgar to emerge from a culture as provincial as the one into which he was born. There was little music at all in the air of the England of Elgar's formative years; only oratorio, four-square in harmony to the world . . . . It is doubtful if anybody would be remembering Elgar as a composer now if he had died at the age of forty. Not until 1899 did he reveal his genius in the "Enigma" Variations. Then, full spate, he produced his masterpieces within a space of fifteen years . . . . In fact in his long life his years of fertility were confined to this short period. His inspiration died in him while he was still in the early sixties. It is impossible to convey to minds formed since 1914 the effect which the A Flat Symphony had on young music-lovers nearly fifty years ago. It extended the national sky. It swept us into the European main-stream. We admired it all the more because it did not remind us of any English music, Victorian or Elizabethan. Strauss took off his hat to Elgar's genius: that was enough for us; we could at last look the world in the face . . .

Many years ago I likened Elgar to Bruckner. But there was an unrest deep down in Elgar never shared by Bruckner. The idea of a complacent Elgar is contradicted at once by the Second Symphony in E flat. The slow movement is a "Recessional". And in the scherzo there is the spectre in the shadows of the wrath to come. He was the music laureate of his epoch. Pomp and Circumstance and the Public Occasion. The Composer Shows His Medals. Church Militant and Whitehall. Cardinal Newman and the Trooping of the Colour. Rand millionaires in Park Lane, a group of gracious dames on the lawn. The drum and brass of satisfied conquest, the unfurled flag and the organ-note of a nation's thanksgiving. Here is the Englishry of the Edwardian Elgar.

There was the other side of him, the troubled soul and the nerve easily tried, the unfulfilled and unhappy sources in him. The full man that Elgar was may be sought out in the symphonies. For all the miscarriages in them, the crotchet-quaver rhythms, the development by sequence and caesura, the over-orchestrated rhetoric, yet here resides the heart of Elgar, with all the secret places. The Violin Concerto no doubt is Elgar at his most resolved and realized. But we need not pick and choose. He left us a body of work, with not a note written for musical effect. "I put the whole of myself into my music", he said. "I keep nothing back."

To sum up: Man of action and private poet and Empire laureate. Austere, vulgar, prosaic, romantic. The Catholic whose oratorios are acceptable to the Anglican Church. English to the bone, and in nothing more than in his quick use and adaptation of the best Continental methods – Free Trade in composition. His music has survived time and changes of fashion for more than half a century. No other English music written since Purcell and the Elizabethans has lived as long as that. We are not honouring a dead language of music to-day by lip-service. There is richness for you in Elgar yet, if anybody still wants richness.

Jacqueline Du Pré

THE 'CELLO CONCERTO

21st March 1962

The most richly gifted young 'cellist I have heard for years played last night in the Royal Festival Hall for the first time. Jacqueline Du Pré was soloist, in the Elgar concerto for her instrument, at the concert of the BBC Symphony Orchestra. Her grasp over the 'cello tone and capacity for flexible movement is pretty complete and absolutely natural. Even when she is attacking – as at the superb admonitory recitative beginning of the Elgar work – there is no hint about her of a struggle against an unyielding medium.

Of not every 'cellist dare we say that they are wed to their instrument without impediments. But Miss Du Pré doesn't inhibit those strenuous characteristics which are essential to the 'cello diction and range of expression. She can be forceful enough and yet retain definable tone. She spares us the familiar wasp-in-the-window buzzings. Indeed a rare point in this performance was her clear playing of the perpetual motion of semi quavers in the Scherzo. The notes seemed to flicker from the strings, animated, and in all the scurry they were endowed with individual particles of tone. And she was swiftly and musically responsive to the sudden change in the hurrying movement when Elgar switches in two bars from allegro to largamente.

Her tone, for so young a player, is good and plastic; though not yet is it warm and mellow enough for Elgar's beautiful transitions, towards the end of the finale, where the refrain of the adagio is recalled after great, daring and touching passages of imitative downward-leaping phrases, none of which are sentimentalized by our gifted young artist. Her playing in the adagio had a most eloquent raptness. She should go far, to our musical enrichment.

193

The BBC Symphony Orchestra conducted by Rudolf Schwarz gave to Miss Du Pré a very sympathetic orchestral background, woven with an intimacy of orchestration which shows all the cunning of Elgar's hand, and none of the fist blows of rhetoric. It is a swan song of rare and vanishing beauty.

Menuhin

THE VIOLIN CONCERTO

12th July 1969

At the concert in the Royal Festival Hall last night, Yehudi Menuhin was soloist in the Elgar Violin Concerto, with the London Symphony Orchestra, conducted by Istvan Kertesz. Menuhin has been playing this masterpiece man and boy for a lifetime. He has made the concerto more or less his own; and it is interesting that two non-English artists, himself and Kreisler, have established the interpretative tradition and touchstone of the work. Only Albert Sammons and Thomas Matthews, of English violinists, have got to the heart of this Concerto.

Yehudi to-day probably doesn't want to lavish on the concerto the ear-catching sensuous tone which, as a boy, he could give to Elgar sometimes, notably in his treatment of the first entry of the violin in the first movement, making the music sound like Max Bruch. Nowadays he thins down his tone, sort of spiritualizes his fiddle, as though searching beyond the material world of sense data to the essential "Substance". The younger critics, poring like a jury of adjudicators over their scores, take note of Menuhin's recurrent lapses, real or imagined, from tonal accuracy, also not overlooking any obvious departures from textual instructions written down in black and white on the said scores, by Elgar himself, who, by the way, seldom obeyed these markings when he conducted his own music.

Yehudi Menuhin is one of the few artists in music to-day who are not conditioned by the pressures of mass communication. Music is for him a way of life; with Klemperer he is one of the few great survivors of the period in which music was naïvely called "Die heilige Kunst" (the sacred art). The advances in technique have been prodigious, in accordance with the demands of a "scientific epoch"; but a high price has had to be paid. Menuhin can still present the Elgar Violin Concerto "in the round", with authority and rare persuasiveness of presence. There is nothing new to say, either of the concerto or of his interpretation – except, for all his technical ups-and-downs, it goes deeper and deeper into the inner chambers of Elgar's mind and imagination. He remains incomparable in the cadenza of the closing movement, playing with a matchless impression of inspired improvisation. In short, when Menuhin plays the fiddle we are attending not only to a great violinist but to one of the greatest men and spirits and cultural forces of our time. I can only say of his playing, at this concert, what I have said before; he convinces us of the concerto's genius. He causes us to realize that the work enshrines a man and an artist who never concealed his limitations. Moreover, Menuhin forces home the fact that the work is a complete exploration of concerto form and technical procedure. The cadenza of the finale remains a remarkable transformation in which the genius of the violin is allowed full and uninhibited play; it sums up the instrument's history and development . . . which, since Paganini, has transcended technical dexterity and struck out combustible imaginative shapes peculiar to the violin: tonal and catgut emanations which seem not born of any one composer but come into the world of music as lovely and thrilling visitations from the independent if adjacent world of the virtues, exulting in his instrument for its own sake.

In the slow movement, Menuhin played with a beauty and a security of tone beyond anything I have heard from him, or any other violinist, for years. Maturity looked back to youth, and found refreshment. At any rate, this is the way the performance affected me. It was much more than a performance; it was an *experience*, enriching life, certainly enriching my accumulation of years.

10

RICHARD STRAUSS
(1864–1949)

25th February 1927

"Strauss has transformed into great music most of the
stuff of life as we know it in the modern world, but the
note of spiritual exaltation has never yet been heard in his
work. The possibility is he doesn't believe in it. His genius
has fed on the cynicism of his own day, its vast energy, its
cruelty and superb waste of powers. His touch is surest
when he is singing not of faith but of disillusion – think of
the sad beauty at the close of 'Don Quixote'."

"Ein Heldenleben"

SELF-PORTRAIT

27th October 1927

"Ein Heldenleben" is, after "Don Quixote", perhaps Strauss's finest symphonic poem; one would be hard pressed to say which work gives us the more masterful blend of realistic narrative and intimate human portraiture. The listener will be well advised not to take too rigid a view of the composer's claim that his music does not depict a heroism of an everyday sort, but rather "a heroism which corresponds to the inward battle of life, and which aspires through effort and renunciation towards the elevation of the soul". The work is personal and particular enough; the energy of the themes, the swift changes of scene, the fierce contention of isolated instrumental groups in the orchestra – you do not universalize ideas and emotions by methods of expression as dynamic as these. "Ein Heldenleben" is one of the greatest of musical narratives; the more single-heartedly one listens to it, for its story's sake, and the less one looks into it for philosophical symbolism, the more will one fall under the spell of art. Strauss was the first of composers to provide a corrective to the romanticism of the great Weber, Schubert, Wagner, Schumann, Liszt, and Berlioz line. This romanticism was beyond full flower when Strauss came into his strength, so much so that seeds of it had been blown even into the Brahms field.

Strauss brought music out of rather remote realms; for him, the proper study of mankind was man, and of course woman. He planted music on the earth of our own sophisticated epoch. Strauss is always a contemporary; never does his art look back to the past or let us hear the strains of half-forgotten traditional cadences. He has none of the true romantic poet's sense of the pathos of distance. The chief note of his music is an astringent criticism of life but bred by contact with our human-all-too-human world. This is not to say that Strauss is without idealism; in "Heldenleben" there is music which aspires as nobly as anything in Wagner. But Strauss's aspiration is not Wagnerian or Lisztian simply because it does not involve a renunciation of the world, the flesh, and the devil – at least, not for long. The idea of redemption became, during the nineteenth century, almost a trick of the poetic and musical trade in Germany. But by the time Strauss grew to mastery this idea had passed out of life and art; the age was now one of new discovery, of a fresh renaissance. The twilight descended on the gods, and Valhalla toppled into ruins. And man's aspiration sought to find satisfaction on his own teeming earth, in its great upspringing cities, in his sudden possession of brave, vaunting, reckless intellectuality. Even the new age's disillusion did not breed nihilism; the Superman counts as a virtue the cynical, all-critical attitude. Strauss in "Heldenleben" certainly does, during one section, work in the old German vein of "renunciation and redemption". He works, though, with proud and not humble tools; the humanist in him suffers no immolation. If his hero at the end of the tone poem turns his back on the world, redemption is not won in an ideal music which, like Senta's, soars upward, and in its flight needs the bright light of string-tone to suggest a more and more unearthly spirituality. No; the hero of Strauss remains to the end part of the passionate dust; the music of the apotheosis seems to return, in spirit at least, to the reliant "hero" motive with which the tone poem begins. And noble though the calm is in which the work closes, we cannot think that the hero has found lasting peace.

Strauss's music never really suggests spiritual fulfilment; it is dynamic in essence, living in a dangerous, leaping melody and contending harmonies. He has written few slow movements of any length; his active, mutable genius flows naturally into variation-form (as in "Don Quixote"), into rondo-form (as in "Till Eulenspiegel"); into symphonic-first-movement-form (as in "Heldenleben" and "The Alpine Symphony"). Strauss has been a Faust in his music, ranging through the great and little world, ever curious and restless, and finding few of those blissful moments in which the spirit cries out "Ah, stay awhile, thou art so fair." He can be, as in his songs, as domestic and *gemütlich* as Robert Franz himself. But in "Salome" he can live more courageously than any other composer of his time; he can look into the heart of lust and see how sadly and pitifully beauty is poisoned there. Strauss has never been afraid of burning himself in the fires of his art.

In "Heldenleben" the first theme bites into the mind the moment the orchestra sends it leaping and surging forward. Strauss's chief contribution to the symphonic poem (as far as expression goes) is the acid quality of his themes. He does not paint but etches, and the graphic effect of a Strauss tone-poem as a whole is that of some giant engraving. This opening theme of "A Hero's Life" draws the typical Straussian superman; the energy is always more than life-size, yet, with all its pugnacity, hardness, and arrogance, the theme is susceptible of sudden turns and declivities, and in these we get a hint of some essential weakness of spirit. Our hero is as easily depressed as he is exalted. The statement of the heroic motive is followed by a stupendous development section in which trombones and tubas seem to vie with each other in telling of defiance of temper and insistent energy towards an announcement of the will to power.

The "Hero's Antagonists" section shows us the hero's critics (that is, Strauss's) making sardonic laughter. It is this passage and the one where the hero contemplates the "works of peace" (which are the works of Strauss) which provide the clue to the personal nature of the music. A composer who is trying to express a "general and free ideal" of heroism would not completely mix up the universal and the particular. Strauss is his own hero, magnificent egoist that he is!

There is a tendency nowadays for criticism to belittle Strauss. His trouble, it seems, is that he has not kept in step with the march of technical progress! He is an avowed enemy of atonalism. It is argued too that he has allowed his style to become standardized. For our part, we have found in "The Woman without a Shadow" and "Intermezzo," that Strauss can still show fresh aspects of his genius. "Heldenleben", at any rate, is alive yet; not for a long time is the work likely to lose a jot of its energy of intellect and emotion – an energy which must be coveted by every other living composer, none excepted, radical or conservative.

"Don Quixote"

MUSIC WHICH TALKS

6th March 1931

The Hallé Orchestra's performance of "Don Quixote" did justice to the definitely musical parts, but the realism was given rather apologetically. We lack, as a people, a German richness of humour in our appreciation of the art which we call divine. At the passage where the sheep bleat, the audience tittered furtively. Why? Strauss intended us to laugh at it, and really the passage is one of the masterpieces of comedy in music. The scoring is a marvel of mutton-headed stupidity. To laugh at it surreptiously is as though we went into a back entry to read "Pickwick". We are, indeed, a solemn crowd in this country when we go to our "classical" concerts. The only defect in the playing of "Don Quixote" was the tentativeness I have mentioned in the frankly realistic moments. Discretion can hardly be counted part of Quixotic valour; and it is not enough when Strauss lets himself go, that the notes should be merely played; we must have bravery, a rhapsodic recklessness. Last week the Berlin Orchestra in Liverpool let us understand how essential to Straussian expression is an audacious sky-rocketing freedom of instrumentation, a relish of hazards; the triumphant power to rise above them is needed to render expression actual in Strauss, and not just potential. Unless every player throws his technique about, not hampered by conscience and the need to read his music to the last note, Strauss can easily sound a composer of frustrated energy in his dynamic and unsentimental periods.

Of all the works of Strauss the symphonic poems will probably fall into disuse first. "Till" and "Don Juan" will survive; and parts of "Heldenleben" and "Don Quixote" certainly. The others seem already like the mammoth top-heavy flying machines of ancient years, burdened with a complicated Heath Robinson sort of machinery. Strauss's trouble, as a writer of illustrative music, has been an inability to reduce his programmes to a consistent musical essence; he has tried at one and the same time to be objective and subjective, to be a painter of the external dimensional world, and a psychologist of the incomprehensible and elusive world of man's mind. The plane of the one activity is aesthetically considerably lower than the other, and that is the reason why Strauss often makes us suffer a sensation of heavy descent from imagination into the cruder region of the prosaic. He marvellously exhibits the sad, mad brain of Don Quixote, a habitation of twisting notions – all suggested by wisps of confused, mazeful melodies or figuration. Then, next moment, his music is depicting the material earth as sane men see it, with bleating sheep holding up the progress of knightly endeavour, and windmills a positive proof of the objective reality of things. Strauss goes as far as human skill possibly could go to make the transitions musical between the shifting planes of his poetic scheme. If he fails, it is because, as I say, his programme seeks to serve two masters; and because the art of music, as Wagner sometimes understood, will not be hurried in its transitions, will not be stampeded from emotional pillar to matter-of-fact post.

Yet is it astonishing even now, at this time of day when Strauss is regarded by the present generation as a writer more sentimental than inventive, to consider the "Don Quixote" score and to realize how nearly the music comes to solving the eternal problem of how far a composer may tell a story without forgetting that music has its own scheme of evolution, and must develop according to a law and order of its own. A symphonic poem must not be formless apart from the clues given by the programme to all of its changes of style or mood. The programme, indeed, must serve only like a plan of a strange and wonderful city, explaining our whereabouts in it, but not at all necessary for the existence of the town's inherent logic of design. Strauss's "Don Quixote" could be enjoyed as an essay in variation form. It was a stroke of genius to adapt the Don Quixote story to variation form – for here we have the one great musical device for the task of expressing the changing fantasies of the Knight's adventure, while at the same time keeping us in touch with a basic common sense.

"Don Quixote" has a certain magical touch which has seldom if ever been discussed. I refer to the uncanny rightness of the atmosphere of the music's setting or environment. The orchestra frequently seems remote in the mists of a forgotten age of chivalry (for that reason the moments of stark realism are all the more disconcerting). At its best the score has a quite conventional, tapestried sort of beauty and grace. The main themes are chivalric. And through all the work we feel an ancient copper-coloured air and texture. Again, there is the masterly touch by which the Don is delineated by the 'cello's antique and courtly tone. The passage where the Knight and Sancho set out on their adventures seems to me one of the most wonderful in music. Strauss unerringly creates the illusion of perpending deeds of the spirit; also the illusion of a spacious world waiting for the Don and his squire. They go forth in a boundless, murmurous land; and the distant peaks are lit with sunshine. The music fixes this old beloved picture from Cervantes so that some of us cannot think of it ever again as belonging entirely to a jealously guarded literature. Or perhaps we do, at bottom, bring to Strauss's music happy associations obtained from an old book with enchanted pictures, which years and years ago we looked at with boys' eyes in the glow of firelight . . . .

Sir Hamilton Harty attended to the score's details skilfully and there was nothing inarticulate anywhere. The strings were not strong enough to give the work its comprehensive sweep; the texture seemed curiously thin for Strauss. But the interpretation had the merit of emphasizing the music's really lasting qualities – its astonishing allusiveness, its many swift points of humorous characterization, its innate style of the *picaresque*.

Toscanini Conducts "Don Quixote"

25th May 1938

Toscanini has conducted a performance which even in his remarkable career must count as one of the finest. The score of Strauss's "Don Quixote" has been known to musicians for forty years; some of us have loved the music and have come to realize, through close study, the genius of it. But in the concert rooms we have suffered disillusionment. The orchestration has been made to sound merely tricky, ingenious, and in places badly written. Toscanini achieved a perfect fusion of parts, and the playing of the BBC Orchestra was constantly eloquent –

now audacious, now vivid, now warm and wise, and always accurate, balanced, natural. The great wheeling of the conductor led the way through the technical maze; a child could have followed him. It is not a "thick" score, in the usual Straussian sense; there is little massing of sound for mere sonority's sake. Faithful to his subject, Strauss reminds us of the old illustrations to "Don Quixote" in the story books of our childhood. Musical cross-hatching abounds – and most times the poor average conductor becomes hopelessly entangled in the interstices, the many entrances "off the beat", the swift recurrences of motifs usually in polyphony, each of them significant and calling for clearness of statement, yet not to be made so clear as to ruin the golden haze of distance which suffuses the work – the most wonderful piece of story-telling in existence.

There is the other and even more important problem too. "Don Quixote" is at one and the same time a descriptive composition, programme-music, and also a set of variations. The truthful performance must appeal to us on two sides of our sensibility – as Strauss's loving retelling of Cervantes (and why should a great composer not live over again in his own art the delight he has received from a favourite book?) and as a developed form of music. The best tribute to Toscanini's interpretation is to say that he seemed to create "Don Quixote" whole while we sat enchanted there. I even asked myself whether Strauss had ever really composed as beautifully as all this. The shape of the composition, its originality of technique in evolution of pattern and in the weaving of a satisfying orchestral tissue – to these musical qualities was added splendour of dramatic and poetic vision. The music sang music and spoke wit and poetry at one and the same time. At more than one point during the performance one's heart filled at the music's affectionate aptness. It was as though Strauss were telling of his devotion to Cervantes' tale and saying, "Yes, remember where Quixote and Sancho did this, or said that."

Nowhere did Toscanini miscalculate the style. The introduction was a quiet statement of the themes, modulating to the rhapsody which tells of Quixote's breakdown of reason. Then in variation the knight and his man journeyed forth. The music's movement here was entirely right – it really was adventuring, going into regions unknown. Toscanini caused the passage of the bleating of the sheep to sound – as seldom before it has sounded – a masterpiece of humorous musical onomatopoeia; we saw the flock standing in front of the knight, sheer mutton-headed immobility. Again in the assault on the army of the Emperor

Allfanfaron, the gorgeous comedy of Sancho's panic-stricken warnings was brought out as never before in my acquaintance of the work. In none of the mainly realistic episodes was a point missed . . . .

The reflective or lyrical moments were dignified always. Emanuel Feuermann, as solo 'cellist, gave a moving account of the Don's music, and though he played with a master's command over the nuances of his instrument he remained part of Toscanini's conception. The death scene, I am not ashamed to say, brought moisture to the eyes; Strauss was made to sound wise and not just sentimental – this was Cervantes as much as it was Strauss. And the gentleness of the coda; Toscanini translated it simply: "Once upon a time – long ago."

The solo viola of Mr Bernard Shore chattered away entirely in character during the third variation, the colloquy between the knight and Sancho Panza; the nicest appreciation was given to the delicious apophthegms, the comfortable old saws and axioms. The more one knows the work here, the more astonished one becomes at the genius that could draw wit and humour so pointedly out of music. Quixote's extolling of the nobility of chivalry was another of Toscanini's strokes of insight into style. There was no exaggeration as the daring sequences were piled one above the other; and the closing emulations of appoggiatura were treated with a rare and heart-swelling beauty of curve.

At the end of the work one conductor of fame in the audience was almost beside himself with admiration. "To conduct such a performance, to make it all so real and beautiful!" The performance justified the admirers of Strauss – and they are running short in this age of "fashionable" reactions. Well, one listener bowed greatly before the art of the music and before the genial humanity of it. How absurd to say that music is belittled where a story is told in a composition! It depends on the composition. Strauss does not merely reproduce in his work a set of episodes of Cervantes. The music is his reflections on Cervantes, with one or two imitative passages playfully thrown in. "Don Quixote" does not ape Cervantes; it adores and extols him. For the BBC Orchestra there is nothing but praise; everybody played like an instrumentalist possessed.

"Der Rosenkavalier"

ONE'S SENSE OF LOVE AND LIFE ENRICHED

25th January 1934

A serious attempt has at last been made by HMV to get the finest parts of "Der Rosenkavalier" on to the gramophone. The records were taken in Vienna, the one and only place for the job; also the one and only orchestra was engaged, the Vienna Philharmonic, which knows the secret of Strauss's enchantments. The cast of singers, too, is ideal; here, after long waiting, is proof that Lotte Lehmann's Marschallin is beautiful for now and for the years to come, not only as sensitive vocalism but as deep, heart-felt understanding of ironic comedy. Her singing, and Elisabeth Schumann's as Sophie must be nearly the best given so far to the gramophone. There is Olczewska's glory and tone of phrase, too, in Octavian's impulsive music. Perhaps best of all there is Mayr's luscious notes, steeped in humour, as he portrays the rogue Ochs; unfortunately much of his part is cut; no doubt the excisions were unavoidable, for Ochs's music more often than not asks for stage actions; it is indeed marvellously wedded to the man's movements and gestures. One or two of the cuts in general are unhappy. After Ochs takes his leave of the Marschallin in Act I the music to the great scene between the woman and the boy is so fine that not a single bar should have been denied us.

But there will be complaints against Heaven itself. Here is the cream of "Der Rosenkavalier", and it is not all merely whipped-cream – Schlagobers. There is an ignorant notion going around this country at the present time that "Der Rosenkavalier" is just a free fantasia on waltz tunes. The work is really a comedy of manners, consummately arranged or patterned, with deep understanding of life to be felt in and beneath all the surface glamour. There is no character in all the

literature of comedy more beautifully drawn than Strauss's and
Hofmannsthal's Marschallin; she is complete, seen "in the round", a
woman of the world and of her sumptuous station; sensitive to the bitter-
sweetness of her lot, she presses her lips like the very muse of tragic irony,
when pain and disillusionment fall upon her; how exquisitely she tells
Ochs at the crisis to think of nothing but his dignity; her language here
cannot be got into English: ("Mach' Er bonne mine a mauvais jeu: so
bleibt Er quasi doch noch eine Stand-person".)

But Strauss tells us everything in his music, tells of the woman's
nature, so sweet but at the breaking point she can turn to the Commissary
of Police and recognize that he once served as her husband's orderly. In
Act 3, when the Marschallin enters the private room of the inn, there to
find out and suffer everything, the music swells and billows with all the
pride and glory and colour of the panniered dress she is wearing. And the
dignity of her presence touches even Ochs, whose music suddenly
softens and flows into the rich humane current of the score at this part.
Strauss was inspired when he wrote "Rosenkavalier"; he missed nothing
of Hofmannsthal's superb text, nothing that goes on in the hearts of the
characters or outside them in the brilliant world which is the opera's
setting.

Strauss's orchestra is a mirror that reflects every movement; or rather
it is a magical glass in which the play is actually happening. When the
little nigger boy makes his bow after serving breakfast, the orchestra
bows too in long-drawn chords which positively taste of eighteenth-
century prettiness and formality. When the Marschallin laughs at
Octavian's despair the orchestra laughs too – with a delicious playfulness
that stuns the heart. When Ochs assures the Marschallin that he comes of
respectable ancestry, that the first of the Lerchenaus was a pious founder
of convents, the music takes on a gorgeous solemnity and unction. When
the candles of the private room at the inn are lighted the wood-wind
flutters and flickers and floats upwards. When the silver rose is an
important protagonist, when a door is open or shut, when the
Marschallin takes a looking glass from her table, the orchestra makes a
noise like a silver rose, like a door opening or shutting, like a looking glass
flashing in the light. A more allusive and more enchantingly allusive
score has never been written . . . .

But the great thing is the full work which Strauss and Hofmannsthal
give us in "Der Rosenkavalier". To know the Marschallin, Sophie,
Octavian, and Ochs, is to have one's sense of life and one's love of life
enriched.

Robert Heger conducts the Vienna Philharmonic Orchestra on these records .... It is a pity the orchestra is so often too much in the background; recording an opera still tends to work on the assumption that we ought to hear only the singers. These singers, fortunately, we cannot possibly hear too much of; never again will such a cast be gathered together for "Der Rosenkavalier".

"Don Juan"

12th June 1939

The month's best publication for the gramophone, qua records, is the HMV "Don Juan", played by the Sächsischen Staatskapelle, conducted by Karl Boehm. Here is a magnificent performance, vividly reproduced, of one of Strauss's really convincing works – it will outlive all the composer's later symphonic poems, with the exception of "Till Eulenspiegel". The technique of story-telling in music has seldom been better displayed than here. Strauss was only twenty-four years old when he wrote "Don Juan", but with it he gave "programme music" an extraordinary urge forward; he left the oleographic romanticism of Liszt far behind; he achieved a remarkable fusion of pictorialism, characterization, and quasi-symphonic order and development. "Don Juan" may be said to contain the essence of all the Strauss of value. The work, indeed, is a grimly ironic anticipation of the course of Strauss's subsequent career as an artist. First, the audacious flight of his young eagles into the sun; the whip-crack attack of the opening of "Don Juan" was a new note in music; the surge of those divided strings swept us to new brave worlds. It was good in those days to be young and to welcome Strauss and to follow him.

But what an old age he has sunk into! – the disillusionment so wonderfully expressed at the end of "Don Juan" is prophetic; how can Strauss himself listen to it nowadays, if ever he does? The hollow, bitter harmony seems to mock the false ends which Don Juan-Strauss came to in his pitifully empty later work – after the great tumult of "Salome" and the allurements of the Marschallin. Not a note is wasted in "Don Juan" except a brief passage where, for the purposes of musical shape, some hint of "joinery" is given. And the orchestration is vibrant and done with the ease of a young giant tossing the instruments about in play. The performance on these HMV records is easily the best I have heard of the work.

"Die Frau Ohne Schatten"

"MEIN MEISTERWERK"

28th April 1966

"Die Frau ohne Schatten" is not known in England though it is the most elaborate of the Strauss-Hofmannsthal dramas, one in which two women would be set into conflict on different psychological and spiritual planes. It would be for the two men a sort of 'Magic Flute' . . . .

Nearly half a century has gone by since this work was finished. Throughout the 1914–18 war the two collaborators worked on the opera with a concentration and loftiness of purpose not sustained, and indeed not needed, in the production of anything else born of their labours. Strauss maintained that "Die Frau" was his masterpiece, in the only conversation I ever had with him. But Strauss himself – always modest about his own music – suffered one of those moments of self-doubt which apparently don't afflict second-rate artists, suffered it while composing the third and closing act. He confessed to Hofmannsthal that "characters like the Emperor, the Princess, even the Nurse are not filled with red corpuscles – like the Marschallin, Octavian and Ochs . . . . Much as I tax my brain my heart is only half in it . . . ."

Strauss's first thoughts in this matter were wiser than his second. As soon as he received the manuscript of the first act from Hofmannsthal, he wrote in reply, "You have done nothing more beautiful in your life, and I am flattered that it has been brought about by our collaboration. I can only hope that my music will be worthy." He admitted he would have to find a new style to suit Hofmannsthal's poem, and its strange blend of fantasy and poignant humanism. He succeeded to a degree not yet appreciated, except by those musicians and opera-goers who have lived with the score for years.

The first stumbling block presented is the story, the argument, usually described as unintelligible or obscure, by critics who are enslaved to the logic of realism. It wouldn't perplex any ordinarily intelligent child, though, of course, the child would miss the overtones of wisdom. The theme of the opera briefly is this: One day a Prince out hunting kills a gazelle, from which springs a beautiful girl. She is the daughter of Keikobad, king of the spirit overworld. She has been given a talisman by which she is able to transform herself to any shape or mode of being. She and the Prince fall in love at sight and "in the ecstasy of the first hour" she loses this transforming talisman. But – an important point – in assuming human life and shape she does not become *entirely* human. She cannot cast a shadow in any light – a symbol that she has no power to give birth to children. The spirit king sends a message warning her that unless in a given time she casts a shadow, the Prince, now her husband, will be turned to stone.

The Princess's Nurse-companion is a figure of "Mephistophelian evil". She knows that in the world below, in the humble house of Barak the dyer, there is a young woman, wife of Barak, who is unhappy and vain for the pleasures of the world. This woman has not used her shadow fruitfully. So the Nurse and the Princess fly down to the lower dimension of earth; and the Nurse tempts the young wife to sell her shadow to the Princess. Barak, gentle and simple, waits patiently for the awakening of his wife to the desire of motherhood. But while the Nurse's acts of temptation, her evocations of sensual appetite and luxury are in process, the Princess, who lives in Barak's house with the Nurse, disguised as servants, sees and slowly realizes the tragedy of the dyer's lot. And a perception is born in her of the mysteries and sad vanities of the human heart.

This conception of Hofmannsthal's alone would have ennobled the libretto above ordinary operatic levels; and it is expressed by subtle changes of mood, consummately embodied in Strauss's music, as the Princess changes from half-spirit to a human and very much a woman. On her first appearance, her music has a bodiless flight, a tremulous *cantilena*. Then, as she slowly comes to an intuition of the world and condition of mortal men and women, with their joys and sorrows, her music becomes humanly poignant too. Strauss, in fact, with ironic prevision of genius, casts her shadow in the orchestra as soon as she appears before us, hinting of her susceptibility, to a pathos beyond her inborn nature.

The opera shows us a dual testing on different planes. At the supreme challenge, the Princess, even as the Prince is being turned to stone (a marvellous scene when by a crescendo with gongs Strauss petrifies the orchestral tone) renounces the shadow. Barak and his wife, spirited to another region and separated by a wall of rock, are at last drawn together. Where is the difficulty in understanding all this? Incidents such as the flight of the fish to the pan, in Barak's house, are not more incomprehensibly fantastical than many an episode which has enchanted the young in the "Thousand and One Nights".

Strauss as we have seen had to find a "new style". At the first rehearsals in Vienna experienced Straussian players in the state opera orchestra discovered that their former methods with the composer's scoring would not serve. One of the most remarkable of Strauss's achievements in "Die Frau" is transition of scene and character; for example, the magical change from the clamour in Barak's home to the loneliness of the Prince's "falcon" scene, introduced by the most haunting 'cello solo in all opera, with the pitiful cry of the falcon, one of Strauss's rarest and most original inspirations. Barak and the Princess are the most poetical and lovably conceived characters in Strauss. The orchestra is used masterfully, varying from a chamber style to full tone voltage, as in the terrific dream of the Princess, the orchestra volcanic of genius.

Only an Austrian-German feeling of fantasy and symbolism could have conceived and shaped this immense music drama. "Die Frau ohne Schatten" occupied four years of the minds of two men each a product and flower of civilization of his day. It was not put together entirely to entertain the every-night operatic ear. Maybe, now and again, it is pretentious to British common sense. Nonetheless it should be taken into serious account – with an end to the persistent chatter about Strauss's "worldliness". He could, and here he did, rise above it.

On His Centenary

11th June 1964

Richard Strauss is rather out of the good books of the avant-garde in the year of his centenary 1964. His ghost is not likely to be troubled by this knowledge from earth because his operas and symphonic poems still bring in the public's cash everywhere. No opera house dare not have a Strauss in its repertory; no orchestra can afford not to play during a season or two "Don Juan", "Till Eulenspiegel", "Don Quixote" or "Ein Heldenleben". If there was such a thing as a music investment my money would be on Strauss as far as "futures" go before it would competently go on any composer now alive and in full fashion.

Strauss would certainly find a rich irony in his present dispossessed chuck'd down position among the highbrows. For it is the comical fact that he is attacked to-day for reasons entirely contrary to those which assailed his music at the rise of his fame. In the late 1890s and early 1900s the name of Strauss was anathema to the Establishment. He was the antichrist, the infidel profaning the sepulchre of absolute music – this same Strauss nowadays spoken of by those who must be "with it" or perish in the attempt as bourgeois romantic old hat. When "Ein Heldenleben" was first heard at a Hallé concert venerable subscribers crossed themselves and put their minds on Johann Sebastian, not realizing in their innocence that Bach also had written descriptive "programme" music in his time. "Programme music" were dirty words in the years of Strauss's first impact. Ernest Newman, champion of Strauss in the beginning, thought it necessary to advise us to listen to the battle section of "Ein Heldenleben" horizontally. Strauss, after Berlioz, broke up the harmonic blocks of prevalent orchestral scoring (so did Mahler but could not get a hearing in the general hullaballoo caused by Strauss). Strauss gave pace to German music, springiness of gait and, in opera, sometimes the quick give-and-take of human conversation. As far back as 1896 Strauss ended a work – "Also Sprach Zarathustra" – in two keys: B major in the high woodwind and violins, C major in the basses. This was going too far . . . "A dreadful battle of dissonances, in which the woodwind comes streaming down in chromatic thirds, while the whole brass thunders and the fiddles rage"; thus Hanslick on "Tod und Verklärung". The Kaiser Wilhelm suspiciously asked Strauss if he was one of the "modern Evil Ones". "The whole of this modern music has no melody," added the Kaiser, "I prefer 'Freischütz.'" "Your Majesty," replied Strauss, "I also prefer 'Freischütz.'"

It is easy enough to be "modern" in 1964 and remain within the pale. The joke of the present position of Strauss is made more and more pungent if the historical point is emphasized, but it was none other than Strauss who prepared the "new paths". Since his first laying of explosive mines of orchestral polyphony and swift photographic orchestral onomatopoeia the going has been fairly easy in open country for the advancing composers of to-day. Strauss broadened the field of action; what is more important he shocked the public mind out of a "classical" complacency. Young men sixty years ago rallied to him. He gave music wings; led music, in this country at any rate, out of the Victorian captivity. It is easy, it is banal, if criticism, aided by hindsight, maintains that Strauss was from the outset a "romantic" (whatever this term may mean as it changes from year to year), a diatonic composer fundamentally, a composer who in his maturity did not shed a skin and grow another. Why should Strauss have tried experiments after mastering his inherited technique and vocabulary? He was the cleverest, most cultivated composer of his time. He could, had he chosen, easily have exploited the newest gimmicks. But instead of changing a superficial surface coat of technical know-how, he went through deeper and truly creative metamorphoses. This is the fact his detractors overlook or cannot see; it is the fact that even his admirers don't often emphasize enough.

In the symphonic poems Strauss was protean enough of imagination to portray "Till Eulenspiegel", then turn to "Don Quixote", subtilizing at the same time the technical procedure of the symphonic poem – a rondo for the mischief of "Till Eulenspiegel", turning on itself; variations followed cumulative fanciful notions of the Don. Strauss then turns from male impersonations to operas, enriching the theatre with women as various as Salome, Elektra, the Marschallin, the Amme, Sophie, the Kaiserin, and, – in his old age – with Madeleine. Women gloriously, sometimes obsessively alive, unmistakably feminine of sex, most of them civilized and alluring, ready for, if not already acquainted with, bed and love. From Salome to Sophie, from Elektra to the Marschallin – which other composer, except Wagner, has equalled these terrific metamorphoses of imagination and characterization? And the changes went on to the end . . . .

It might be argued of Strauss's characters and characteristics that the more they changed after having got so far, the more they remain the same – Madeleine, a daughter of the Marschallin, the Amme (in "Die Frau") sister to Elektra; and so on. But similarly, the Flying Dutchman could have been father to Wotan, Radames father to Otello. Even a genius's growth is conditioned by a certain germ-cell. Also it might be argued that I am begging the question of Strauss's creative range and supposing that his characters have living and separate identities. But it is the fact that for more than half a century reasonably intelligent men and women have come to know Strauss's people and have had civilized and entertaining experiences in their company. Strauss was himself a civilized and widely cultured man. He didn't house a daemon; he enjoyed composition and enjoyed being enjoyed. If he enjoyed equally his share of the box-office returns he freely admitted it. Kaiser Wilhelm was sorry when he heard "Salome". He had liked Strauss so far but he was afraid this ultra-modern opera would bring injury to his reputation. From the injuries "Salome" brought him, admitted Strauss, he was able to build his beautiful villa at Garmisch.

He was at the extreme of our latest idea of an artist. He didn't trouble whether he was "committed" to society or to Freud or to sex or to anything except his own way of making music. Stylistically or technically he remained absolutely true to himself. From "Don Juan" onward – the work of a young man in his early twenties – the sound of Strauss's music, the thinking and shaping processes of it, followed a line of evolution which we could well say was predetermined. After all a pioneer doesn't go on advancing – he consolidates, if he isn't merely an opportunist.

It is nonsense to maintain that he wrote himself out too soon. Working within the scope of his own musical language, and ripened over a long life time, he undoubtedly achieved astonishing and fruitful modulations and extensions. It is a far cry from Don Juan to Ochs, from Elektra and Clytemnestra to Oktavian and the Marschallin, from Till Eulenspiegel to Barak, from Salome to the Kaiscrin in "Die Frau", from "Don Quixote" to the "Four Last Songs." He could be called on this day of his centenary, the last of the great humanist composers, the last to appeal to a full man and a woman of experience. He was of the world we know, little concerned as artist with the better spiritual world. Since most of us belong mostly to this same world we should sensibly make the best of it – and of Strauss.

II

SIBELIUS
(1865–1957)

Symphony No. 5 in E Flat

25th October 1929

This symphony had a surprisingly warm reception last night – surprisingly, we say, because the composer does not budge an inch to meet a common approval. We had expected that the work would win deep respect, for only a dullard was likely to miss the music's independence of thought, its strange but sincere speech. But frankly we never looked for the warm appreciation it received. The cry was for "More – more of this Sibelius!"

A more manly music than Sibelius's has never been heard since Beethoven. It disdains the petty emotionalism of fashionable art; it avoids the personal note, and, by doing so, achieves epic grandeur. The closing section of the last movement, with its superbly measured sonority, is kingly, royal as anything in the music of our period. It sings as ancient bardic strain, the strain not of man only, but of a whole race that lives near to the earth. The very subtlety of Sibelius's mode of musical development is a mark of the "natural" as distinct from the civilized composer. The mannered logic of symphonic form, with its artificial statements, workings-out, and recapitulations – this formal logic would tie the tongue of Sibelius, who, like the true primitive, is direct and concerned only with essential things.

Since Beethoven, whenever have we heard plucked strings as ghostly as those we hear in this work? And since the last quartets of Beethoven whenever have we heard music so independent as this of a deliberate sensuousness. Sibelius strips the orchestra of all reach-me-down tricks of emotional and pictorial suggestiveness. This orchestra is capable of giant dynamics, but never of the sound and fury that signify nothing. Sibelius's orchestra bursts out at full strength only when the man is thinking and feeling at full strength. He is never emotional only; his feeling is the result of his aesthetic reactions to ideas conceived musically. And out of a few ideas, morsels of melody, his symphony is grown, not "developed". Sibelius is probably the most original composer since Berlioz. His orchestra is of normal scope, the curve of his music classically symphonic. Yet his syntax, the order of his musical thoughts or imaginings, is a matter entirely belonging to his own psychology. The course of his music is continuous; we intuitively believe that the logic is right – because power comes through.

There is no art without power, and if we can feel the driving force of creative energy in Sibelius then we must needs accept the logic. What is not organic cannot be powerful – a point occasionally forgotten by the modern composers. At times you might think that Sibelius is keeping his music on the move by the trick of thematic repetition. But every figure, as it is repeated, is either heard in a new rhythmical harmonic context, or it is subtly transformed. Compared with the Fourth or the Seventh, the Fifth Symphony of Sibelius is positively companionable. One hearing, though, carries us only through the skin of the work. In view of the interest and pleasure it gave last night would Sir Hamilton Harty and the Hallé Concert Society entertain the idea of repeating the Fifth Symphony at the next concert, in place of the Second Symphony of Borodin?

Symphony No. 7 in C

11th December 1931

This Symphony was finely conducted last night by Sir Hamilton Harty, who by his every gesture let us all understand that the music contains rare qualities worth digging out – and they have to be dug out and no mistake. It is in a single continuous movement which lasts only twenty minutes. It begins with a big ascending scale, then by part-writing that would be commonplace from any other composer the music sings a noble song of national praise. A middle section chatters loudly and not very convincingly. Then by means of his favourite device of getting sonorities by accumulating notes added by the horns and brass on top of one another, with a persistent ground bass lending a steady rhythmical

continuity, Sibelius builds up his climax – and without warning snaps it
off and leaves us, so to say, standing. Abruptness could go no further
than Sibelius's brusque way of writing a full-stop. And though he is the
most personal composer of the day and the hardest to classify, his
language, his vocabulary – as distinct from his form of syntax – is quite
familiar. All his music in this symphony is made up of common devices
– simple scale-passages, insistent rhythms that anybody could beat out,
primitive cadences in the horns, thrummings in the violins, rapid swirls
in the wood-wind, sudden and violent pluckings of the bass fiddles, all
of it music raw and ungarnished, yet somehow original and at times
powerful and stimulating.

The form of the symphony is almost naïve in its disregard of the
customary divisions and key relationships. It is a symphony composed
in music's state of nature. Sibelius breaks clean away from the classical
device of two contrasting themes. Try to analyse the melodic,
rhythmic, and harmonic germs of this Seventh Symphony and you are
in the position of a man in search of unknown bacilli; the music is
evolved out of itself and is indivisible.

Sibelius is not one of the modern composers who, in order to find new
modes of expression, have tried to invent a new alphabet. Beethoven
himself would have understood the vocabulary of Sibelius. Beethoven
might even have grasped Sibelius's concentrated and elliptical use of
the symphonic form: he was reaching towards something of the kind in
the last quartets. Sibelius ignores the usual divisions of the symphony,
compresses the logic, and gets rid of the conventional divisions and
repetitions. In effect, he says to us: "The term symphonic has come in
our time to mean not a formula of musical style, but an attitude of mind,
a degree and order of aesthetic emotion. It is possible to speak of a
symphonic novel – Hardy's 'The Woodlanders', for instance. You can
even speak of a symphonic meal – a Lord Mayor's Show dinner, for
instance. If I can make my music produce its symphonic effect, a sense
of unfolding bigness of idea and feel, with unity in variety and contrast
and development, then there is no reason in the world why I should
rigidly keep to the old verbose tricks . . . . I see no reason for bridge-
passages or repetitions as such; they only perpetuate the ancient
patterns. I propose to cut out the trimmings: I will telescope the usual
'episodes', so that you won't know where one ends and another begins."

There is, of course, great danger in plain and economical speaking if
you happen to be an artist. To say a thing in the fewest and simplest
words is all very well for the uses of the everyday affairs of life – if you

are talking over the telephone, say. But in the arts the man of few words is usually the man of few ideas. Suppose Shakespeare had been under the ridiculous but common delusion that good literature means plain language, with the fewest and simplest words – if he had thought that he would have made the dying Hamlet say to Horatio, "I'm counted out; drop a tear for me now and then," and not "Absent thee from felicity awhile." The energy of genius is not parsimonious – and it does not mind a mixed metaphor or a gigantic redundancy now and then. Sibelius, in his first two symphonies proved himself a fulsome, big-breathed melodist, who possessed the power to throw a tune about like a giant. In his Seventh Symphony has he not gone too far in his rejection of some of the ample juice and rich blood which really belonged to him? Ought such a full man as Sibelius not to have said, like Falstaff, "I will refine myself no finer than I am"?

The Seventh Symphony is great stuff, no doubt. But let us enjoy our Sibelius sensibly – he is in danger of becoming an unintelligent fashion. I, who have perhaps helped in the bringing about of this fashion, cannot believe that the meagreness and frequent aridity of Sibelius's present period is altogether a thing quite normal to the style of the composer of Sibelius's Second Symphony, a work of guts and sinew as well as of fundamental brainwork. I do not mean that the Seventh Symphony is cerebral and nothing else; that is a mistake which Sibelius critics are always making. Because he does not spill the Rimsky-Korsakovian paintbox over the orchestra, Sibelius is constantly called grim and drab. No, my own feeling about the Seventh Symphony is not that Sibelius has lost his true masculinity but that in this Symphony he is dealing it out to us on a surface too small for his natural freedom of stride . . . . The transition of the Sibelius of the first two symphonies, full of long-spanned tunes, to the sparse commentator of the Seventh Symphony, makes a fascinating problem.

He justified the austerity of his old age by saying that while other composers, post-Wagnerian, were occupied in manufacturing cocktails and heady wines, he was offering the public pure cold water . . . .

Symphony No. 2 in D

1962

In some ways the Second Symphony always appeals to me as the most comprehensively humane and characteristic of all his symphonies. He is, maybe, more interesting to the critics in his later works, because of his experiments in concentrated logic and symphonic structure. But the fact is that music lives not on those intellectual points which provide material for the critics to engage in forensic analysis; nothing counts in the long run but the *music*, the tunes, the rhythms, the power through tone, to express genius.

The Second Symphony glories in excess of melody and accumulating exciting rhythms. Critics have described the finale "banal". In my ears it crowns the previous three movements by its gathering momentum and swinging marching song; the movement emerges from the ghostly will o' the wisp landscape of the scherzo. Sibelius wrote a composition, as we all know, called "En Saga". The entire output of his genius could well answer to the same description, with all the associations of a remote legendary world, timeless, and in the truest sense, national. Sibelius remained aloof from the dominating musical and aesthetic movements of his long-lived period; he kept apart from the romantic back-wash of the tidal waves of Wagner and Liszt; he was unaffected by the French "Impressionists", and the Straussian "programme" orchestral illustrators. He was unmoved by ethical connotations; he does not address the "umschlungenen Millionen" of Beethoven's heart's desire. Nor does he woo the *salon* of civilized men and women of the culture of Chopin; Debussy, Stravinsky. His music, in fact, does not even postulate, or seem to be aware of, an audience. The Sibelius symphonic world leaves the habitations of everyday multitudes, cities and cosy interiors; leaves men and women and their "values", leaves sex and society altogether.

The music in these symphonies is as though the sights and sounds of Sibelius's homeland of Finland had been transmuted into orchestral sound in the light and darkness, the air, the legend and the history – it is as though nature and the backward abyss of countless years had been made audible, in terms of rustling violins, horns that loom through the orchestral texture, visitations of tone; brass that comes to us in sudden gusts, oboes and flutes clucking like wild fowl, bassoons croaking like frogs in the mist. But, an important point, this is not, and never is, "programme" or pictorially descriptive music. Sibelius draws all his material, tone evocations of the landscape he loved, through his imagination, expressing everything in a style, a technique, which – qua music – is unmistakably Sibelius, his own voice, his very image.

. . . . The exposition of the first movement is a superb example of his power to play off, one against the other, two theme groups; the dancing woodwind theme of the initial bars, and the supposedly second "subject" – the main point is that every bar is germinal, breeding the next. The bassoon takes over an oboe figure, and at once it is changed, "translated". Again, consider the beginning of the slow movement: merely a sequence of plucked lower strings, yet the observant ear will recognize and delight in the symphonic, and dramatic, uses Sibelius makes of a device as old as the hills – or, at least, as old as Beethoven. From the groping twilit motion of the opening of the slow movement, after emphatic assertions, convulsive upward leaps, as though confidence and conquest are hard to come by, a long-phrased tune, a sort of national anthem, wins through for a while, only to suffer primeval interpolations of brass, belching out the crucial significant downward leap. The movement goes to a quite unexpected and catastrophic collapse, the entire orchestra falling into the void; then a wail of wind, sinister plucked strings and a mournful echo of the anthem.

The scherzo, in the outer movements, is almost Beethovenish in its vigour, elasticity and abruptness. Beethoven could have listened to this Second Symphony without perplexity concerning vocabulary and diction. Sibelius did not explore new tonal territories. His *daemon*, his genius, would allow him no freedom to go in for the "latest" experiments. Only the second-raters, the merely talented, are at liberty to invent new musical ways of saying things. The mature genius needs to involve himself, mind and imagination, in a known established language – to which, of course, he introduces new twists, nuances, implications.

The trio, or middle section of the scherzo, is a sad lonely song, a folk-song, you would say. Sibelius made use of no Finnish music; he himself created his own "folk" music. From the scherzo the symphony climbs, without a break, to the finale, by means of a familiar Sibelian bridge, to a clinching last movement, a mounting sequential device. Now occurs the tune which the egg-heads think is banal. It is merely familiar, in Hazlitt's sense of the word, rendered Sibelius's own by his genius. The finale marches in, legend and history hand in hand. Hurrying strings, far-off martial echoes, a momentary remembrance of old unhappy battles, now triumphant brass, now the forbidding plucked strings, now the hymn; and another determined climb, grip by grip, now a rest for lyrical refreshment, and, at last, over running purposeful strings, the national anthem attains mastery, crowned by vibrant brass and a fist-shaking peroration.

Sibelius doubtless composed finer-grained and more elliptical symphonies than this Second but none truer to the man himself. In fact, such music impels me to misquote, and adapt a saying of Walt Whitman: "Who touches this Second Symphony does, indeed, touch a *man*".

12

TOSCANINI
(1867–1957)

Toscanini's Art and Influence

AN APPRECIATION

7th June 1935

The concerts of the BBC Orchestra conducted by Toscanini are the most important events that have occurred for years in the musical life of this country. He has come to us at the right time. For years we have made much of the orchestral conductor; we have allowed him to take the place and to gather unto himself all the spell-binding powers of the old actor-managers, political tub-thumpers, long-haired musical virtuosi, and other exploiters of personality. In most callings there has been a distrust of the individual; but at concerts the orchestral conductor has wallowed in the limelight, and we have approved.

His sway and dominance happened, of course, as a mere matter of cause and effect. The history of music in the last fifty years is mainly (though by no means altogether) a record of the growth of the large concert and of the development in it of the orchestra. The present age will be called by the historians The Age of the Orchestra. Obviously the opportunities have for long been tempting to all manner of musicians to stand on the rostrum and take advantage of the vast public desire to have its music provided in terms of histrionics, vivid physical gestures, to "see" an interpretation as well as to hear one. Nearly all the celebrated conductors of the present day win their reputations in the concert-world – where they can be seen – not in the opera-house, where, though their work is much more difficult, it cannot be seen. The astonishing fact is that the public has not been imposed upon more than it actually has been by adventurers, not to say charlatans. Fortunately, it is hard to fool an orchestra all the time; many an instrumentalist has winked at his colleagues as the hall has sounded with the crowd's tribute to the latest "reading" of the Fifth Symphony.

The genuine virtuoso conductor came to a head, so to say, a few years ago – I mean the conductor who, possessing genuine gifts and temperament, uses music first of all as a means of self-expression. These artists have often given us powerful experiences; we have thrilled to feel that in music they have come to a full life; they have delighted us and impressed us. But recently some of us have wished for some escape from the "personal" conductor when we have gone to orchestral concerts; memories of Richter's honest objectivity have come back to mind, and though we have not wished for a return to his unyielding and rather narrowly German mastery, we have had an instinct that the moment was ready for a conductor who would combine with the so-called classical sanity of vision all the tenseness of a musicianship born of experience in the dynamic world of a modern orchestra.

Toscanini is the conductor of our present need – other lands, of course, have known him for years. Thanks to the BBC and their resources he is with us to-day, deepening our sense of music's beauty, of the orchestra's scope as a medium, and – best of all – of the essential dignity of the office he is filling. Many of our great conductors owe nearly everything to the fact of their genius; if they were not geniuses they would be nothing. Toscanini is a genius, but even without genius he would be a great musician and, what is more, a great and high-minded man. His pursuit of beauty is fanatical; he suffers for beauty – and that he is able to suffer for beauty is his first asset. Many artists, gifted and sincere, simply cannot suffer. Toscanini has been known to go away into solitude after a great concert that has brought him praise from the best minds; he has gone away feeling he has missed his way, touched only the outer door.

The measure of idealism is his passion for rehearsal. He has no use for the dilettante's trust in the "inspiration of the moment". No conductor can by sudden gestures, no matter how vivid, compel a hundred instrumentalists to do things "on the night" which they have not been trained to do before the concert. Imagine it; an orchestra is playing a quick movement; each man is occupied with his own technique. And the conductor makes a few swift flutters with his left hand as though rubbing something out, and the orchestra responds immediately without the suspicion of a jerk or jolt in the rhythm. Obviously the miracle cannot be performed. It is at rehearsal that the great conductor gets his work done; the dramatic gestures are often for the benefit of the audience; or perhaps they have a psychological value for the "impressionistic" conductor – by means of them he may be able to work himself up, like the old actor who before he went on the stage to express the rage of Shylock took hold of a pole and shook it vigorously.

Toscanini's technique is simple. He beats time continuously with his right hand, and he uses it from the shoulder. He has no wrist or finger work; he does not "play" on the orchestra in the familiar picturesque way. His left hand gives a few very broad directions, a lead here and there, or a gentle but spacious sign to the subsidiary instruments. He turns to the places of the main interest, and he is facing them with expressive eyes well in time for their entrances. Never do you see Toscanini giving a direction in a hurry; his conducting has plenty of energy but it is a deliberate energy. He knows exactly what he wants and how to get it.

Technically the only things that matter in conducting are rhythm and tone. The score definitely states a composer's rhythmical needs, and it gives all the information needed to obtain the balance of tone heard in the composer's imagination. Conductors are fond of telling us how such and such a composer "did not know how to write for the orchestra and we have occasionally to help him out." But in every case where the composer is a master it will be found that he knew all that it was necessary for him to know of the tone-values in an orchestra. In any case, it is not the conductor's business to improve the masterpieces, no matter how capable he feels of putting them right here and there. The trumpet parts in Beethoven may often offend his susceptibilities; but the point is that we want to listen to the music as Beethoven conceived it.

Toscanini makes us believe in the objective reality of the score; he observes the markings diligently, and the effect we feel, if we know the score well, is that the performance is giving life and motion to a perfect photograph. This act of re-creation could not, of course, be done by pedantry; many musicians can set out to follow the score faithfully and achieve in the end only a museum piece. The truth is that only by vast knowledge quickened by an imagination which kindles as the composer's own imagination kindled can a conductor read a score. His understanding of style is knowledge plus imagination. Culture and the study of the musical life in all its changing periods will tell him that music has sounded differently in different generations, and that a tempo instruction from Beethoven does not mean the same thing as an identical marking on a score of Brahms.

Toscanini's art combines knowledge and vision. Reverence and love of music and long experience at his job – and genius for it from the beginning. He does not conduct for our entertainment; he does not seem aware of an audience at all as he goes through his work. His white hair and dignified bearing suggests the professor. "Arturo Toscanini" has a vivid sound; it brings to mind the familiar passionate Italian, hot-blooded and violent of gesture. The expectations of the picturesque are disappointed by Toscanini; I imagine that Einstein would conduct in this simple and drastic way. The effect is everything, the sound – and the responses of our hearts. Toscanini brings back sincerity and truth and charm and beauty to the concert-hall, and dismisses rhetoric and showmanship. It is difficult to believe that he will not leave behind him a strong, lasting influence on our standards.

Toscanini and the BBC Orchestra

4th June 1935

Tonight Toscanini has given his first concert with the BBC Orchestra, and it has been a musical experience of the rarest and finest kind – not, indeed, merely a concert but a revelation of the wonder and nobility of music and genius. In a later article I will try to make a measured statement about the art of the greatest conductor of the age.

In Toscanini we have a paradox. Here is the most powerful and personal, not to say tyrannical, conductor of them all, a man whose command over the orchestra is greater than that of all the virtuosi put together – and yet he is the one conductor in the world who is never an exhibitionist, never concerned more with Toscanini than the masters whose works he serves like a priest. It is profane almost to speak of Toscanini's Brahms, of Toscanini's Wagner, and so forth. He does not give us anybody's Brahms or anybody's Wagner, but Brahms's Brahms and Wagner's Wagner. The world's acknowledged master conductor is the very man who never stands between us and the music, never plays tricks with it, never uses it as a sort of private and personal confessional.

Toscanini has the keenest sense of musical style. He sees into a composer's mind because his knowledge of music and its development and its relation to the period of its composition is unrivalled. The basis of his art is rhythm. He makes no unnecessary gestures. On the whole he gives his leads by his quick and expressive face and he does not dance. He is at one and the same time a master and a servant – master of the technique of the orchestra and a servant of the genius of the music. He has a perfect ear for balance and, of course, he is in a position to get as many rehearsals as he feels he needs. Music with Toscanini is usually spacious and rounded yet absolutely clear in its paths. His clarity of rhythm and figuration gives to his work a classical stamp. I can understand the point of view, although I cannot share it, of those who sometimes feel that Toscanini lacks the half-lights of the romantic.

Tonight he gave the fullest Brahms conceivable, his interpretation of the Fourth Symphony was eloquent yet direct, beautiful in its balanced line and energy, but always human and many-sided. Here was the masculine Brahms, and also the Brahms who had a love of the tender things of life. The andante was gorgeous in texture, richly sung during the half-teasing 'cello theme, which was for once in a way absolutely right in tempo, and also decorated with a sensibility which more than ever exposed the fallacy that Brahms was not an artist in his instrumentation. The scherzo was lusty, genial and exultant, and not for a moment over-emphatic. And the finale had an explosive and generating energy which recalled the interpretation of this movement by Nikisch.

Toscanini and Beethoven

15th May 1939

At the third of the Toscanini Beethoven concerts the symphonies were the "Pastoral" and the Fifth. The "Pastoral" was given with rare beauty of tone, phrasing and balance; the harmonies have a fullness seldom achieved by orchestras in this country. The rich easeful sonority was not obtained at the cost of any individual part; details in the orchestration which we have always known were there from the evidence of the score now came to natural musical life, all flowing along on the current of Toscanini's incomparable rhythm . . . . He relaxed genially enough in Beethoven's most naïve and gracious work. Perhaps the mood of the opening allegro was scarcely lazy; a sleeping sort of grandeur should lie over it, and Toscanini cannot, for all his culture, get away from the fact that by temperament he is Latin. Toscanini took us a country walk, true; but I could not escape the feeling that we must never dally uselessly, and that not far away a resplendent car throbbed as it waited for our return to a more austere environment. The realistic touches of the symphony were treated as essential parts of the music; they were not exaggerated and made to seem childish. The storm was vivid and as finely a composed tone-picture as any extant. The rare quality in Toscanini's interpretations, indeed, is the way they seem to add to a composer's stature and genius; at each of these concerts of his we have been made aware that Beethoven's music is even greater than we have hitherto known – certainly better composed. The breadth of the melodies of the andante of the "Pastoral" was something to remember for a long time to come, the songfulness of them. The interpretation compelled the listener to sit back and say, "What a lovely work!"

The Fifth Symphony was a model of integrity. The four-note attack on the first movement had no portentous "fate-knocking-at-the-door" nonsense about it; the quavers were announced in strict tempo. And once the rhythm began there was apparently not a single let or hindrance. Toscanini's rhythmical subtlety sometimes seems in danger of defeating the composer's purpose in changing rhythm at all. Toscanini so despises exaggeration that his scheme of dynamics is extraordinarily economical. Also his scale of tone is jealously guarded; he gives us no extremities of softness or of loudness. As a consequence I felt at the end of this magnificently musical performance of the C minor Symphony a slight disappointment. I may have been badly brought up by more superficial readings of the work. Anyhow, I missed the sense of being present at a cosmic process; I was given no glimpse into Beethoven's forge. This C minor Symphony had come out of the forge ready for a consummate finishing process. There were wonderful features of musical control – for example, the transition from the coda of the scherzo; the forty or so bars of pianissimo were incredibly shaded, and the change from minor to major touched the imagination without need of any extra-musical property. But the scherzo in the main lacked chiaroscuro; it was too musical, especially the fluency of the treatment of the 'cellos and basses in the C major elephantine rumblings of the trio.

Toscanini's treatment of Beethoven is without doubt the most musically comprehensive of our time. But in fairness to other conductors, some protest should be made against the growing fashionable idea that Toscanini's view of Beethoven is also the most poetically comprehensive. He is a great artist from his own point of view of music. Let us be content with that, and cherish him with some sense of proportion.

Toscanini and the Ninth

24th May 1939

For most of us the Ninth Symphony of Beethoven is a concert in itself, and a vast enough experience to get through in an evening. But on this occasion the Ninth Symphony was preceded by the third "Leonora" Overture, an extract from the "Prometheus" ballet music, and – incredibly – by two movements from the Op. 135 Quartet dressed up for orchestral strings. I am astonished that a musician of Toscanini's sensibility could have considered for a moment conducting such a programme. I timed myself to arrive at the concert during the interval. I would not wish to go to "Hamlet" or "King Lear" and have to sit through a curtain-raiser, no matter how good. The audience, it must be admitted, found no difficulty in coping with this enormous and curiously diversified spate of Beethoven. They crowded the Queen's Hall corridors saying, "Marvellous!"

The performance of the Ninth Symphony was, as usual with Toscanini, terrific in its rhythmical urgency. During the first movement the playing of the BBC Orchestra was so uncertain of touch that for one listener at least the symphony failed for the first time in a long experience of it, to hold him in a prophetic grip and to make him tremble as though revelations of unspeakable awe were about to happen. The BBC Orchestra is apparently feeling the strain of Toscanini's uncompromising idealism and also of his uncompromising rhythm. These fine players have been considerably worn out on the Ixion wheel of Toscanini's right arm. It is not simply that his tempi are on the quick side; a severer test of an instrumentalist's skill comes from Toscanini's disdain of nuance, except in so far as the instrumentalists can lend light and shade without much prompting, while the great wheel revolves, sometimes metronomically – in my ears, at any rate. The argument has been advanced that Toscanini possesses the purest musical sensibility of anybody born for a century or so. For that reason, it is said, he abhors anything in his interpretations that can be called extra-musical. It is a curious view to take of a conductor who made his name first in opera – and in Italian opera. And a conductor of so "pure" a musical sensibility would be the last in the world to reveal the whole content of Beethoven, especially the Beethoven of the Ninth.

The conception behind the performance of the work last night was undoubtedly sublime . . . . Toscanini may in heaven find the orchestra which will be able to give him all that he increasingly wants as, in his old age, he searches farther and farther and goes beyond poor mortal susceptibilities and weaknesses. The BBC Orchestra could play little but the notes at this earth-bound concert; the first movement lacked (for me, let me repeat, and I know I am in an overwhelmed minority) mystery, the sense of the subterranean, the sense that we were in the world's womb. The scherzo rattled on, chattered and bustled, with no perceptible change of mood and tempo in the trio. Toscanini's stresses in these two movements were severe; he builds the form of Beethoven consummately, moulds nobly the architecture of the temple; but O for some time and place for communion within!

The adagio, which is a terror to conduct because of its winding ways, its tendency to lose itself and sound a series of what are known as "joins" – this movement was a masterpiece of logical connection in Toscanini's far-reaching control. The orchestra, now given breathing space and Lebensraum, revealed their ability to phrase expressively and to touch the poetic imagination. On the whole, though, the interpetation appealed to one's respect for ordered prose rather than to one's sense of inspired poetry and revelation. The choir rose, as they say, to the occasion; the noise was inclined to deafen – one listener once coughed, just to reassure himself that he could still hear everyday sound. The soloists were Isobel Baillie, Margaret Balfour, Parry Jones, and Harold Williams.

Brahms's First Symphony

AN ELECTRIC EVENING

30th September 1952

From the moment when Toscanini walked slowly to the conductor's place tonight in the Royal Festival Hall it was certain that the evening would be electrical and creative. The atmosphere was ready for him; we were all of us, in the packed audience, capable of and determined upon ignition. He might have conducted at less than his usual vantage; the effect would have seemed the same. Here is the irony of Toscanini's position today. He is not among the accredited prime donne of the orchestra. The tireless seeker after the objective value of the score as written in the lifetime of the composer is fated always to receive the tributes of thousands temporarily rendered uncritical and facile.

The force of his presence is to be felt instantaneously; many forces, some of them extra-musical, have contributed to his power to hold us in thrall. On the face of it, before the event, few of us would expect even a great Italian interpreter to give us Brahms "in the round". Age and culture do not necessarily subdue race, and Toscanini would not, if he could, wish to neutralize the Italian in him by too intensive a study of objectivity. The performance of the C minor Symphony of Brahms at this concert was superb in musical flow, shapeliness, and a forgetive and plastic energy which moved onward, moulding periods and phrases in its course, to an end foreseen in the first bar's beginning. Notes and figures not revealed in average good interpretations were given life, individuality, and relevance; and no part was allowed to impose on the greatness of the whole.

It was as though a light or glow of a clarifying and comprehensive mind were illuminating the symphony to its depths, an imaginative X-ray! Now and again the question boldly came halfway into the surface of my consciousness, and would not be pushed down, whether the Brahms of the C minor Symphony gains all the time by a treatment as masterful, as lucid, as healthy and vital as Toscanini's. In the first movement there is more than a hint of those noble strivings, sometimes pathetic in their aspiration, which Nietzsche misunderstood when he charged Brahms with impotence. There is a dark and backward abysm in this first movement out of which come a bodeful pluckings of strings, with woodwind reaching upward as though with blind eyes. There are gaps in the rhythm suggestive of a sudden sight of the void.

Not once but twice and even thrice I felt that Toscanini was endowing the movement with a resolution and grasp of rhythm or pulse which, though the music grew consequently in godlike stature and competence, diminished the poetic reflection of pathos momentarily, and also the sense of life's frailty and ineffectuality which, as I like to think, the movement can express with rare humanity and poignancy. It is not easy for Toscanini, so masterful is he as to embody the godlike, to relax into a vein of the pathetic, even poetically or musically felt and conceived.

The andante was pure song, with the simplest phrasing of the melody in the first dominant section; the warmth of harmony compelled unusual admiration for the beauty of Brahms's scoring. Even here there was more of magnificently controlled musical art than that of tenderness which so movingly could emerge from the masculinity and strength of Brahms. The allegretto was not allowed to reduce the stature of the performance in the slightest; this was not an escapist intermezzo; the energy remained purposefully directed and there was no hiatus at the descent to the trio.

And all was a preparation for the finale, where the plucked strings now came tragically out of the darkness; then the horns announced the solemn sun-awakening melody, followed by the great heartening song, supposedly emulative of Beethoven in the finale of the Ninth, but really as genial as any in a German students' community concert. The presto dance, in a variation of this tune, was gigantic in its stresses, and in itself was enough to make nonsense of Wolf's taunt to the effect that Brahms could not exult . . . .

The playing of the Philharmonia Orchestra was apparently beyond fair criticism . . . it was a magnificent, ripe, and full throated performance, recreated by a great and wonderful old man.

13

FURTWÄNGLER
(1886–1954)

With the Berlin Philharmonic Orchestra

23rd January 1934

An enormous audience packed Queen's Hall tonight, and once again the playing of the Berlin Philharmonic Orchestra provoked scenes of wild enthusiasm. The splendid tone, the precision in every part, the ideal balance – all these excellencies were praised even by those critics who dislike Furtwängler's conducting. But they forget that the Berlin Orchestra is Furtwängler's creation. They should not allow differences on the point of interpretation to blind them to Furtwängler's genius as an orchestral builder . . . . The D major Suite of Bach was given a thoroughly musical performance, though it is one of Furtwängler's defects that he lacks geniality. A tremendous amount of labour was put into Schumann's D minor Symphony, which took on a grandeur not often, if ever, heard in this country. But something of romantic graciousness was missing, and also some spontaneity of rhythm.

The Berlin Orchestra's strings are as good as strings well can be, for, if they lack the vivacity and bloom of those of the Vienna Philharmonic, they have their own incomparable breadth. The woodwind is blended equably, though in parts it is not better than that of Sir Thomas Beecham's orchestra, if as good. The brass is dignified, if not always golden. The horns are a model of accuracy, if now and again a little dry. The drummer is a joy.

At the moment there is reason for a word or two about Furtwängler. Nothing is more certain in the world than that his conducting will be attacked by the London musical critics – according to their annual custom.

Furtwängler might well wonder at the anomaly of his position, which is surely without equal in the history of music: accepted as a great musician and as a master of the orchestra in all the countries that are musically cultured, and mainly rejected in England! The joke about the London musical critics' view of Furtwängler is that they condemn everything he does. Whatever the work, he conducts it badly. He cannot succeed, even by accident. He guarantees the second-rate, so to say, and we are all of us free to make up our minds in advance about his work and to get on with our notices. Obviously, there is a heap of nonsense in all this. Even certain English conductors have been known now and again to achieve a piece of good conducting. The common complaint against Furtwängler is that he does not give us a score as the composer himself wrote it down on paper, that he is intent more upon Furtwängler's Beethoven than on the Beethoven of the printed and published score.

Well, let us suppose these are true charges. Are they not true of Sir Thomas Beecham's conducting, which is never found fault with in any detail once in a blue moon? Are they not true of every other great conductor that has ever lived in this world of relativity? I can anticipate the answer to these questions. "Ah," comes the reply. "What about Toscanini? Doesn't he give us the truth, the score as in itself it really is?" The last time I heard Toscanini he conducted a beautiful but almost unrecognizable "Enigma" Variations and a thoroughly Italian "Meistersinger" Overture. But if it is admitted for the sake of argument that Toscanini is the perfect objective conductor, what of it? Who is to tell us what the score on a Beethoven symphony amounts to as part of objective reality? The essence of things may be our capacity to perceive things. If Beethoven himself were alive to-day, would he interpret his symphonies every time in accordance with the dynamics adumbrated in his markings of more than a hundred years ago? Anyhow, there is as good a case to be made out for subjective idealism as there is for objective reality. The time may shortly come, indeed, when Toscanini is regarded temporarily by the fashions as a dull routiner, simply because of his belief in an unchanging and fixed Beethoven, a Seventh Symphony entirely realized in the printed score. The thing-in-itself, positive and permanent, in a world washed round by the waves of relativity!

Furtwängler is at the extreme to Toscanini. He is for ever seeking a deeper significance in music as he feels it. I am told that every summer he departs for the quietude of the hills and looks into his scores again, and then returns to his orchestra with different conceptions, determined to "hammer it out", like Richard the Second. For him, the truth and beauty of music are infinite; there is no "so far and no farther". It is a fine but dangerous belief. It is responsible for the excesses in Furtwängler's conducting, the restless probings which can so easily suggest egoistic mannerisms. I myself do not "like" some of Furtwängler's italics any more than Furtwängler's severest critics do, but I do not feel that an artist should be dismissed because we do not "like" his methods, or that we should write him down as a humbug because he does not share our views of the truth of things as they are, now and for all eternity. Furtwängler possibly regards the printed notes of a score only as so many finite symbols of an infinite inexpressible vision. If it is argued that only a vain man will take upon himself the task of showing us the one true way, the answer must be that if we are going to protest against vanity in the artist, we had better get rid of all art at once. And if this doctrine of mine suggests that any presumptuous charlatan is free to pull Beethoven about in the sacred name of interpretation, the answer must be that indeed he is free. But he will find it a difficult job to get all Europe to accept him as a great conductor.

The Berlin Philharmonic Orchestra in Manchester

5th December 1935

A large audience attended the concert in the Free Trade Hall last night, and at the end there was a scene which recalled a revivalist meeting. That is the effect Furtwängler's conducting is always likely to have on a great crowd; he is the most possessed of conductors, a vehement searcher after the ultimate secrets of music. His exaggerations are the consequence of a vision which tries to go beyond the commonplace, and has no use for the plain man's "objective score"; truth is not as easily found in the greatest art as all that. None but a superficial view of Furtwängler has ever attributed his excesses of tempi and shading to showmanship; you have only to look at him to realize the tawdriness of this accusation – the man is austere, and has none but the politest recognition of his audience. His reading of the C minor Symphony of Brahms at this concert would no doubt have kept all the Beckmessers of the world busy with their chalk and crosses; but in only one instance –

243

the long diminuendo and pause towards the end of the last movement –
did Furtwängler's underlinings or licence go contrary to the music's
implications. The work was grandly presented; a tragic note of it has
seldom been so nobly struck in the present writer's experience. The
genius of the work was vast and rich; for this was not the "comfortable"
Brahms against whom many musicians of this country are reacting at
the moment; the symphony we heard now was, to use the old term,
titanic. "Er kann nicht jubeln," said Hugo Wolf of Brahms. Wolf
should have heard the mighty dance which sent the symphony to its end
with a giant's humour and energy.

The chief points of the Berlin orchestra's playing have been familiar
in this country for many years . . . it says much for Furtwängler's skill
as an orchestral builder that he can mingle into a harmonious whole so
many artists who are individually distinguished and equal to the
dizziest of virtuoso flights. Has Manchester, or anywhere else, heard a
more breath-snatching tour de force of orchestral technique than the
performance of Stravinsky's "Firebird" Suite? The colour, verve,
precision, and the unfailing instinct for beauty – nothing could have
been more remarkable or ravishing. The Haydn Symphony was manly
and firm – and a little unsmiling. Furtwängler does not easily smile. He
is a great romantic; and humour does not always go well with the quest
for the absolute. But it was refreshing, once in a way, to hear a Haydn of
some girth.

The impressions carried from the concert on a cold night were mainly
of a truly symphonic orchestra controlled by a conductor at the extreme
of Toscanini but just as great. Furtwängler is bound to perplex the
school of objective score-reading which is fashionable at the moment (is
a conductor's score really a sort of architect's blueprint?). Furtwängler,
being a German, could probably produce arguments well based on
metaphysics to demonstrate how difficult it is to chase objective truth
save by help of the variable sense of the subjective self. And when
Furtwängler is taken to task by the objective critic for a pianissimo
which that critic says is softer than the one marked in the score the
retort might easily be made, "Are you sure your ears are objectively
acute tonight? And is your position in the hall the very throne and seat
of objective truth?" Furtwängler was once told in Berlin that the people
in the back seats were complaining that they could not hear some of his
soft passages. "It does not matter," he said, "they do not pay so much."
Last evening my seat was conveniently close to Dr Furtwängler and the
orchestra.

Furtwängler lives in the music he conducts; one might even say he battens on it. In it he seeks a way of living passionately, a means of freeing the imagination. There is room in the world, surely, for the romantics and their strivings as well as for the realists and their firm foundations in fact. All is irrelevant but greatness. At this concert Furtwängler's power, culture, mastery, and love of music were as strongly to be felt as those temperamental characteristics in him that sometimes challenge criticism severely. And his superb orchestra is his own creation; he has reason to be proud of it.

Beethoven

FURTWÄNGLER'S LAST VISIT TO LONDON

15th March 1954

Furtwängler and the Philharmonia Orchestra gave a Beethoven programme on Friday night at the Royal Festival Hall and at the end the scene was quite emotional: time after time Furtwängler was called back to the platform to make his modest, almost apologetic bow, to turn to the orchestra as though to distract our attention from him: but the orchestra joined in the general applause to a man and woman. It was, indeed, a great concert nobly conducted, nobly played. Best of all, it caused us, more than ever, to wonder at the genius of Beethoven, to revere it, and to count ourselves fortunate ever to have been born to know or get anywhere near to knowing it.

Furtwängler has mellowed with the years, a statement which is not confidently to be made on behalf of all conductors. The old nervous, spasmodic movements of the head and right hand have gone; more important, the tempi are less arbitrary and more related in detail to a ripened conception. His rhythm, always unshackled by accentuation, is free enough to contain intimate shadings of melody and harmony; but to-day Furtwängler's grasp on the main outlines is firm and his vision far-seeing. It seemed to me that here was the ideal (in our time) blending of classic and romantic characteristics in a conductor. Furtwängler does not present music to us so strict to the letter of the score that the spirit is, so to say, embalmed: he is never mechanically objective. Though he is master of the orchestra, he does not whip his players along; he gives them scope for pleasure.

Music for Furtwängler is, of course, an art of expression, related note by note to the mind and bloodstream of the composer, conceived as a symbol of his period as well as man and spirit. There is no room for an impersonal commentary here. So Furtwängler brings even to the Fourth Symphony of Beethoven the cast of constant thoughtfulness. The accompaniment of fourths in the introductory bar of the adagio, for example, were not taken trippingly and the sudden changes as the main melodies go their ways of key and pulse were touched with a dramatic menace, gripping to the musical imagination.

The beauties of this perfect symphony were unfolded with a devotion born of a lifetime's experience. Nothing ran to waste and we could always appreciate the marvellous economy with which Beethoven lavishes over the orchestra his largesse of ideas, so that every instrument can share the delight and go into the sunshine of the general scene; although Furtwängler sees to it that shades and half-lights come into the picture, proportionately and pertinently.

In the scherzo of the Fourth Symphony, Furtwängler brought solemnity to play on the quick contrasts and alterations of strings and wind; and the trio was quite contemplative, not to say stolid. The finale was not whirled along at a pace defying precise and musical execution; something of the movement's divine "spin" was missing but, all in all, the performance and the interpretation were a tribute to one aspect of Beethoven's genius which is often overlooked: his fineness of art and his stylish invention, when these things suited his purpose.

Another of Furtwängler's great strengths was the quickening of tempo and the masterly diminution of it in the adagio of the same Fourth Symphony, also his strong control of the stupendous descent of the orchestra, where the main theme is miraculously transformed in sforzando chords. If Furtwängler here and there departs from the gospel according to the metronome it is not, as one or two of his critics appear to suspect, that he has never seen or read the score and therefore needs didactic correction.

He knows, we may be sure, that the pauses in the scherzo of the Fifth Symphony should be made after a "poco rit". By slowing down more perceptibly at these points, Furtwängler no doubt weakened the dramatic tautness and urgency; he certainly did not match in this movement the mystery and subterranean chiaroscuro of Toscanini in the same music.

Furtwängler's interpretation of the Fifth Symphony is, in fact, symphonic rather than dramatic: it is reflective, contemplative, and exalted in its gathering musical momentum, but not so epical that the humanity of Beethoven cannot be felt. However Furtwängler, as we know, can be dramatic enough when he thinks the occasion calls for drama: his conducting at this concert of the Second "Leonora" Overture was highly concentrated in its rhythmical energy, so that for once in a while we could realize or recollect that dramatically this Second "Leonora" Overture is more apt for its purpose in the theatre than the musically greater Third.

The Philharmonia Orchestra played for Furtwängler with heart and full technique: the performance was truly magnificent, yet all this excellence and executive musicianship was put to the service of Beethoven, so that we could realize his stature in the full and in the round.

A Conversation with Furtwängler

7th May 1955

On the only occasion I met and spoke to Furtwängler he complained of English critics, who attacked him because year after year he included in his programmes the same Beethoven symphonies. "But they are never the same to me," he replied. "Each time I lived through them I seemed to get closer to the heart – but it is still far distant!" Furtwängler sought a solution for all his problems of spirit; he even believed that by the power of music he could defend Germany against the Nazi ideology. "I did not directly oppose the party," he said . . . "because I told myself this was not my job. I should have benefited no one by active resistance. But I never concealed my opinions. As an artist I was determined that my music, at least, should remain untouched. Had I taken an active part in politics, I could not have remained in Germany. I knew that a single performance of a great German masterpiece was a stronger and more vital negation of the spirit of Buchenwald or Auschwitz than words. Please understand me correctly: an artist cannot be entirely unpolitical. He must have some political convictions, because after all, he, too, is a human being." (The naïveté here is quite touching!) "As a citizen it is an artist's duty to express these convictions. But as a musician I am more than a citizen. I am a German in that eternal sense to which the genius of great music testifies."

Furtwängler's unfulfilled wish to compose was no doubt the cause of his extremely personal treatment of a well-worn masterpiece. He was trying to share the processes of creation. Never did he conduct in a routine way. A player in the Berlin Philharmonic Orchestra has said that Furtwängler conducted like a sort of musical vampire. "He draws the blood and life out of you, so that we can't make music for ourselves – after a concert with Furtwängler I can't even take part in a chamber quartet for days and days."

It was as absurdly narrow to think of Furtwängler mainly as a conductor as it was to think mainly of Schnabel as a pianist. He was an artist for whom music was the chief mode of consciousness, a necessary way of life. Like any other artist, he enjoyed the public's admiration and support, but he did not set himself to serve them or any critic or fashion. As a conductor and artist who seemed to go into the creative forge, he must be counted the greatest since Mahler, and Nikisch. There is only Klemperer left to us from this Faustian tradition. It is a school with limitations, maybe – but, as the greatest of Faustians has told us, it is within limitations that the master finds himself.

14

BRUNO WALTER
(1876–1962)

Bruno Walter

AN APPRECIATION

16th February 1962

Of the great conductors of his long career, Bruno Walter was first in a command over the affections of a large public in most parts of the world. He lacked and never sought after the imperious authority of Toscanini. He was, in fact, less the maestro than the chevalier or grand seigneur. And he was not obsessed by the intense nervous romanticism of Furtwängler.

Nothing about Walter's conducting removed him from the sensitiveness of normal musicians and music-lovers; his culture was wide and he kept a psychological balance for the most part, mingling classic feeling for form and deep understanding of the emotional content of a work. During a certain period, after the tragic death of his daughter Gretl, his rhythmical grasp weakened into sentimental delays and hesitations, so much so that a performance of "Zauberflöte", directed by him at Salzburg in the 1930s, was so weak of pulse that I could not sit it out. The recovery of mental equilibrium was quick; Walter emerged from the greatest affliction of his life stronger in his art than ever before, and reassured those of us who had long regarded his conducting of Mozart as the best of our time; he reassured us by an unforgettable performance of the "Jupiter" Symphony.

He himself wrote in his autobiography of the existence in his nature of a dualism, "a Dionysiac and an Apollonic side which apparently had enough breadth to grant both sufficient room for mutual tolerance." His interpretations never suggested labour or struggle; and his German feeling for fundamental tones prevented superficiality. When he returned to Covent Garden in 1924, after 14 years' absence from this opera house, he conducted the memorable performances of Strauss's

"Der Rosenkavalier" with two young singers in the cast: Lotte Lehmann and Elisabeth Schumann. Lehmann had sung and played the part of Sophie at Covent Garden in 1913, but now London had heard her, and what is more London saw her, as the Marschallin. Schumann was Sophie and the Oktavian was Della Reinhardt, with Mayr as Ochs. Temptation must be resisted to describe those presentations of "Der Rosenkavalier" as the best, the handsomest, the most brilliant, and most finely poised of all.

Walter was a student at the Stern Conservatorium in Berlin, and he was born in 1876 into a "modest Jewish family". His father was a bookkeeper in a silk firm; his mother played the piano "nicely". The boy took to music instinctively. At the Stern Conservatorium he advanced rapidly enough to appear at one of the "popular" concerts of the Berlin Philharmonic Orchestra in 1889, in his thirteenth year. But his parents would not allow exploitation of the boy as a "prodigy" so he continued his studies with zeal until one evening he heard Hans von Bülow conducting. At once he decided to become a conductor too. After some four years of severe work, including an attempt at composing an opera, he was recommended coach to the Municipal Opera of Cologne in 1893.

The rest of his 'prentice years was easy. Everything favoured him: good looks, presence, and natural aptitude. At the right moment he left Cologne for Hamburg where he met Gustav Mahler, then director of the opera there. "So you are the new coach?" asked Mahler. "Do you play the piano well?" "Excellently," said the young man. "Can you read well at sight?" "Yes, everything." "Do you know the regular repertory operas?" "I know them quite well." Mahler gave a laugh, tapped the youth on the shoulder, saying: "Well, that sounds fine."

The influence of Mahler on Walter in his impressionable years was crucial. After two years at Hamburg he went to Breslau as one of the reserve or "second" conductors. The routine disillusioned him, but the experience was priceless. And Mahler wrote to him: "Have courage . . . remember you are carrying your marshal's staff in your knapsack." From Breslau to Pressburg and Riga; then back to Berlin at the Royal Opera. And at last came the call, apparently predestinate, to the Hofoper in Vienna, in 1901, as assistant to Mahler, at the age of 25.

For a while some necessary adversity had to be coped with by the young musician. Anti-Semitism in Vienna, ricocheting from Mahler, raked Walter at once. And Mahler did nothing to help him resist it, for Mahler was now lost in his courtship of the beautiful Alma, whom later he married. There was nothing for it but self-help.

As he grew older Walter tried not to remain confined in familiar musical grooves. But he could not respond to the contemporary percussionists and tone-rowers, not even to Schoenberg, one of his Viennese friends and contemporaries. He was even late in life discovering the greatness of Bruckner. In his ripest years he was incomparably the best Mozart conductor; he corrected the current tendency to "prettify" Mozart and emphasized, without endangering the style, Mozart's seriousness and vigour and power of dramatic expression. He, of course, knew the Mahler language by heart. At Salzburg he conducted a perfect "Don Giovanni", with Pinza; also at Salzburg he conducted the most poignant "Tristan and Isolde" I have ever heard. His conducting of Hugo Wolf's "Der Corregidor" was another masterpiece of creative response and interpretation, and of course Schubert came to him as though by second nature; nobody has excelled the beauty of his conducting of the great C major Symphony. He ripened without softening to any weakness as his years accumulated; the tempo of life in America did not harden a warm poetic and musical nature.

"Music," wrote Bruno Walter on the last page of his autobiography, "has as an element an optimistic quality." We might add, quoting from a source he would easily have recognized: "Die liebe Erde allüberall blüht auf im Lenz und grünt aufs neu!"

The Vienna Philharmonic Orchestra

LE GRAND SEIGNEUR

30th April 1934

This afternoon, in Queen's Hall, the Vienna Philharmonic Orchestra, conducted by Bruno Walter, have given a very beautiful concert. During the interval I heard one or two people comparing the horns and the oboes and the violins and the timpani etcetera with the same instruments in the London Philharmonic or the Berlin Philharmonic Orchestras. These opinions were born of a sporting and not a musical instinct; the folk who expressed them should have been not at Queen's Hall but at the Cup Final. A great orchestra is an indivisible whole; you can no more compare any instrumental group in the Vienna Orchestra with any instrumental group in another orchestra than you can compare the petals of one flower with the petals of another. We English apparently cannot forget sport and competition even at a concert as stylish as this one given today . . . .

The playing was the warm bloom of orchestral art; the present writer has seldom experienced in this country a purer musical pleasure. Usually an orchestra is an affair of rhetoric, aiming at an "effect" on an audience. Most orchestras would have little meaning unless related to an audience; virtuoso brilliance is a kind of histrionics, and has no significance apart from that which is flashed back from the mirror of public acclamation. This afternoon the Vienna Philharmonic Orchestra played with an absorbed modesty of art; each instrumentalist drew his beauty easefully, without demonstration, out of an instinctive love and mastery. Riper orchestral playing could not be imagined; the skill was taken for granted by the musicians themselves; nothing was forced upon us to astonish the senses; the orchestra as a man devoted himself to the interpretation of the music; it was presented lovingly, with the connoisseur's taste and quietness. I cannot recall an orchestral concert that protested so little, that was so intent upon the proportions of true culture, and that was so blissfully regardless of spectacular values.

This was orchestral playing which we, the audience, seemed to intrude upon; the fine shades of chamber style could be discerned and enjoyed everywhere. Even in the Bacchanale of Wagner's "Tannhäuser" there was no vulgar noise, no empty theatre, no really sensational appeal. The music possessed texture; the expression of frenzy was achieved by observance of a great composer's written indications based on a feeling for dynamics and contrasts of colour. Wagner's instrumental style was honoured; the consequence was a Bacchanale which did not abuse beauty, even while beauty was ravished. And the dying down of the excitement was rich with a stained sort of disillusionment; the dying form was misty and langorous.

Bruno Walter was in a restrained mood for the most part. His treatment of the Second Symphony of Brahms had a restful evenness of tempo which probably seemed tame to many listeners brought up on the modern English view of Brahms. It was as though Herr Walter was glad to give himself up entirely to the gorgeous cushion of this orchestra's tone, content to lie upon it, and recollect music in tranquillity. The E flat Symphony of Mozart was clear in every part; the melody floated; the harmonies were round and unforced. Now and again a fault of chording lent the touch of enthusiasm to fine art; the Vienna players, unlike the Berlin players, are not tyrannized by their own technical perfections. The Brahms symphony, if it lacked variety of tempo, delighted us with many miniature graces. Herr Walter can so frequently achieve the note of exultation that we must suppose he aimed deliberately at the gentle impeccable Brahms we have heard to-day. The combination of 'cello pizzicato and wood-wind melody at the beginning of the allegretto was for once in a way made to sound absolutely felicitous; the movement as a whole was charmed into musical porcelain. In the last movement Herr Walter gave the orchestra its head and the music danced and bubbled – what wood-wind, what flutes!

The Vienna Philharmonic Orchestra simply cannot be analysed down to so many instrumentalists, this man a perfect player, that man not so good, if very good. No; the Vienna Philharmonic Orchestra is the full flower of a long and proud culture – plus a musical temperament softer and more sensitive than any generally known this side of Vienna.

Brahms and Bruno Walter

NEW GRAMOPHONE RECORDS FROM NEW YORK

19th February 1955

If such a gramophone album as this is the harvest of the sowings of the Sinatras and the Crosbys, all power to them. On four long-playing discs, superb interpretations are preserved of the four symphonies, the "St Antony" variations, the "Tragic" and "Academic" overtures and four Hungarian dances. The Columbia Company of New York deserves warm congratulations. It presents the conducting of Walter at his ripest in a composer always dear to his heart. A year ago Toscanini recorded the Brahms symphonies, and I ran into some slight trouble when I described them in the New York "Saturday Review" in these terms: "They are rather terrific records, so realistic in suggestions of orchestral attack and sonority . . . . Whenever Brahms calls for stern measures and uncompromising directness of utterance the records seldom fail to ring true – perhaps truer to Toscanini than to the music . . . . Toscanini is here greater as a formalist than as a poet . . . ."

Walter is, of course, at Toscanini's extreme as man and artist. He is the only musician of European origin and culture who has lived long in America and remained absolutely untouched by the American aesthetic and way of life. He mingles classic and romantic elements in proportion. His interpretations have never hinted of labour or struggle. There has always been courtesy in Bruno Walter's conducting. The driving force of Toscanini, hardening in rhythm in his old age, has often seemed tyrannical; he has bound composers, notably Brahms, to the Ixion wheel of a relentless if great orchestra. Walter's conducting of Brahms is autumnal, yielding. There is no hurry, no pressure, nothing that is not ripe. A life-time of masterful musicianship is warmed by love. Each of Brahms's most songful phrases is caressed, sometimes lingered over, without the slightest hindrance to a flowing abundant rhythm. Walter's treatment of Brahms's writing for wood-wind is subtle and exquisite in its variety of inflection; I am reminded of Langford's lovely sentence: "Brahms, though not a Wagner or a Strauss, had secrets of his own of which these masters of the orchestra knew nothing . . . . If a half-close of music ever died in the heart with ineffable sweetness it is the second phrase" (he is discussing the second movement of the C minor Symphony), "whose minor third of the key the composer presses against his heart, as the nightingale presses the thorn." The analytical school of music criticism will probably fight shy of Langford's metaphor; but as a fact it is one which enables us to pierce not only to the heart of Brahms's style and musical meaning but reveals in a flash the technical ways and means, the technical rationale. People who imagine that music, or anything else, can be understood or described in terms of itself should embark on a simple elementary course of metaphysics.

In his first symphony Brahms scaled the heights of the heroic-ethical symphony conquered by Beethoven; but he never again ventured into realms as austere and storm-tossed. The older he grew the more he mellowed into an avuncular sort of romance, Mittel-Deutsch and bourgeois. It is easy to understand why certain musicians of to-day dislike Brahms, even while feeling sorry at their loss. Brahms did not protest or rebel after the C minor Symphony. Hamburg joined hands with Vienna; in Brahms classicism and romanticism alike are fused in an urbane bloodstream. The tough-minded among our contemporaries find Brahms too tender-minded. They also object to his solemn, thorough-going German way of getting through his development sections, falling back on "reach-me-down" formulae. Bruno Walter beautifully balances the essential Brahmsian characteristics – poet and pedant!

Compare the tranquil course of the first movement of the Fourth Symphony, as it goes a Vallombrosian way and course under Walter's direction, with the almost inimical tautness of Toscanini's rhythm and beat. Walter's interpretations show us Brahms entwining more and more romantic garlands on the classic trellis. Every note is related to a various, humane, and lovable art. He does not etch with Toscanini's Olympian objectivity. He paints, his brush is soft and his colours are subdued, yet the musical outline and shape are respected. As he approaches his eightieth year Bruno Walter remains young at heart. Of him we may say, as of Brahms, that youth in him looks ahead to age and age finds another impulse as wisdom glances back over the years. This is an album to procure by hook or crook and to cherish.

Post Script:

Orchestral players, as a rule, do not enjoy conductors who talk, instruct too much by word of mouth, at rehearsal. A famous conductor rehearsed the New York Philharmonic in Mahler's Ninth Symphony. At the end of the final rehearsal he addressed the orchestra: "On Saturday, gentlemen, when we play at the concert, in the audience will sit Alma Mahler. I want the performance to be more than a performance. I want it to be a – *visitation*, so that Alma Mahler will feel the presence of Gustav Mahler in the hall. So I ask you now for any advice, to make this performance truly a creation. Any advice, about bowing, phrasing. I am prepared to have another rehearsal, at my own expense. So *please*, gentlemen, any advice . . . ." Not a word from the orchestra. "Come, gentlemen," implored the renowned conductor, "don't be shy. I am waiting – any advice, *please*." Then, from the brass. "Well, Professor, send for Bruno Walter."

N.C.

15

BEECHAM
(1879–1961)

The Memory Lingers On

8th March 1971

Beecham has been dead these ten years – and the eclipse goes on. Other conductors shine planetarily in the musical sky, also a comet or two flashes away into the outer darkness. And one of them, a master, remains with us, Klemperer. None of these shares Beecham's secret, his capacity to make music rise and fall and flow as though fresh-born. He had the gift of improvisation. A final rehearsal by Toscanini was indeed final; the concert itself was a sort of tonal photostat of the final rehearsal. With Beecham, a rehearsal was a tuning-up of the orchestra, so that at the concert he could play on it, even as Cortot could play on a piano. Music is an art of motion, must go up and down, must not ever be static. "Look for the melody," was Wagner's advice to conductors. Beecham, by no means a Wagnerian, followed the advice of the man who first changed conducting of orchestras from metronomic control to personal interpretation.

His baton technique, often unpredictable, depended much on the watchful responses of his first desks. I have seen Beecham's baton fly from his grip high into the orchestral empyrean. I have seen it entangled in his coat tails. In a symphonic development passage, when frequently he became impatient (if the music wasn't Mozart's), he would point his baton rapidly down to the floor of the platform, like a musical water-diviner.

He was the product and fine fruit of a more leisurely and aristo-cratically-minded age than ours. He mingled, in his art, the amateur or connoisseur relish with professional experience. Toscanini, at Beecham's extreme temperamentally and by aesthetic, called Beecham a "great mountainbank", his translation of mountebank. Beecham could be naughty. If he didn't like a composer he suffered no pains over him.

261

He was not concerned overmuch with harmonic subtlety; a Hallé player, who adored Beecham, called him a "top-line" conductor. Beecham maintained that music should present itself with style, should appeal first of all to the cultivated ear. He could not involve himself in a polyphonic texture. He was gorgeously outrageous about Bach – "too much counterpoint; what is worse, Protestant counterpoint."

He once ruined a beautiful performance of "Siegfried", at Covent Garden. He conducted the first and second acts with a memorably sensitive control, and then rushed the third act at so reckless and headlong a tempo that the singers could scarcely breathe. I took him to task, in these columns, because he so deliberately spoiled the perform-ance. He spoke to me on the telephone. "I see from this morning's paper that you are more than usually fatuous. You say that I ruined the performance last night by my reckless tempo." "So you did," I retorted. "You critics are indeed inhumane," came his suave voice over the telephone. "When the third act began, I took note of the time. It was twenty minutes to eleven. My orchestra had been in the orchestra pit since half past six. The 'pubs' would close at eleven. And many of those dear people in the audience had to get back to Woking and Pinner. So I said to my orchestra, 'Whoops!'" Incorrigible, yes, but imperishable . . . .

He was himself, for all his sharp piercing wit, entirely humane. And with music after his heart he could be as scrupulous as Toscanini. He never was naughty in Mozart. His "Figaro" was champagne; his "Zauberflöte" incomparable for dignity of carriage, and heartfelt poignancy. His interpretation of Verdi's "Falstaff" had a sunny brilliance compared with which Toscanini's treatment of the same young-old masterpiece was brittle. It has been said that Beecham was at his best as conductor in composers of the second order. True, he avoided the Ninth Symphony of Beethoven. He found Bruckner rather a bore.

He seemed to me many times to conduct "by ear", by born musical instinct. For years he dispensed with the musical score. In his old age he actually used a score for a performance of the overture to Mozart's "Marriage of Figaro". "You used a score," I said to him, with pointed astonishment. "Yes, my dear fellow," he replied. "I have been going through my scores lately. And I find that they hold my interest from the first page to the last."

His range was wide, in spite of his dislike of music of any didactic implication. His Delius, of course, was as though he had collaborated in the conception of it. Poles apart from Delius, Beecham presented

Sibelius powerfully and in the round. His conducting of Berlioz was as authentic as his conducting of Mozart. He could take a hackneyed piece, such as Sibelius's "Valse triste" and magically cause it to sound haunting, evocative, original. His Haydn has seldom been equalled for geniality and period graciousness.

He came to British music at a time when it was, as Oscar Wilde said, speaking with a heavy German accent. He transformed music of his period into the "gay science" of the forgotten Nietzsche's dream. He led us out of the German captivity. When he was in charge of opera in these isles, he produced works of fascinating differences of style, form and procedure; Charpentier's "Louise", "Boris Godounov", D'Albert's "Tiefland", Delius's "A Village Romeo and Juliet", Bizet's "The Pearl Fishers", Stanford's "The Critic", Ethel Smyth's "The Wreckers", and "The Bosun's Mate", as well as the customary repertory. Richard Strauss thought Beecham's conception of "Elektra," and his deliverance of it, the most powerful of any in his experience. The Russian ballet, too – stars danced when Beecham was born. Since his death, as I say, the eclipse has scarcely moved. One of my most affectionate remembrances of Beecham was his appearance, during his last years, at a Sir Robert Mayer's Children's Concert. It really was an audience of children. I sat next to two rosy-chubby-cheeked of the cherubim. Sir Thomas walked very slowly to the conductor's chair. Arrived there, he addressed the children – "Ladies and Gentlemen" –an adorable touch – "My slow progress to the conductor's desk was due not to any reluctance on my part to conduct before so distinguished an audience. My slow progress was due entirely to the infirmity of old age." A pause, then "And now, Ladies and Gentlemen, our first piece is by Mozart. It was composed when he was at the age of – er – at the age of – ," he pointed to a small boy in the front row: "at *your* age, sir."

He was mixed in the elements, kind, generous, recurrently intolerant, witty yet given to most robustious humours. By Falstaff, out of Toby Belch . . . . He would talk to a taxi-driver as to the next belted Earl. Kindly and touchy, aristocratic by emulation. None the less, he was "Tommy Beecham" as orchestra players called him. He was born, after all, in St Helens, Lancashire, a fact he would recall from time to time, with satisfaction.

London's New Orchestra

ITS FIRST CONCERT

8th October 1932

Tonight the new London Philharmonic Orchestra triumphantly began its career in Queen's Hall. It is the creation of Sir Thomas Beecham, who at last is in charge of a band of his own. Continental musicians have often expressed astonishment on hearing that Beecham did not conduct any one English orchestra regularly; but in England we are wasteful of genius, and some of us even begrudge recognizing it when it is given us. The London Philharmonic Orchestra has been elaborately rehearsed, and this morning Sir Thomas Beecham put the finishing touches on an eager and dexterous team of instrumentalists. "There is no rank and file – they are every one of them leaders" – this despite the presence amongst the 'cellists of a promising lad of about eighteen who, no doubt, will shortly become a leader.

It is at rehearsal that Sir Thomas, like every great conductor, gets his work done. His genius is histrionic as well as musical. He lives the score, acts it, dances it, absorbs it, before passing it on to the players in the many vivid gestures and motions – now down to the ground with a crouch, now up straight as a guardsman. He shouts and sings; he is at one moment ecstatic with satisfaction, then suddenly he will stop the orchestra, clutch his head as though in horror; his body reels and threatens to totter. Anybody who thinks that the gestures of Sir Thomas Beecham are excessive at a concert really does him an injustice. In a public performance he must suffer a martyrdom of self-denial. Every orchestral player will tell you he plays "50 per cent" better under Beecham than under anybody else. Sir Thomas can persuade us that a flute was played well when actually it wasn't. This morning he said with immense pride in his men: "They know the music backwards; they couldn't play a wrong note if they tried" – this statement not long after an instrumentalist had wavered slightly in "Brigg Fair", and had requested, at the end of the rehearsal, that Sir Thomas should go over the passage just once more. Here is a subject for Bateman's next picture – "The English orchestral player who at twenty-five minutes past one asked for another run through of a doubtful passage."

The enthusiasm of the new orchestra is its great asset, and, of course, the inspiration comes from the most vital and persuasive of living conductors. The leader, Paul Beard, is also keen and sensitive. The fiddlers are lithe and always true to string tone and style. There are flexible wood-wind, including Léon Goossens, and though the brass is not yet distinguished it probably will become so before long. The first horn played beautifully in "Brigg Fair". At present the orchestra is like a new machine – a little too crisp and polished. In a few weeks the mellowing will begin. And all the time Sir Thomas will be exercising his influence. A Continental saying is that there are no good and bad orchestras, only good and bad conductors. By this argument the London Philharmonic Orchestra ought soon to rank with the best in the world.

Tonight's programme was ideally chosen – the "Carnaval Romain" Overture of Berlioz (given with an almost sensational verve), the "Brigg Fair" of Delius, the "Prague" Symphony of Mozart, and Strauss's "Ein Heldenleben". The music was nicely calculated to exhibit the finest of Sir Thomas's qualities. He made a glowing enough texture of "Brigg Fair". He gave us the wit and the poignancy of Mozart's masterpiece, though in the slow movement there was just a hint of overstressing, as though the conductor and players were too anxious to show off their beauties; as a consequence we lost a little of the modesty of nature. "Heldenleben" came in time to crown the evening; the performance was magnificent; nothing more sumptuous and daring in orchestral playing could be heard in more than three other places between New York and Vienna. Strauss under Beecham is a far greater composer than Strauss under Strauss. And Paul Beard's interpretation of the love music was the most poetic I have heard. The evening was musical throughout – and a significant occasion in the records of English orchestral playing.

The London Philharmonic Orchestra
in the Free Trade Hall

30th October 1933

Sir Thomas Beecham leaves us with little to do but praise. It may be that occasionally we do not agree with his interpretations, but what of that? It is not the business of genius to agree with us. He places the stamp of his own style on everything, lightens everything with the glow of his own personality. He creates the standards and laws by which we must judge him. The only fault a genius can commit is an error of disunity in his own style. Sir Thomas never is guilty of such an error; we must accept him, then – remembering Carlyle's warning to the young lady.

At Saturday's Brand Lane concert Sir Thomas conducted the London Philharmonic Orchestra. The playing was better, more finished, and more distinguished than any the present writer has ever heard in this country. The strings were always musical and in admirable unison, with no false accentuation and no loose ends. (Mr Paul Beard is an artist as well as an orchestral leader.) The special glory of the orchestra is the wood-wind; it is perfectly tuned, and, though Mr Léon Goossens is so fine and individual an oboe player that he must be difficult to match, the wood-wind is blended with a nicety that is not excelled even in the Vienna Philharmonic. The first flute is delicious; in the last movement of the "Eroica" Symphony his playing gave to his music a joyousness which seldom before have we heard. The brass is reliable and yet capable of considerable nuance; the attack of a chord is strong – the close of Berlioz's "Carnaval Romain" Overture at this concert was a magnificent example of harmonious brass playing. The double basses are good enough, and so are the 'cellos, though here and there on Saturday the orchestra's lower strings seemed to need more body. The horns are not a strong point, and the brilliant drummer miscalculated more than once the Free Trade Hall's acoustics. The orchestra is the most stylish this country has produced; if Sir Thomas were to take it abroad he would, by his own powers, do greater good for English music than all the exported Elgar and Vaughan Williams in the world. But, here again, when we praise the London Philharmonic Orchestra we are merely praising Sir Thomas.

For delicacy of touch and ensemble, one of the choice things of this concert was the performance of a suite arranged from Bizet's "The Fair Maid of Perth". Here was music distantly removed from the heavy didactic schools which went so far, during the nineteenth century – indeed too far – in the forming of the general orchestral style and technique. One of the services done by Sir Thomas can be described in words which Nietzsche used in praise of Bizet – he has Mediterranean-ized music, given warmth and clarity and poise to it, taken it out of the Northern mists and doldrums. Yet it is a mistake to persist with the old notion that Sir Thomas is merely a tasteful and cultivated conductor. His interpretation of the "Eroica" Symphony on Saturday was big and noble – it was, in fact, the most possessed piece of conducting I have experienced since Nikisch; it made the symphony sound the greatest symphony written by anybody; it made the heart to throb and the mind to thrill with delight at the invention, the marvellous mutations, of the music; it made us love Beethoven and bow the head in gratitude that we have had the blessed fortune to become acquainted with the genius of the man. (Think of it – many people, many cultured people, have never been in the world of Beethoven!)

Sir Thomas gave the first movement pace, and he pointed the rhythm in a way which with other conductors might have diminished the stature; but Sir Thomas has his own intensity, which ran through the transitions like a current of electricity, so that the great wheel of the first movement never stopped. The sense of immediate fitness was in every bar, and an immediate grandeur, a controlled excitement and anima-tion, with no obstacle to high moods or fine thinking. The second movement was grave and eloquent and never portentous; the scherzo was perhaps more of a dance than the spirit of the grotesque calls for. But the fourth movement crowned the interpretation. I have known no other conductor give to this movement the unfolding grandeur of variation-form which we could feel in every onward course of the music on Saturday. The emotion, the heart of the work, was there, beating stupendous, but, rarer still, the musical art was there – the transform-ing force and shapes of music's most wonderful device, which is variation-form. This is Sir Thomas's way with Beethoven – to shut his mind to all the accumulated weight of extraneous, non-musical significances which have been dumped upon Beethoven by the metaphysical commentators. The "meaning" of Beethoven, his "philosophy" and all the rest of it, are in the music and need not be brought to it. Being in the music, this "meaning" can best be expressed by playing the score with an entirely musical intensity which penetrates to all parts. When everything is said about great conducting, it boils down to close knowledge of the score, personal force of suggestion, an ear for orchestral effects – and a lifetime's love of the music, a passionate activity in it day by day. A column of musical illustrations would be necessary to show half of the felicities of this reading of the "Eroica": I will mention just one of them: the treatment of the fugato section of the closing movement, the strength and clearness of the parts, the growing climax, and then the transition to the andante division – all was natural, inevitable, creative. There is a rather shamefaced way nowadays of paying tributes to the artists who move us profoundly; it is a weakness of small men to praise with small words.

Saturday's audience did not hesitate to acclaim Sir Thomas a great conductor. The present writer has spent a lifetime in music and has learned his standards from Richter, Nikisch, Mahler, Toscanini, Bruno Walter, and Furtwängler. There is no reason for thinking that Sir Thomas Beecham is not of this company. But though his genius is known and truly estimated, his devotion to music, his labours in the cause of music behind the scenes, is a matter which will probably have to wait for proper recognition until biography makes Sir Thomas into a legend. The audience on Saturday would not leave the hall until Sir Thomas and his orchestra had played "The Bartered Bride" Overture as an encore. After the colossal energies of the "Eroica" the musicians might have been spared this abrupt transition to brilliance.

Sir Thomas Beecham and Mozart

PLEASURE-SEEKING CONNOISSEUR

18th October 1935

The season of the Royal Philharmonic Society began tonight with an outstanding concert. Sir Thomas Beecham was at his best, which means he was at his most persuasive. Under his leadership the London Philharmonic Orchestra played with a superb verve and precision. When Sir Thomas is in this form we can only say, "For all his faults we love him still." He tries us in many ways, he pulls our legs, he sometimes keeps us waiting, he outrages us and tantalizes us; but the moment he ascends the rostrum – a good word for the place and position he fills at concerts – he has the means of enslaving us in a moment. Genius is better than the power to convince us by appeals to reason. Sir Thomas can put his spell on us even when our better understanding feebly whispers that he is doing things with music which are against the common canon His secret is to delight us on his own terms. The pundits may argue till they are hoarse that he over-phrases Mozart, that he lends to all music the same rhythmical formula, that he draws the most diverse composers into the same dazzling world – nothing matters while Sir Thomas is conducting but his own allurements. And what a rare quality he brings to English music. He expels plainness. The merely respectable and competent perish in his presence. No other English musician to-day shares his élan, his pagan enjoyment of vivid colour, vital pulsations, dancing musical epigrams. He sometimes misses the divinity of Mozart, the unselfconscious pathos, but no conductor living can express for us as Beecham can the joyousness of Mozart with Mozart's own bubbling prodigality and, at the same time, his miraculous clarity of form, his breeding and his pride of carriage.

269

Tonight the performance of the third and fourth movements of the E flat major symphony of Mozart made moisture come to the eyes because of the sheer happiness of the music and the incredible accuracy and bloom of the playing. To hear this music played to perfection was to escape from the material burden of the world for a while. We could feel for a blissful moment that felicity is the only reality, the Thing-in-Itself. When Mozart is in this heavenly mood it is as though he were saying to us: "A star danced and under it I was born." Yet when the work was composed Mozart was a harassed mortal man afflicted with responsibilities and griefs which would send the average man of "Big Business", or the average politician, staggering into the nearest nursing home. The creative spirit in genius seems to owe nothing to the support of the flesh or to those facts of life which most of us imagine are worth worrying about. Mozart's music is the answer to the theory that art must wait upon the external universe and serve it by indulging in what Matthew Arnold called the "criticism of life". All true art is above and beyond reality, a thing sui generis, a platonic idea and ecstasy.

The paradox of music is that it can achieve its moving eloquence and significance when it means nothing that words can say, when it is, as Schopenhauer said (in the best prose ever written by a German), an idea of the world. All modern art is reacting against the tyranny of the representative and the real. It is reaching out towards abstract patterns. But there is nothing new under the sun; the movement is a return to the idea of a universal harmony of members – it is as old as Pythagoras. And in Mozart we find the idea set forth once and for all. The highest praise that could be offered to Sir Thomas tonight is that he made us feel more than ever that Mozart's music is the music of the morning stars and the Cherubim.

Sir Thomas with Isaac Stern

BRAHMS'S VIOLIN CONCERTO

7th November 1952

The Royal Philharmonic Orchestra, conducted in the Festival Hall last night by Sir Thomas Beecham, more than maintained the high level of play recently heard from this same platform. The string tone was brilliant and varied in temperature, so to say; the wood-wind were beautifully in tune; indeed the balance of every part was a sign of fine musicianship and mature and masterful direction. Sir Thomas has apparently opened yet another vein of musical energy and delight. No other conductor expresses as much as Beecham's enjoyment in his work; he is like the connoisseur, savouring vintages from his own cellar; he is not expertly selling them to us. His and the orchestra's performance, at this concert, of the "Haffner" Symphony was of the kind properly described as a "spirited rendering". There was nothing aloof in the poise of style of this Mozart! From Mozart, Sir Thomas modulated easefully, and without score, to the Sixth Symphony of Sibelius, and the interpretation was so beautifully spun or woven in its texture that I could not have wished for music more engrossing in its content. Once we had become accustomed to the Sibelius way of putting together his limited material, his tiny scale-passages, his persistent string thrummings, his sudden and resolving brass cadences, the imagination craves for a larger and more changeful world. The later Sibelius symphonies are very much like jig-saw arrangements in the same tone material; whichever way the bits and pieces are put together we get the same picture, the same misty monotonous Finnish landscape, streaked intermittently with noble gleams of light from somewhere. The chances are that we may have over-estimated Sibelius; I doubt if he can fairly be said to possess more genius and a larger stature than Dvořák's – to name another composer often called "nationalist" or regional.

After Mozart and Sibelius Sir Thomas turned to Brahms – the Violin Concerto, with Isaac Stern the soloist. Seldom have I heard the work sound a fuller symphonic note than now, in the orchestra. Sir Thomas let us hear all the noble resonance of Brahms's D Major as the first movement was unfolded: such a canvas might easily have reduced to insignificance a violinist of less than Stern's reserves of tone and his strength and superb technical domination. It is hard at the moment to think of Stern's equal to-day as a violinist who draws from his instrument all its natural beauties and bold, proud manifestations of dexterity. He has, I think, a finer fancifulness than that of Heifetz, and a warmer romantic glow: and though he is essentially the virtuoso he is never straying outside the realms of music. There was in fact a certain sedateness of rhythm in his treatment of the sequences of figuration in the first movement, where he was so scrupulous as to endow every swiftly touched note with an individual quality. Now and again he dwelt on a phrase with a solicitude and relish quite extraordinary in an artist nurtured mainly in America.

Stern missed nothing of the great expansion which occurs after the rhapsodic attack on the first movement; and there were some magnificent chorded notes, vehement as military trumpets. The slow movement was remarkable not only for the flawless quality of Stern's tone, the delicacy of his transitions, the lovely flights at the end to the upper ether; also we heard the proper romantic twilight grey and gold of the orchestration: the mingling of wood-wind and horn at the beginning was another proof of rare technical skill and the finest musical sensibility. At times it seemed that Stern was playing the concerto for us more beautifully than anybody else since Kreisler. But there was not, as I remember well, the Kreisler impulse of melody, nor the Kreisler dual control over classic outline and romantic freedom. And, of course, Stern could not match the intensity of Huberman's piercings into the heart of the slow movement; he is so richly blessed with the fiddle's musical allurements that he could not, even if he would, enter the non-sensuous chambers where Huberman held sessions of not exactly silent thought.

The Rondo finale was vigorous and big: Sir Thomas almost himself danced to the rhythm he established. Stern's power and attack were strenuous enough, but at no danger to articulation. The change to the flowing middle-section transcended the directions of mere tempo indication; the Rondo changed imaginatively by an appeal to the sense of the picturesque with its dancing gipsy lilt and echoes. The tremendous applause for Stern at the end, from a hall crowded to the gangways and doors, was thundered proportionately at Sir Thomas in turn. What other conductor of the present day is equal, at one and the same occasion, to doing justice, with a personal relish, to Mozart, Sibelius, and Brahms?

Beecham and Delius in Rehearsal

1959

Sir Thomas conducted a Delius Festival in London thirty years ago. Delius, who was living in France, came to hear it. He was then 67, and a complete cripple, blind and paralysed. I saw him in the old Langham Hotel, and his Swedish valet carried him and dumped him on a couch like a rag doll. But his mind was keen as a knife. It was at this Festival that Sir Thomas while rehearsing, without a score, stopped the orchestra and asked the oboist whether he hadn't played A flat instead of A natural. The oboist replied "It's written A flat in my part, Sir Thomas." Whereat Sir Thomas turned to Delius, sitting hunched up in the Circle: "I am having some controversy with my oboist," he said. "Perhaps you can help us, Frederick. Shouldn't he play A natural?" And Delius replied, "Well, Sir Thomas, it sounded all right to me." So Sir Thomas addressed one of the attendants of the hall. "Go across the way to my flat, and bring the full orchestral score". The man departed. In a quarter of an hour he returned with it. Beecham turned over the pages. Then he spoke to Delius: "A natural, as I thought. I say, Delius, I wish to God you would take the trouble to learn your own music!"

At His 70th Birthday Dinner

Telegrams and congratulations were read out from famous names. "Finally," announced the Chairman, "my warm felicitations – Sibelius."

Immense applause, after which Sir Thomas Beecham asked, with a pained expression on his face, "Nothing from Mozart?"

273

16

KLEMPERER
(1885–1973)

The Interpreter

8th July 1973

Otto Klemperer was one of the last great conductors nurtured in the nineteenth century, when music was regarded as expressive of matters human and spiritual. Born in 1885 he studied at Frankfurt and Berlin. Mahler encouraged his first efforts as orchestral interpreter and recommended him for his first post at the German Opera in Prague in 1907. For long – well into his years of maturity – he was fated to work in the shadows cast by Bruno Walter and Furtwängler in Europe, and when he went to America his methods were at the extreme of Toscanini's. Not until he directed the Kroll Opera House in Berlin did he rise above a prevailing level of importance . . . .

My own first experience of him was in Vienna, more than a quarter of a century ago. He conducted the Vienna Philharmoniker in Bruckner's Ninth Symphony. He was in his prime, tall, upright, and handsome in an aquiline, not to say daemonic way.

Klemperer waited long for recognition outside Germany and Austria. In England, he remained more or less unknown until after the second world war, although he conducted at a Courtauld-Sargent concert in London in the 1930s, when the late William Turner was perhaps the first critic here to get an idea of his potentiality. In Klemperer's ripe maturity he became accepted as the most authoritative orchestral interpreter of Beethoven, Bruckner and Brahms. This country's misfortune was that only seldom did our concert promoters allow him to conduct Bruckner, whose symphonies he encompassed with a grip and vision which saw the end of a large musical shape in the beginning. He knew the secret of rhythm that can go on and on and on, evolving bar from bar, phrase from phrase, with no hiatus, yet not burdening a curve of melody by too great a stress. Towards the end of his life he became more and more unyielding. Never a colourist, his treatment of texture tended to produce a black and white neutrality of tone. He almost took the schmaltz out of Mahler; and one of his driest witticisms was that, though he admired Bruno Walter's interpretations of Mahler, they were for him "too Jewish".

It is a paradox that Klemperer, a nineteenth-century romantic at bottom, lived to serve as a rallying point for the young music-lovers who reacted against the subjectively expressive schools. But Klemperer's austerity at the end came as a natural development in his deeply experiencing nature. He was above all sway of fashion. He suffered physical hardship and pain, and seemed thrice to rise from the grave. In exile from Germany, he was affected by a tumour of the brain. Then he broke a femur. Next, and after he had passed his seventieth year, he was nearly burned to death while bedridden. Poverty was his portion at a period of his high-noon of achievement – thanks to Hitler. In music he found refuge and clarification. He was a religious man, in spite of, or because of, his knowledge of the flesh and the world. He was Faustian, with a tincture of Mephisto thrown in.

In character and method he stood poles apart from his great contemporary, Bruno Walter. Klemperer had about him nothing of the grand seigneur charms. Unaffected and simple, he dominated orchestras by direct unobtrusive indications from baton and left hand . . . . His eyes pierced the orchestra to the last of the back desks. The timpani was as much under the spell of his presence as the first violin, who at a rehearsal, determined to let Klemperer know that time was up and everybody was anxious to get away and enjoy Saturday afternoon, kept pulling out his watch and very pointedly looking at it. For a while Klemperer took no notice, then asked, "Is it going?"

Many musicians were not happy about his manner of conducting Mozart. It was not for him the *galant* Mozart presented by Sir Thomas Beecham; far from it. Klemperer's Mozart was made of sterner stuff. But some years ago he set in motion the "Nachtmusik" with one liberating beat of the baton. He could then have sat back in the audience, so it seemed, for the patterns of tone gravitated to their places in the harmonized sky as the stars in their courses . . . .

Klemperer's integrity was something nearly obsolete among conductors to-day. It is because he would not trust a merely personal indulgence in music that he was perpetually returning to the forge and the anvil and the hammer. He did not set out to woo the senses: his intention was to get at the truth. In his martyred old age he could well have often uttered to himself (probably he did, for he was a Goethean), the words of the blinded Faust:

> "Die Nacht scheint tiefertief herein zudringen,
> allein im innern leuchtet helles Licht."
> (The night seems deeper now to press around me,
> but in my inmost spirit all is light.)

The Noblest Roman of Them All

26th March 1947

Doctor Klemperer last night conducted the Philharmonia Orchestra in the Royal Festival Hall . . . . The evening began with a stupendous performance of the Great Fugue, designed originally as the finale of Beethoven's B flat Quartet. A string-orchestra version is justifiable for the voltage of the music strains painfully at tone capacity of four fiddlers only. Klemperer moulded the shape with terrific grip; the clearness of parts was astounding, considering the intensity of dynamics. And out of the giant strength came a certain poignancy, as though the music were aware that for all its effort it was trying to express something beyond the scope of music to express at all. We could no doubt make out a case supporting the view that in this colossal movement Beethoven was occupied mainly with tonal, textural, and rhythmical problems; but Klemperer's treatment of it dismissed such a conjecture as flippant, not to say sacrilegious.

Klemperer is apparently the last of a school that regarded conducting as a vocation. His approach to music is constantly serious, one might say devout. It is an approach in fact which suggests that an ethical sort of integrity is behind it in stronger force than a truly artistic, or aesthetic, activity or concern. His interpretation of the Seventh Symphony of Beethoven at this concert scorned delights and lived, if not laboriously, at any rate strenuously throughout.

Many of us have loved to think of the Seventh Symphony as one of Beethoven's relaxations. After the tumult of the Fifth, the comparative relaxations of the Sixth, Seventh, and Eighth Symphonies prepare us to open our imagination as we come to the titanic challenge and wrestlings in the Ninth; and as we hear Beethoven at work on that heroic announcement of faith, beaten out by hammer on anvil, we can look back and come back all the more affectionately to the preceding symphonies, in which the mightiest heart and nature ever known in music rested for a while. But there is no release from stress in the Seventh Symphony as Klemperer conducts it. The hammer and the anvil are here again; and the wonder grows whether the anvil will prove hard enough to stand the impact of the forceful, relentless blows.

There is, of course, tremendous energy in the Seventh Symphony, however yieldingly it is treated. It is, as the old saying goes, the apotheosis of the dance. Klemperer takes no mortal view of its exuberance and seven-league boots. The violence of emphatic loud tone in persistent rhythm threatens to exacerbate the ear. It was undoubtedly a great performance, great in conception, great in execution. But it protested too much. The allegretto was Olympian, too; austere and detached in its beauty, a beauty which did not touch the heart. The lovely episode in the major was not allowed to woo us with any appeal, even to the impressionable senses. The movement was taken at an unusually stately, not to say portentous, tempo. As Donald Tovey pointed out, Beethoven could never have called it allegretto if he had not thought it too fast for an ordinary andante.

The mastery of Klemperer is not equalled by any conductor now living; but it is a mastery which seems to be under the compulsion of being not only eternally vigilant but eternally at full tension as well. His integrity is something very nearly obsolete among conductors; it is because he will not take on trust any personal musical reaction that he is perpetually returning to the forge. An action of Klemperer at this concert was revealing of the man. After the performance of the Great Fugue, volleys of applause went to the platform. Klemperer at once motioned to the first violin and the whole of the Philharmonia to stand. When he was recalled to the conductor's desk, he remained slightly in the rear of the violins' front row. He is now the noblest Roman of them all. Age has much to do with it.

A Conversation with Klemperer

Otto Klemperer has the reputation of a man hard to approach, sometimes ill-mannered, unsympathetic, and incalculable – a Mahlerian, in fact. This legend is as misleading as the one about Mahler himself, who was usually kind and helpful to serious young musicians and a terror to all people of pretension. It was with some understandable nervousness that I met Klemperer for the first time, face to face. To my dismay he had arrived at the restaurant arranged for our meeting in advance of the agreed time, and he was waiting for me. He waved my apologies into the air; at once I found the wavelength to his nature. In less than ten minutes I was talking to him as freely and intimately as if I had known him for years. His austere face, with strong jaw and penetrating eyes, is no guide to his simple modest friendliness. I found it hard to believe that this was the same Klemperer generally feared by orchestral players, the Mephistophelian being who, so the story goes, postponed a rehearsal with a famous orchestra because the first trumpeter was late, having lost his way in a fog. "He will be here in half an hour," Klemperer was assured; but Klemperer stamped from the platform. "Rehearsal this afternoon!" he grunted. At 3 o'clock that afternoon the orchestra was assembled in full. "Ah," said Klemperer, "we are all here. The first trumpet? – ja so! Wir beginnen rehearse! 'Eine kleine Nachtmusik'!"

Klemperer did not talk until I began. In fact he mostly listened. When I spoke of the seldom-played Sixth Symphony of Mahler he refrained from telling me how often he had conducted it. He merely said. "Not one of Mahler's best." I deliberately, to draw on the egoism which most times is the orchestral conductor's most unmistakable point, reminded him that when he was a young student of twenty-two he made a two-hand piano arrangement of Mahler's Second Symphony. I also reminded him that Mahler was very much pleased with it. "He was always kind to young musicians," was Klemperer's comment; simply that and nothing more. He changed the subject, which was the only instance in our conversation where he steered the course of it.

He has a quite sardonic, yet not ungenial humour, and he actually laughed audibly when I told him of the first concert I ever heard him conduct, in Vienna one Sunday morning twenty-three years ago. He was about to begin the Ninth Symphony of Bruckner; he stood arms outstretched before the Vienna Philharmonic Orchestra, baton poised. The concert hall was hushed and tense, next to me was sitting a middle-aged Viennese, and before Klemperer moved his baton, before a single note of Bruckner was attacked or heard, this middle-aged Viennese burst into tears, and buried his head in his hands. "You need not have played the symphony at all," I said to Klemperer, who replied, "It could not possibly have come up to his expectations."

He did not think too highly of the music of the later Strauss, though he agreed that "Metamorphosen" was a finely composed work and the "Four Last Songs" were beautiful. In his opinion, Strauss's best ideas ran out after the composition of "Ariadne". I asked if he did not have a good opinion of "Die Frau ohne Schatten". No, not really; but he admitted that some of the melodies were "attractive"! I then had the temerity to tell him that my first impressions of "Die Frau" were, like his, not altogether favourable; but closer study of the opera had now convinced me that it contained some of Strauss's greatest music. "So," said Klemperer, "Then I will look into the score again." Imagine the average maestro responding to any suggestion of prompting that he might change his mind.

He was not "against" tone-row composition and the latest experiments. He had in his own lifetime waved the flag of the avant-garde. But after long study of the "new" music he had not yet come to an understanding of its ways of organization and its implications as expression, which was very modest of him, a musician of the rarest culture and experience; compared with the quick-minded young music critics of the present day (who also know all the "classics" upside down) Klemperer might even be regarded backward in his comprehension of the contemporary masters, of whom I gather there are at least a dozen – up to the moment of writing.

Klemperer has needed to battle hard to get recognition in this country. As recently as 1947–8 Klemperer was given belittling notices in London, though about this same time he made musical history in Australia by means of a superb interpretation of the Second Symphony of Mahler, played by the Sydney Orchestra on four consecutive evenings to packed audiences. Today Klemperer can do no wrong in London; he could very well echo Schnabel's remark: "They always applaud – even when it is good."

Klemperer and the Ninth

THE PHILHARMONIA'S CONDUCTOR-FOR-LIFE

12th November 1957

On Friday the Klemperer cycle of Beethoven concerts was crowned in the Festival Hall, London, by a performance of the Ninth Symphony. It was strict of tempo and rather dry of tone, with few moments of pianissimo and with no great hush or holding of the breath even in the slow movement or at the moment of adoration in the finale, when all the music kneels before the mystery of creation – "Ihr stürzt nieder, Millionen!" Klemperer seemed a tired man, and at his age no wonder, after his recent prodigious labours. The performance was, of course, authoritative and far-reaching, scarcely a note unheeded, and all given their proportionate places.

It was a superb exposition, not from the heart to the heart (in Beethoven's own phrase), but from the musical intelligence to the musical intelligence. There was one tremendous stroke in the first movement, the manifestation of D major, omnipresent for long but invisible; but on the whole it was a fairly analytical treatment of music incredibly subterranean and creative. The scherzo was noon-day clear and very percussive, with few half-lights. But the trio was a marvel of clear part writing. Klemperer held the adagio logically together, an achievement possible only by the greatest conductors: for the great mind of the composer turns inward and on itself in musings beyond these voices. Klemperer drew phrase from phrase, link from link. The only thing missing was the ease of an unselfconsciously working imagination. With the advent of the finale and a noble piece of declamation by Hans Hotter, the Philharmonia Choir crashed upon us like the dawn that comes up like thunder.

This choir is Mr Walter Legge's latest contribution to our music, and none better or anywhere near its equal ever before. The tone and attack were fresh, terrifically competent and accurate, with, apparently, power in reserve. In fact, I was given the impression that, really, this Philharmonia Choir needs more scope than the finale of the Ninth Symphony provides. Many of the singers sang unburdened by scores, from memory, and the men stuck out their breasts, clenched their fists, and showed Hans Hotter where, so to say, he got off. The women soared to the high As with mouth so wide open that I feared for cases of lockjaw right and left. At the concert's end Klemperer was tumultuously applauded and repeatedly recalled to the platform; but always he remained in the rear, as though one of the orchestral back-desks.

Klemperer's Beethoven

30th October 1961

Last night in the Royal Festival Hall, Dr Klemperer took his seat and expounded the "Missa Solemnis" of Beethoven through the agency of the superb Philharmonia Orchestra and the equally superb Philharmonia Chorus, and four soloists. By experience, knowledge and musical wisdom, Doctor Klemperer conveyed to us the immense reach and power of the work. Occasional insecurities of pitch, not actually "off the line" but threatening to leave it momentarily, mattered not at all.

The Mass is much more than so much musical art. Indeed as musical art it has its brusque imperfections. A hint, a mere hint, of virtuosity in the performance of the Mass would defame it. The terrific technical difficulties presented to the singers were possibly essential to Beethoven's purpose, which went far beyond a conventional eloquence of tone, even as it went far beyond a conventional ritualistic or liturgical significance. The Philharmonia choir actually met the challenge in the heights of the "Credo", where there is struggle enough. This is a Mass for all who have for a moment pondered the mystery of creation and the relation of man to eternity, as he conceives it; a Mass for Everyman. For whatever this or that individual's faith or church, he and all of us must here and there stop to think – we are alive now and none can escape death. Not much room in the Mass for vocal or orchestral complacency.

Maybe this profoundly moving performance missed sometimes a note of mysticism and the throb of terror in the sudden dynamic contrast. It is easy for a conductor, as he attends to Beethoven's treatment of musical stuffs and elements, often simple, to understress and consequently take away a little from sharpness and intensity of utterance. Even as he announces faith, Beethoven is occasionally rebellious. He won't "believe on compulsion".

Dr Klemperer's rare virtue as he interprets this, the most humane sacred music in existence, is that he is direct and humble, yet authoritative. The shattering fact of the work is that in it Beethoven retains a quite naïve piety, for all its range, heaven to earth. His faith is not argued by dialectic. "From the heart to the heart", he wrote on the score of the "Kyrie". He pondered the Latin text from his own point of view, a view he could not always make verbally intelligible. And in music, too, he had to "hammer it out".

The performance really left this critic with little to say or do, except bow the head. The choir's singing was truly magnificent. So high does much of the vocal music aspire that the singers may well be half-way to heaven when they get to the notes. Thus, on the afternoon and evening of the same Sunday, the Royal Festival Hall has witnessed within a few hours Beethoven and Stravinsky and Klemperer in conjunction. Another "fall-out" on the way?

Birthday Homage to a "Rock of Integrity"

15th May 1970

Klemperer celebrated his 85th birthday in the Royal Festival Hall last night. He was helped to the conductor's seat and, having modestly bowed to the audience, sat down in it, while everybody stood up and rendered to him homage, homage probably seldom lavished upon a musician since Hans Sachs. Then, silence obtained, Klemperer with the least obtrusive motion of his baton, set into motion "Das Lied von der Erde" of Mahler, with the New Philharmonia Orchestra and Richard Lewis and Janet Baker as soloists.

Klemperer's baton, once it had announced the "Fiat Lux", seemed to free the players and the singers to proceed by their own experienced volition to the work's end, the end apparently seen in the beginning by Klemperer. His authority is, of course, sure, comprehensive and, so to say, invisible. He almost clarified and diminished the overscored tumult at the outset of the first section, "Trinklied von Jammer der Erde", so that Richard Lewis's vibrant tone could be heard as, maybe, never so clearly and pungently since the voice of Patzak. And Lewis most sensitively modulated to the "Traumerisch", nearly Schmalt-zisch, interlude, with the violin allurements, of the passage about the "eternal Firmament". On the whole, though, Klemperer kept "Das Lied" very much on and of the earth, except when the music, in the "Abschied", the "Farewell", was lofted on high on the wings of song by Janet Baker. She has not quite got the thrush-in-the-throat throb of Ferrier; she cannot soar with the incredible disembodied sound of Kathleen at the line "blueht auf im Lenz"; none the less, Janet Baker in this marvellously original music can respond subtly to Mahler's twilit implications, notably in the eloquent (I almost could say incomparable) recitative: "Er stieg vom Pferd," a recitative which causes silence and loneliness to become audible. Janet Baker was like a medium through which Mahler spoke, a vessel of grace. She sang as an artist anointed – and Mahler was well equipped with oils and unguents. In a word, Miss Baker gave me an experience, an incorporation of the essence of a composer – my second such rare experience in the same week, for on Monday, in the Purcell Room, Else Mayer-Lismann evoked the presence of Mozart, in a talk (*not* a lecture) informed by imagination, devotion and understanding, with unselfconscious power of communi-cation. And here is Janet Baker's precious secret – an unselfconscious power of communication, in an age of more or less musical salesman-ship.

The evening was naturally Klemperer's, and tribute to a great musician and man, Faustian (with a corrective Mephisto at his shoulder), a rock of integrity in a rocking sea of the arts. Klemperer, now the last of the authoritative interpreters and prophets of Beethoven and the so-called "classical", also was one of the avant-garde . . . . He has himself recently composed a symphony in which he experiments with the latest tonal know-how. He will rise early from his bed in the morning to attend a rehearsal of the latest music – not as conductor but as ever-searching mind. A true Goethean, he has renewed himself day by day through trial and error and appalling physical suffering. He has been faithful to the commandment of Goethe – "Die and become!" . . . .

17

BARBIROLLI
(1899–1970)

"Glorious John"

30th July 1970

Barbirolli was born just over 70 years ago in London . . . . He could well have become renowned everywhere as a conductor of opera. In the 1930s, he conducted Strauss's "Der Rosenkavalier" in Manchester, one of the most understanding interpretations I have heard of this score.

Environment and musical necessity compelled him to concentrate on concert work. He had the confidence in himself to go to New York to take charge of the Philharmonic Orchestra, which was as though a cricketer had chosen to go in to bat after Bradman. He did not lack a certain faith in himself; on the other hand he was not vain in an irritating way. He would tell me: "I have just been to Berlin conducting Brahms. And they told me they'd never heard Brahms in Berlin before." From the mouths of other conductors, this would have sounded unbearable; Barbirolli's naïve charm could be disarming. If I happened to mention to him that I had been looking through a score of Bruckner, he would at once remark: "Yes – I gave the first performance of Bruckner's Fifth in Houston."

Yet he was never arrogant; indeed, he could be embarrassingly sensitive to criticism. Sir Thomas Beecham would ring me up saying: "I see from this morning's paper that you are more than usually fatuous" – his comment on an adverse notice, a comment which let me know exactly where I stood with him, as critic and friend. Barbirolli could be so much hurt by a review that he would say: "I won't touch that work again," almost with tears in his eyes. He was not so much the conscious egoist as the artist who could scarcely believe that the boy in him had truly grown up and that he, Barbirolli, was now a Maestro.

He was admired throughout Europe as one of the most illuminating of Mahler conductors. In New York, Alma Mahler was not only satisfied with Barbirolli's conducting of Mahler. She declared that he somehow "*looked* liked Mahler"! It was when he was in Australia that I suggested to him that he should turn his attention, as a conductor, to Mahler. At this time he confessed that Mahler was more or less unknown to him.

He ripened his talent by observing – whether he learned it or not from Goethe – his limitations. He frankly was not the ideal Mozart conductor. He was not, in my hearing, consistently convincing in Beethoven. He was drawn to music of openhearted, and all-too-human, humanity. The manliness of Vaughan Williams stirred responses in him not less quickly than the highly strung mental and nervous system of Mahler.

Last year, at the Edinburgh Festival, Barbirolli conducted one of the Chopin piano concertos with Claudio Arrau as soloist. The orchestral scoring of Chopin has never been a conductor's delight; but on this occasion, Barbirolli somehow changed the neutral, ill-woven texture into a sort of velvet in which the pearls of Arrau's piano tones could beautifully repose. Arrau was enchanted. "I don't think," he said to me, "that you, in Britain, quite realize what a wonderful conductor Barbirolli is." Barbirolli, for sure, was endowed with one very rare gift from the Muse – the gift of the magical touch. He was happy, too, to have at his service an orchestra ready to fall under his spell.

He was a fully equipped musician; he knew the orchestra from the inside. He knew his music backwards. It is true that he invariably conducted with the score in front of him, on the desk. He appreciated my story of Knappertsbusch, the Munich conductor, who in his old age was asked: "Why do you always have a score when you are conducting? All the conductors today – Karajan, Maazel, and so on – don't use a score." And Knappertsbusch replied: "Why should I not use a score? *I* can read one."

It was Vaughan Williams who first called Barbirolli "Glorious John". He will be missed sorely. And he will be admiringly and affectionately remembered.

The Hallé and Mahler's Ninth

"AT LEAST ONE LISTENER HELD UNDER A SPELL."

13th May 1960

On Friday and Saturday the Hallé Orchestra and Sir John Barbirolli made excellent music in the Royal Festival Hall playing Wagner, Mozart, Beethoven, and Tchaikovsky; but it was the interpretation of Mahler's Ninth Symphony that crowned this visit to the capital. The Hallé players know the work so well that Sir John can straightway go into its great complex of expressiveness, certain that the instrumentalists are not likely to allow technical difficulties to detract their minds from what Mahler is saying, and saying with no inhibitions.

This was an interpretation which could have been given with pride anywhere in the world. For my own part, I have never before heard this Ninth Symphony explored as comprehensively, as poignantly, as on this occasion; the gathering tension was quite tremendous. Extraordinarily eloquent were the wood-wind, especially the bassoon, in those pathetically exposed soliloquies in which Mahler seems to grope or commune in a sudden orchestral vacancy. I particularly admired the treatment of the passage in the "Rondo Burleske", where the main theme of the adagio finale is conceived; it was entirely Mahlerisch, with the clarinet's leaping quirk absolutely right in tone and pointedness, with the general orchestral texture pungent with the flavours of refined "Schmalz", during the dream-like interlude coming between the movement's brusque sardonic emphasis. Sir John very persuasively conducted the inner movements, which in many performances have sounded diffused and repetitive . . . .

It is a terrific thought that the wonderful tone-world of the Ninth Symphony – and of "Das Lied von der Erde" – was heard only by Mahler's inner ear, heard only in the murmurous silence of his imagination. How modern the symphony is in feeling and sometimes in technique! It is prophetic not only in its musical language, but also of the world we are now living in, disruptive, complex, and unsure, with our inverted sentimentality and our haunted sense of the subconscious. The music lives on its nerves and at the end, wins through to some peace, if it is only the peace of submission and resignation. But though Sir John forced home every blow, every stab of poetic pain, though the crack of doom in the first movement's crisis – "Wie ein schwerer Kondukt" – threatened to shatter the concert hall, he did not lose grip of the shape. The fierce logic and inevitability of the music's onward course held at least one listener under a spell.

The string-tone in the adagio had the right sonority, the right choral emphasis, and also the violins reached up to the Mahler altitudes of aspiration, while the lower strings wrung out the lees of appoggiatura. The tempo of the first movement, marked "andante comodo", risked a certain slowness which might have hindered the impression which it should convey of peripatetic motion; but the phrasing, the varying tone pressure, and the masterful grip of the texture, now fully scored and dynamic, now thinning to a tragic sort of vacancy and emaciation, allowed no impediments to our imaginative perceptions and reactions. Perhaps the most praiseworthy characteristic of Sir John and the Hallé's presentation of the masterpiece was the way Mahler's thinking processes were emphasized. Much too much is made of Mahler's nerves and emotions, his pathologically subjective expressiveness. His brain was one of the most subtle and keenly textured ever to find a way of life in music. The Ninth Symphony is the work of a thinker as much as it is the work of an imagination possessed by the power to experience and suffer and wear itself out. And, as I say, Sir John did not miss the irony and the humour of revolt.

I suppose I shall be told that I praise the Hallé Orchestra with the prejudice of a man born in Manchester. Maybe. But I know my Mahler more or less backward and inside out; and I would not spare the rod against any performance of Mahler that did not do him justice. I count this unfolding and emptying-out of the Ninth Symphony one of the best, truest, and most Mahlerisch in all my experience of the composer.

Twenty Years with the Hallé

28th September 1963

Tomorrow Sir John Barbirolli will be presented with the Hallé Gold Medal to commemorate 20 years of service to the orchestra and to the Society. The award has a deeper significance than most of its kind.

We all know the dramatic circumstances of Sir John's appointment in the summer of 1943. The world was in the melting pot of the war. The Hallé Orchestra was in extremis. Philip Godlee authorized the famous telegram to Sir John in New York. Barbirolli had conducted the New York Philharmonic since 1936. The telegram read as follows: "Would you be interested permanent conductorship Hallé important developments pending."

Barbirolli returned to a bomb-racked country, in which few men, women, or children could be sure that they would be alive this time next week. Moreover, he returned to find a skeleton of an orchestra; he had to begin from scratch, to conjure instrumentalists almost out of vacancy. "Good heavens!" people said, "A woman trombonist! Even a woman timpanist!" (And what a timpanist she was – one of the best since Gezink was the unparalleled master of his battery from the time of Richter to Harty.)

It is a compliment to the Hallé Orchestra that every permanent conductor has proudly taken it upon himself to call it his own, bestowing upon it his own name. Harty could well be turning in his grave if he could know that anyone other than himself had done so, since Charles Hallé himself presumed to call the Hallé "my orchestra". But nobody has held the position of conductor-in-chief of the Hallé longer than Sir John. None since Richter has shared his influence, not only over performance but over musical policy.

He is regarded in certain quarters, notably in the south of England, as

295

something of a square, because he won't encourage experimental composition to take place in public. He won't conduct a work if he doesn't understand its language. Why, if a conductor is honest, should he?

In any case, a conductor takes little risk to his reputation as interpreter with the newest music, since no standards of performance have been established for it. Barbirolli is admired throughout Europe as one of the best Mahler conductors extant. The players of the Berlin Philharmonic Orchestra have assured me that the name of Barbirolli is as alluring to the public of Berlin as that of the imperious Karajan.

Sir John has the forcefulness and tenacity of most men of his physical stature. He can assume a Napoleonic aspect as he walks to the conductor's rostrum, left arm consciously hooked across his shirt front. He has an Italianate look, the dark complexion, the gleam in the eyes. He was called at the baptismal font Giovanni Battista, and was the son of an Italian father and a French mother. His father and his grandfather were players in Italian orchestras – his father, in fact, played under Toscanini.

But Sir John is a Londoner as much as he is an Italian; for he was born in Southampton Street, near the Strand, learned to cope with the 'cello at Trinity College of Music, and played in the Queen's Hall Orchestra under Henry Wood and Beecham. Could Sir Thomas, in his most whimsical fantasies, have dreamed that the day would come on which an obscure 'cellist in his orchestra would follow after him as director of the Hallé, and, more or less, keep him for long at a distance from it? A pretty irony.

What manner of man is this benevolent dictator of the Hallé? Vain? Well, to change a famous saying of Sir Winston Churchill about a contemporary statesman, Barbirolli has much to be vain about. He is, and there is little use or point in arguing about it – our most interesting conductor, the most artistically temperamental of them all. For he certainly is the artist with the accompanying irritants that go with power of personal expression and imagination.

Frankly I like his pride in himself, his constant and delighted discovery, moment by moment, of new aspects of Sir John Barbirolli. He is really hurt by a critical doubt about the excellence of any performance given by the Hallé under his baton. In a way, this susceptibility is not vanity at all. He feels an injustice has been done. This is a trait in his make-up that deepens my affection for him.

In most artists worthwhile at all there is a certain naïveté. Sir John will turn round halfway through a Hallé performance of the National Anthem and conduct the audience (and most times the audience won't sing, creating a sense of anti-climax). Here is a gesture easily but mistakenly identified with showmanship. But Sir John really wishes to get the audience involved, part of the concert's creative activity. Any conductor is bound to exploit his own mannerisms. He is a kind of actor. Sir John has a prettily sardonic comment about the sort of conductor who is complimented by critics by some such remark as that he allows "the score to speak for itself". "Yes," says Sir John, "he just beats the time, up and down, left and right. I know that kind."

The paradox about him is that he, the perfect egoist, forgets himself fairly completely, as soon as he begins to conduct. He utterly absorbs the music, identifies himself with it. But the technical control is not thereby weakened. The disinterested spectator of Diderot remains in charge, watching the score from a detached seat of judgment and experience. I have seen tears in his eyes as he has conducted the Ninth Symphony of Mahler. But not a sparrow of a falling demi-semi-quaver has gone unnoticed by him.

He is too notable an artist to be treated as a prima donna for whom only praise is good enough. Consistency is a reasonably sure sign of mediocrity. Sir John often puts so much "expression" into a phrase or period that he allows the arching, forging-ahead rhythm to falter. He is a man of feeling, nurtured in an epoch of music now unintelligently called "romantic".

Naturally, with his unusual complex of blood, brain, and nerves, he is happier in music that touches him from a near distance than he is, say, in certain of the classics. In whatever he touches he is true to himself. That is as nice a compliment as I, personally, can make to him as he receives the Hallé award tomorrow.

Music and the Money-Bags

21st January 1969

A crisis occurs in the existence of any orchestra whenever a long established conductor retires from the rostrum; it is worse than a change of jockey half-way through a Grand National – if such a change were permissible. The Hallé Orchestra is approaching a sort of Becher's Brook in its career. Sir John Barbirolli has for a decade or two made the instrument his own.

The trouble nowadays is that conductors aren't willing to settle and commit themselves to one place and one orchestra, not in Europe at any rate. They fly here and there, each a nocturnal Fledermaus, mingling love of music and the money-bags with equal and remarkable impartiality.

Crises of this kind have happened more than once in the annals of the Hallé Concerts. Not even Sir John was obliged to cope with obstacles as difficult as those which confronted Sir Hamilton Harty. Sir John at least has enjoyed control of a permanent ensemble of players. In Harty's day the Hallé disbanded (a good word!) every March until October . . . . Most concerts were performed on the strength (or fallibility) of one rehearsal. For a new or unfamiliar work two rehearsals might be practicable; in fact Harty gave one of the first, if not the first, interpretations in this country of Mahler's Ninth Symphony after only two rehearsals. And a superb interpretation it was, wonderfully nuanced, with the Hallé strings unequalled anywhere in this country. There was in those days an active and fruitful tradition of string playing in force at the Royal Manchester College of Music, inherited from Adolf Brodsky. No English orchestra of the present epoch, not even the LSO, can produce string players commanding the tone and flexibility of phrase of Harty's Hallé Orchestra. The players were then proud to belong to it. The orchestra was as institutional in Lancashire and Manchester as the County Cricket Club, Manchester City, Peel Park and the Whitworth Art Gallery.

There was no television. Radio was an empirical affair depending on a "cat's whisker". A Hallé Concert was an event, an experience. I remember the years of the "Depression", when the mills of Lancashire were closing down bankrupt. At Hallé Concerts I would see worn men and women listening with closed eyes to Schnabel as he played in the D minor piano concerto of Brahms – what trills at the beginning of the first movement, recalling the terrific word used by Goethe in the Prologue in Heaven of the first part of "Faust": "Donnergang" (pitifully translated into English by "Thundertread"), a German word stolen for his purpose by Goethe from Schiller.

The Hallé under Harty watered every week the musical wasteland and desert; each Thursday was a mirage of refreshment to mind, ear, and spirit. No music "on tap" follows them. No mass production of Beethoven and Mozart; the Hallé Concert came to us as a rare and home-made privilege. Harty, like Barbirolli, was an artist; he found his way of life with the Hallé players. He was the first of our conductors to understand Berlioz, and to reconcile this genius's dichotomy of style and purpose: the romantic of his living environment, and the classic composer deep down in his subconscious metabolism.

It was good to be youngish and sit at the feet of Harty, one rehearsal or two. We weren't aware of periodical tonal miscarriages, just as we were not conscious of Schnabel's occasional wrong notes; because he, like Harty (and like Sir John), took us behind the written notes, led us to the essence, to the "Thing in Itself", to the "Ding an sich". That's why critics like Langford and Newman (and myself) seldom, if ever, tried to read a score and, at the same time, give our ears to the music – a difficult dual occupation, if not impossible. Yet today nearly all the London critics bury their heads in the score the moment a concert begins, even if the music is the "Eroica" Symphony, or, if it comes to that, the "Oberon" overture. I recently sat next to a colleague who endeavoured to "follow" with a score Rossini's "Barber of Seville" overture. When the overture arrived at the *crescendo*, he was turning the pages over with so much rapidity that he caused a draught, and I was obliged to turn up my coat collar protectively. Only once did I see Langford poring over a score. It was during a performance of a chamber quartet by – well, never mind. In the concert's interval I told Langford I had never before seen him absorbed in a score at a public performance. "Ah," he said, "it was such a boring piece that I was looking through Beethoven's Opus 135."

There is still, in Manchester, close communication between audiences and the Hallé. The orchestra remains an Institution. I cannot imagine that the Hallé will ever decline into merely one channel of musical provender amongst many. But the city, and those responsible for Manchester's and Lancashire's cultural welfare and character, should see to it that a conductor is found and secured who will dedicate himself.

He need not necessarily be a Harty, a Barbirolli; the crucial thing is that he must *belong*, and not go here and there serving dispassionately Bach, Beethoven, Britten – and Mammon.

Barbirolli Conducts Richard Strauss

26th September 1969

The concert of the London Symphony Orchestra last night, conducted by Sir John Barbirolli, was mainly concerned with Richard Strauss; in fact it more or less boxed the compass of his range of talent and genius. From "Ein Heldenleben" to the "Four Last Songs" is a metamorphosis in creative imagination and in its duration and development.

Elisabeth Schwarzkopf, superfluous to say, was irresistibly alluring in the songs. Her presence on the platform is, in itself, enough to draw one's entire awareness into a visual channel, leaving the aural chamber quiescent and untenanted. Criticism has to be gallantly on guard against these allurements. She satisfied ear and eye alike singing "Frühling"; her voice gloriously if rather breathlessly endomed the orchestral sky in "Beim Schlafengehen"; and she caught at the heart as she intoned the rising semi-quavers set to the word "sehnliches," and paused adorably after the interval drop following "freundlich". Sir John and the LSO obviously revelled in Strauss's silver-and-gold-dusted scoring. Miss Schwarzkopf did not quite give us the note of autumnal resignation called for in the poignant valedictory "Im Abendrot", Strauss's farewell to his wife Paulina, and to his world and mellow-tired self. "Through privation and joy we have travelled, hand in hand." No composer has more beautifully bowed his way out than this. Schwarzkopf is not essentially an artist of introspection. She is vividly active, rapturously extrovert, vitally present and not naturally nostalgic; this is why she is the greatest Donna Elvira of our time. Her vocal swell at the words "So tief im Abendrot" was sufficiently proud and heartfelt, but the tone scarcely pierced with poetic pain. The use of the spotlight was vulgar. Sir John and the LSO gave Schwarzkopf the ideal environment and atmosphere with the horn doing honour to Strauss's genius for writing for the instrument.

"Ein Heldenleben" is music very much after Sir John's temperament, dramatic, richly lyrical, communicative, kaleidoscopic, even at times operatic; and Sir John could easily have developed into one of the most commanding opera conductors anywhere and at any time. He lingered lovingly over the love music, too much, and took the giant-stride and climb of the preludial section, pointed emphatically the snap and snarl of the "Adversaries" section, and relaxed indulgently for the closing scene and its comfortably house-slippered sentimental fade-out. The LSO's first violin played the cadenza missing no wit or persuasiveness of some of the most volubly communicative recitative ever composed, representing the "Hero's" wife and Consort (and Paulina), as she teases, caresses, and argues with the "Superman", until he is reassured – after some self-pitying grunts in the tuba and trombones.

It is ironic to bear in mind that, once on a time, "Ein Heldenleben" was avant-garde stuff. This work, and "Elektra", burst and exploded in nineteenth-century music like nuclear bombs, compared with which the disturbance caused by Stravinsky's "Le Sacre du Printemps" was as a firework set alight any Fifth of November. Strauss himself was described by a critic of renown as the "Buddha" of music, and Strauss replied to the effect that he didn't know who really was the Buddha of music, but he had a shrewd idea who was the Pest. Today Strauss is regarded by the latest avant-garde (which is always advancing from all directions) as "old hat". Well, Sir John and the LSO put a fascinating fresh gloss on "Ein Heldenleben" at this constantly engaging concert, except for the spotlight.

The "Four Last Songs" are not exactly televisionary.

31st March 1969

Neville Cardus,
"Musical Critic"

Dear Neville,
Critic you certainly are, but bless you, amongst that fraternity you are unique in being wholly and completely "musical". It is this, I think, which has drawn us together outside our professional duties. A lover of beautiful things, be they on the concert platform, in the opera house, or on the cricket field; and, happily for us, endowed with a gift amounting to near genius for making them re-live for us in exquisite prose. Prose full of searching imagery, and at times deeply moving.

It seems strange that these few words of mine are being penned to you as a greeting on your 70th birthday, for you still have all the enthusiasm and exciting response to beauty that belongs to flaming youth. In your debt for many things, one in particular will make me everlastingly grateful to you. Your insistence that I was by nature a "Mahler-Man". In these days when the production of great music is a rarity, you have sent me to music virtually unknown to the general musical public that will occupy and enrich me to the end of my days.

May you live long to continue to delight us and to pursue your mission of humanizing a difficult profession.

Affectionately,
John Barbirolli.

18

KARAJAN
(1908–)

With the Philharmonia

12th May 1952

As a preparation for a distinguished European tour the Philharmonia Orchestra has given two concerts this week in the Royal Festival Hall, and the playing, conducted by Herbert von Karajan, has been unusually fine, with splendour of tone and a masterfully controlled scale of dynamics. Karajan in fact occasionally seems too deliberate in his transitions from loud to soft, one or two pianissimi in the First Symphony of Brahms lent to the composer a self-consciousness which he might well have rejected with some gruffness.

The interpretation of the symphony as a whole was impressive for its high seriousness. Mr Karajan is able to combine with a virtuoso concern for technical polish a true musician's feeling for content and substance. But his tempi do not convince us that the music is always unfolding from an inner cell but rather is being manipulated, sensitively enough, from the outside. This was a Brahms of arresting prose, with a few italics thrown in, a Brahms of culture and a good wardrobe. The symphony satisfied the ear and, by its masculine stride and carriage, satisfied in the end one's sense of the classical symphonic style. But the heart was not touched; I missed the sensibility in the slow movement of Furtwängler, with whom von Karajan occasionally invites a not obvious comparison by reason of his tendency towards changeful rhythm.

He is, of course, a superb opera conductor – his interpretation of "Die Meistersinger" at Bayreuth last year was superb – so naturally enough he revelled in "Don Juan" of Strauss; here the Philharmonia Orchestra played with a most stirring freedom and a sumptuous range of tone. The attack on the opening of the symphonic poem was exactly right, a reckless plunge into a welter. There was also the right romantic glow in the "Donna Anna" section and the lovely coda to it came as an afterthought of perfect misty-eyed German sentiment.

There was again a want of nature in Mr Karajan's treatment of the "Water Music" of Handel in Hamilton Harty's arrangement; it was beautifully played, but it was not music fresh from the great original fount; it was as though laid on in streamlined conduits from a resplendent reservoir.

Music by Mozart

IMMACULATE CONDUCTING

8th February 1956

Another Mozart concert in the Royal Festival Hall on Monday night was conducted by Herbert von Karajan and played by the Philharmonia Orchestra, with Clara Haskil the soloist. Mozart was inexhaustible, but not so the critics, who toil and pant after him in vain; and Karajan at this concert certainly caused one or two of us, short-winded perhaps, to feel a certain tightness of breath. The Philharmonia Orchestra, as usual, was musically very satisfying, in tone, balance, accuracy, and freshness of spirit. But the critic, bankrupt of language applicable to Mozart after the bicentenary celebrations, must now take refuge, as far as reference to Mozart goes, in the silence which at all times is the most eloquent tribute to his genius, and sign of our adoration of it.

It is hard not to admire Karajan's conducting up to a point; he is without affectation, yet he has personal appeal, a virtuoso with manners. Nonetheless I found his treatment of Mozart lacking ease and elasticity of rhythm. Sometimes, too, the conception of a work is not integrated rhythmically; for example, the "Jupiter" Symphony's slow movement had little relation in inner pulse and feeling to the brilliant, precise Finale, in which Mozart (of all composers) was made to sound in a hurry. But Karajan is hard to fault by the Beckmesser test. His performances are as a rule immaculate, beautifully shaped in their various parts. And they are vital enough.

The trouble, as I feel it, is that they do not go deep enough in imagination, or if the surface is seen through – for Karajan is not superficial by any means – what is revealed is not expressed with enough poignancy. The most eloquent passages in this programme happen during the Adagio of the heavenly A major Piano Concerto, with its ineffable melancholy – but the term "melancholy" is vile, in a Mozartean context, for it implies self-indulgence. And Mozart's melancholy, a sudden visitation, is all the more exquisite, because he himself seems touched by it as though by grace.

Clara Haskil, a beautiful, sensitive-fingered pianist, raptly lent ears to this other-worldly music. In the outer movements, rhythm and tone in the orchestra were much too brisk and bright. The introduction to the first movement was so stiffly precise in its phrasing, so staid in fact, that the adorable graciousness was nearly, but not altogether, put out of countenance. As the concert went its way to the end, always musically well dressed, I had the curious notion that we were all being recorded.

More Beethoven at the Festival Hall

7th November 1958

The Berlin Philharmonic Orchestra is still magnificent, if not quite as easefully sonorous as in the Furtwängler days. In the climaxes during the "Eroica" Symphony the texture hardened, and even the lithe and round-toned strings tended to sharpen under the sometimes stressful, urgent beat of Karajan. But it is an imposing body of serious musicians who obviously regard music as much as a vocation as a profession. Each player devotes himself wholly to his part, though listening and tuning himself to the whole.

Extraordinary point and clearness were given to the "Pastoral" Symphony so that its manifold beauties of instrumentation came to us in a bright light. Details of happy figuration had abounding life, details which in most performances are left to fend for themselves. Karajan adopted a quick dancing tempo which dispelled a reflection or any sort of sleeping grandeur over the landscape. All the same, this was a delightful and thoroughly musical interpretation which looked at nature through eyes of the present day, as we glided on smooth cylinders through meadow and by the running, not to say ornamental, brook. The performance felicitously made the most of the "Pastoral" Symphony's picturesque features. There was little suggestion, underneath the finely spun musical surface, of an almost religious conception of nature – which of course a deeply penetrative treatment of the symphony reveals. Moreover, there was a want of humour in the trio of the scherzo. The rustic bassoon was most modestly "refeened".

I do not agree that Karajan is an exhibitionary conductor mainly. He is undoubtedly a master of the orchestra, sure of himself. Whatever we may think of an interpretation of Karajan, he himself has thought it out to the minutest note. He does not lose his way or relax his grip. His control of dynamics is perhaps too deliberate. To obtain the axed forcibility of the opening chords of the "Coriolan" Overture he doubled himself up with the violent abruptness of a boneless wonder. His beat is long-armed and extensive. He is either bowing the music into our presence, or embracing it, or, from a sort of position of "point duty", directing it purposefully on its way.

There are no unnecessary motions. In fact the general impression got from Karajan on the rostrum is of competently conserved energy. Between movements he stands quite still, arms folded, apparently relaxed and thinking. There is missing from his conducting a feeling of spontaneity. As a consequence, the wonderful changes in the "Eroica" sounded sometimes less breathtaking than usual. The symphony was presented as a strongly shaped example of musical art, not entirely as a force beyond music yet compact of and contained in music. The truly great interpretation of the "Eroica" does take us beyond music, while remaining true to the art of it all. The deliberation of Karajan made rather a laborious climb of the mounting climax of the Aeschylean fugue (Weingartner's term) of the slow movement, and the same scrupulous care kept away the melting benediction of the coda of the closing and crowning movement.

Karajan is still young as conductors go (50 years). He has gifts and possibilities seldom shared. At present he is an interesting mingling of virtuoso and serious musician, brilliant and occasionally and paradoxically even pedantic in contrasted sections, especially when coping with a development section. Naturally he conducts the classics without score and seems to see into every part of the orchestra. His command and personal power are obvious and potent. Whether in a period of incessant traffic in concerts and opera houses his gifts will mature to some philosophical vintage and depth is for Karajan himself to decide.

A Compliment to Debussy

15th January 1962

In Debussy's centenary year the Vienna State Opera has paid the first tribute to the unique genius of "Pelléas and Mélisande" by means of a truly beautiful presentation – an evocation rather – in French, conducted by Herbert von Karajan as the last conductor to enter the habitation of silences which is the world of this music-drama. For isn't Karajan a man of our modern world, a musical apotheosis of it, with a flair for glamour, closed eyed in his personal appeal, master of the spectacular, and a sort of Svengali brought up to date, an exhibitionist *au fond*? What is Karajan to "Pelléas" or "Pelléas" to Karajan?

The Vienna performance gives the astonishing answer. Karajan goes to the heart of the work and plays on the superb orchestra – yes, superb – yet with penetration and subtlety of nuance. Debussy does not allow the conductor of "Pelléas" an extensive dynamic range. But Karajan, within the proscribed gamut, obtains a wide variety and reach of tone – a pianissimo which is warm and eloquent, not merely a matter of diminished sound. Also the climaxes were beautifully proportionate, the texture fine, and intense at the right moments. Karajan conducted Debussy with obvious devotion. Moreover he knows the difficult score – difficult to memorize – apparently by heart. More important, he responds to the inner drama and does not meander in a loosely controlled wash of modulating harmony. He kept the thematic connections and relevances clear and pertinent. Such an interpretation made nonsense of two fallacies about "Pelléas" (but they will persist, all the same!).

First, it is still taken much for granted that "Pelléas" is not a "dramatic" opera, that though the music ravishes the senses, the characters and action are unreal, without flesh and blood, shadows in a

309

passing dream. To my own way of thinking, it is the average opera that is "unreal", undramatic, a convention of pasteboard characters non-existent outside the theatre. "Pelléas and Mélisande" is a drama of the inner, the really "real" world, a drama of implications, of psychological conflicts too secret to concentrate into the obvious attitudes of life, exhibitory and active. Here is the drama of things that cannot be spoken, passions, fleeting happinesses, and eternal sorrows, not of the transient day, but all enveloping night. Sometimes the suspenses are quite unbearable, the music holds breath. Mélisande is so much "alive" –fragilely "alive" – that I often think that a poor performance of the part might do it a physical hurt. In fact a poor performance of "Pelléas" seems to me to inflict a pain on the score which, surely, it feels. "Atmospheric"? "Vague"? – why, the score is a marvel of fineness of touch, of imaginative aptness and relevance.

The most isolated tone in the woodwind is a cry in the night. A string tremolo is fateful. The night is omnipresent. A gleam of instrumental colour is a dramatic visitation – not a piece of mere orchestration. "Abstractions" – it is Titurel, not Arkel, who is "symbolic" and not "dramatic". Arkel is old-age poignantly particularized. The music by which Debussy gives him grief and wisdom is bowed in its sombre slow-moving phrases and harmonies, so pathetically in contrast to the golden-throated lyricism of Pelléas; the innocent youngness – but older in herself than she knows – of Mélisande; and the simple manliness of Golaud, that unfortunate horseman.

All these people are pulsatingly themselves. But we see them from a distance: they move in a permanent timeless dimension. It is ourselves, watching and overhearing from *our* clock-measured, active, merely phenomenal world, who are unreal. Debussy does not describe, he evokes. His orchestra, unlike Wagner's, does not *point*. It covers everything, a veiled unheard, yet heard, presence – omnipresent. A score entirely original which came from nowhere and has – greatest sign of its genius – had no "progressive influences". It is a prosaic view of a work of art that it serves a purpose in a "development" or evolving series, logical and sequential as science.

I can make no better compliment to Karajan, the Vienna State Opera Orchestra, and the singers than to say that all these intrinsic qualities of the work, not generally understood, were brought home. I confess that more than once I came near to tears, eyes as misted as the beautiful stage settings of Gunther Schneider Siemssen. The opening forest scene was an endless world of high trees, alluring and mysterious. The fountain in the park was an enchantment, with the orchestra at the beginning spray iridescent in the bright light, all seen in a reflection from afar. What magic of tone-chemistry is here! Different but in perfect harmony was the grotto scene, dark and the darkness more and more revealed when a glow of the outer night entered. The settings mingled with Maeterlinck and Debussy invisibly; the whispering of wind, echoes and shadows, all the invisible shaping powers in a love tragedy that comes to a cruel climax because of the chattering of an innocent child, Golaud's son Yniold.

To give the right stage gestures and movements to this opera sets an almost insoluble problem. Operatic attitudes and any rhetorical action of body or arm would be blasphemous. On the other hand a stilted rigidity should be avoided at all costs. In this performance a more or less happy balance was found, though Eberhard Waechter's admirable Golaud became overemphatic and even a little spasmodic and melo-dramatic in his scene with Yniold. But his singing and acting on the whole were eloquent and natural. The voice of Henri Gui was Pelléas's own, and I shall not soon forget the impulse and ecstasy of his rapturous "Je les nous" outburst. No melody in *"Pelléas and Mélisande"*? The scene is full of melody, but it is melody refined to an essence of the French language and its intonations.

As Mélisande, Hilde Gueden was extremely engaging to ear and eye alike, her song-speech nuanced sensitively, her voice in the proper tonal scale. Perhaps a Mélisande too immediately lovable. But this was highly intelligent singing by an artist of extraordinary versatility. Elisabeth Hoengen, as Geneviève, made the magnificent most of her one great opportunity when she intoned the heartbreaking recitative of the letter: *"Un soir, je l'ai trouvée tout en pleurs."* Here is another artist of fine musical and poetic sensibilities. The Arkel of Nicola Zaccaria had patriarchal gravity and a voice that may be a little too assured and firm. We of course don't want an Arkel babbling, but even without whiskers we should know him at sight as a man well past the age of, say, Pogner.

The orchestra, though, provided the long-to-be-remembered experi-ence. It was a pretty irony to hear this moving presentation of a music drama in which Mélisande never closes her eyes, or seldom, directed by a conductor who doesn't often open them. A triumph for Karajan, the Vienna, all concerned, in a worthy tribute to the most sensitively poetic of all composers of the last century and a half.

Superlative Music-Making

2nd November 1962

The Berlin Philharmonic Orchestra, conducted by Herbert von Karajan, packed the Royal Festival Hall last night. All the "top" people of London's concert public were there – and most of them had absented themselves the night before from Norman Del Mar's and the BBC Symphony Orchestra's superb performance of Mahler's Sixth symphony. I listened to the Berlin orchestra's rich and balanced tone with admiration and pleasure, as Karajan directed the players in a thoroughly musical unfolding of Brahms's Third symphony; but frankly it all seemed in my ears so much beautifully composed music-making, after the ranging, reckless, uninhibited Mahler Sixth. Mahler comes close to our troubled and complex and far from refined or gemütlich civilization. Young folk to-day find in Mahler some affinity of mental and spiritual texture; also they find his language, his technique, far removed from pomposity, something that comes home to them.

Brahms, in his third symphony, is the *mittel-deutsch* symphonist to perfection, the ripe craftsman, the mild-spirited romantic, approachably avuncular, and a thorough composer, attending conscientiously to established procedure. Karajan and the Berliners presented the Brahms symphony "in the round". A striking instance of Karajan's interpretation, and of the quick response of his players to his directions, was the changes of orchestral colour at the different changes of key – for instance, the modulations to D flat at the beginning of the first movement, and the more unexpected (for Brahms) transition to the graceful second theme. Karajan, master of the orchestral palette, ranged easefully over the spacious canvas before him, and within broad outlines missed no opportunity for showing us finely-finished details. Such a performance prompted me to remember that once on a time, in the long-ago, Brahms was regarded as an orchestral composer of dull, drab, or neutral colours!

Karajan is the virtuoso conductor of our glamour-hungry age. But also he is a musician of much understanding of style. His Brahms is perhaps a shade more well-turned-out than Brahms (or Furtwängler) ever imagined he could be made to appear, or sound. None the less, the performance gave constant musical satisfaction. The brilliant strings, playing as one, sometimes broadly bowed, were a ravishment to the ear, especially as they floated upward on the beautiful phrase at the end of the Andante. Maybe the Berliners' woodwind is not individually superior to ours, but it is chorded and blended, instrument matched to instrument, as ours seldom is. The colloquy of clarinets and lower strings at the opening of the slow movement was enchantingly done, also the solemn first entry of the trombones . . . .

Virtuoso instrumentation and ensemble are the first needs in any performance of the Concerto for Orchestra of Bartók; and the Berliners played it with a perfectly mingled solo brilliance, and unity of part-writing. The balancing of short sections in the second movement was another demonstration of Karajan's musicianship; so was his grip on the superbly contrasted phrases and textures of the haunted and nobly tragic "Elegia". This was the evening's most impressive music.

There are periods, maybe, when Karajan very obviously is standing between us and the music, exhibiting its glories – and the orchestra's. At times, indeed, he seems to be under the impression that also he is composing it. But there is no questioning his command. And there is no arguing against the tonal and musical attributes of the Berlin Philharmonic.

Karajan and Berlioz

12th May 1967

Superb playing was heard in the Royal Festival Hall last night by the Berlin Philharmonic Orchestra during a performance of Berlioz' "Symphonie Fantastique", conducted by Herbert von Karajan. A crowded audience packed seats and boxes; on the whole it appeared to be the sort of snob audience which stays away if one of our best English musicians is conducting the same masterpiece; moreover conducting it in his own less spectacular way, as masterfully as any Karajan. Karajan's advantage comes from the wide range of expressive nuance which the Berliners can cover. British wind-players in brass are second to none, but frankly, we cannot compare favourably with the rich gutty string-tone at Karajan's command, string-tone strongly characterized, from the flexible sonorous double-basses to the violins, which in the highest reaches remain musical and firm. Tension is the first essential of great violin playing; tension (and no flatness) even during relaxed passages. And tension, plus range, is Karajan's individual asset.

Before he liberates music from silence, he stands before the orchestra, waiting for the right moment to announce the Fiat Lux . . . . Without a score he encompassed the whole of the "Fantastic" symphony, missing hardly a point, the orchestra clearly contained by his grasp, yet never tightly held or overridden. Karajan has a keen ear for the sorts of music which appeal to and engross his temperament. He reconciled the "classic" to the "romantic" in Berlioz. In the short preludial Largo, leading to the Allegro, the tone and diction were absolutely true to the style – a marvellous suggestion of stillness over Virgilian fields. The waltz had swing and animation, with no alien aromas from Vienna; and the "Witches' Sabbath" achieved instrumental brilliance at no dissipation of the macabre mockery – where the hero's *idée fixe* is metamorphosed with incomparable irony and *diablerie*. Every time I hear this "Symphonie", I am astounded to remember that it was composed by a young man not yet thirty, a few years following the death of Beethoven. No subsequent orchestral work has seen as far into the future as this one, especially the "Witches" movement, prophetic of Stravinsky (at his most real), and a host of others called "modern" to the present moment.

A rare virtue of Karajan's interpretation of the "Fantastic" symphony is that, though vividness of poetic and dramatic point was omnipresent, the approach was definitely musical all the time. Berlioz, in advance of Wagner, strove to follow Beethoven's lead and fertilize music with drama and psychological identity. He could not quite equate the two aesthetic viewpoints which, in his day, were regarded as almost mutually exclusive. In the "Fantastic" symphony the motto theme, the idée fixe, is sometimes dragged in too obviously. The genius of Berlioz was perhaps a little in advance of his time. Towering genius it certainly was, for all the recurrent short-circuitings and frustrations.

This performance by the Berlin Philharmonic Orchestra brought out this genius, actual and potential. I can say nothing more complimentary than that.

The evening began with the Mozart Divertimento K287. Again the playing was fairly flawless, yet something of inner warmth was missing. The flowers in it seemed wired.

Karajan and Bruckner

7th June 1969

Last night, in a crowded and ravingly vociferous Royal Festival Hall, Herbert von Karajan conducted the superb Berlin Philharmonic Orchestra in and through the Seventh Symphony of Bruckner, prefaced by the first Brandenberg Concerto of Bach. Not so long ago, within living memory, Karajan conducted the Vienna Philharmonic Orchestra and the Seventh symphony of Bruckner was his main occupation in this same Hall.

These continental conductors forget nothing. It would be a refreshing change if, for once in a while, one or two of them turned attention to, say, an Elgar symphony; after all, Sir John Barbirolli was bold enough, and persuasive enough, to conduct Mahler in, of all un-Mahlerish places, Rome. Perhaps Karajan doesn't know the two Elgar symphonies – Bruno Walter didn't when I asked him to perform some Elgar in the mid-1930s. Elgar might suit Karajan; at any rate, he has conducted a wonderfully vital performance of Holst's "The Planets".

Karajan doesn't change his view of the Bruckner of the Seventh symphony. He emphasizes the not generally well-known fact that Bruckner really could score richly, evenly sensuously, for the orchestra. The Berliners' strings revelled in the gorgeously written part-writing in the adagio.

Karajan remains for me something of an enigma. He is an orchestral master, comprehensive and sure of himself. He has the score in his head, and can send waves and pulsations of his personality into the instrumental ranks, generated from his inner dynamo, enforced by drastic commanding shoulder action, and the arms thrust down from on high; then, at a transition, the hands suavely shape a phrase, almost kissing it goodbye on its way. He is obviously dedicated – whether to music in general or his own aesthetic reactions in particular, I couldn't say. The Berlin Philharmonic respond as one man to his promptings with full and gutty yet incisive violins, velvet violas, rich brown 'cellos, and basses of vintage in the cellarage. Maybe the brass gets out of focus at times; and no horns or woodwind can surpass our native own. But Karajan worries me as an interpreter; he tends to endow all composers with the same sound.

This performance of the Bruckner Seventh, for all its delights to the orchestral ear, made Bruckner (of all composers) appear rather self-conscious of the effects he was making on the audience. There is hardly a hundred bars in all Bruckner's output which postulate an audience, least of all an audience which is considerably a by-product of records and television. Here and there, for all Karajan's fine artistry – and he is an artist – the symphony didn't quite get off the ground, a phrase which, I think, will come home rather meaningfully to Karajan. Yet the performance had its memorable periods: the spacious opening-out of the first movement, broad and far-reaching, and the truly valedictory coda of the Adagio, lamenting the passing of Wagner, echoing Walhall.

Maybe the Scherzo needed more of geniality; I have never suspected Karajan of having an inexhaustible vein of humour. It is superfluous to report that the Berliners gloried in the Bruckner unisons; and in the angelic rise and fall of melody during the slow movement Karajan again levitated the phrases beautifully, sensitively timing the woodwind responses, and getting the exquisite catch of breath at the entrance of the three-four violin seraphic song at the beginning of the Adagio.

"Exquisite" may be an odd word to apply to Bruckner, or to Karajan. In the context of this performance it falls, as a description, trippingly from the pen. Moreover, I have heard Karajan conduct Debussy's "Pelléas et Mélisande" with a touch of quite exquisite fancy unequalled in our time. He is our most enigmatic and compelling conductor – almost *capable de tout* – capable even of making Bruckner sound, at times, aggressive, noisy, almost a Berliner himself.

Karajan the Spectacular

17th May 1972

The Royal Festival Hall was again crowded last night to hear the Berlin Philharmonic Orchestra conducted by Herbert von Karajan. ("Demn the 'von'" as Mr Mantalini would certainly say.) The main attraction for the public was, of course, Karajan himself. He is the master of all he surveys from the rostrum; from the first violins, sitting at his knees, he dominates his empire to the farthest-flung outposts of timpani and triangle. But he is occasionally quite a benevolent dictator, granting a certain autonomy to his instrumentalists, also granting a certain autonomy to the composers he absorbs into his kingdom.

His control over his orchestra is manifest as soon as he lifts up his baton, sometimes bringing it down pugilistically. His left hand religiously follows his right; whither the right hand goeth, so goeth the left.

The Berlin orchestra has a gorgeous richness of tone, rich enough, indeed, to warm the usually chilly acoustics of the Royal Festival Hall. At most concerts its acoustics reject the sound of music, unlike the old Queen's Hall, where the plushed acoustics welcomed and retained the sound, and harvested it.

Perhaps the rarest possession of the Berlin Philharmonic are the double basses. Karajan has so strong a sense of full and deep-rooted harmony that the balance of tone, from high to low, is maintained. Though the ranks of the orchestra are full of instrumentalists gifted with solo capacity, each plays to the other, achieving a wonderful ensemble.

Karajan began the evening with the "Pastoral" symphony of Beethoven. It was not exactly a pastoral performance. There should fall a sleeping sort of grandeur over the music as a whole, especially during the andante, that marvellous example of extended sonata form. Karajan was too deliberate in his transitions; and he treated the capricious figure of the opening movement too quickly and too precisely. Also, Karajan, too squarely, even ponderously, controlled the murmurings of the brook in the slow movement. The storm was terrific, banally fit for television. But altogether this was a "Pastoral" symphony severely man-controlled; nature did not naturally expand. The landscape seemed scrupulously mapped, according to the Ordnance Survey. Clouds were ordered into place as though by Karajan-Zeus; the winds were held in thrall as though by Karajan-Aeolus. A rather empty and prosaic "Pastoral".

Much more suited to Strauss's "Ein Heldenleben" was Karajan than to the "Pastoral" symphony. This was a staggeringly virtuoso orchestral performance, if sometimes overdone. The introductory section, envisaging "The Hero", stormed upwards, not a note wasted, horns, violas, 'cellos and violins rampant and challenging, all culminating in the emphatic blows of assertion, ending with the dominant seventh pause, leading to the section depicting Strauss's "Adversaries" – the critics.

Karajan took this satirical section too seriously, missing the sharp irony of Sir Thomas Beecham's incomparable conducting of "Heldenleben" (Strauss himself thought Beecham's understanding and vivid handling of "Heldenleben" the best in his experience). The cajoling violin portrayal of the "Hero's Helpmate" was superbly done, followed by a too deliberately curved love apotheosis. But the "fade-out" at the end was entirely satisfying, winning the impressionable senses completely.

The only thing lacking in this generally spectacular presentation of Strauss's Hero and his Life was the Beecham *panache*. I wish, though, that the great orchestras of the Continent that visit us would, once in a while, do homage to a British composer. When our orchestras go to Berlin or Vienna, they often play Mahler and Bruckner, as well as the established "classical". I'd go a long way (and be prepared to pay for a ticket) to hear the Berliners coping with an Elgar symphony. Does Karajan know of them – the entire two?

19

THE LAST MOVEMENT

The National Youth Orchestra at the Edinburgh Festival

27th August 1971

The thunder of applause at the end of the concert here of the National Youth Orchestra threatened to bring about the fall of the Hall of Usher. The programme was much the same as the one performed two nights ago at the London Promenades, except that Yehudi Menuhin gave us his incomparable interpretation of the Alban Berg Violin Concerto.

The work of the National Youth Orchestra goes beyond a mainly musical estimation. These amazingly gifted young instrumentalists are being prepared for a civilized way of life; the value of the work of the Orchestra is as much sociological as musical. It matters little that many of these young music makers may never become professionally and financially secure as orchestral players (though I see no reason why they should not). The great fact is that at a critical time of their lives they are being initiated into discipline and devoted service and to territories of the mind and spirit not generally experienced nowadays, and not to be discovered by ordinary educational processes.

We take many marvellous adventures of the imagination for granted at the present time. For myself, the transformation by the National Youth Orchestra of the magical score of "La Mer" into vital luminous tone is an achievement of human skill and intelligence compared with which the shooting of a mechanical missile to the moon is a prosaic and predictable procedure.

It is always a moving experience to see and hear the National Youth Orchestra, and to know that here, at any rate, is youth momentarily taken out of the world of getting and spending, the world of protest and do-it-yourself. Only after hours and hours of severe study and practice and discipline could these juveniles make an orchestra which is a marvel of tonal range, style, individuality, so unified that no part is greater than the whole . . . .

The striking quality of the National Youth Orchestra, as I have known and heard it for some 25 years, has consistently been a spontaneity of approach, and a completely unstrained expression . . . .

As astonishing as any of the performances of the NYO has been that of Webern's Six Pieces Opus 6. The young instrumentalists produced every essential nuance of these orchestral bowel releases (without odour).

On Over-Production

23rd March 1974

"The average professional actor offends us with his roughness and readiness. His experience is such that he never has to think out freshly for himself. He repeats mechanically the tricks he has played before." So wrote Max Beerbohm 70 years ago; and what he wrote then about actors applies to-day with emphasis to most performing musicians. During the few last decades, distribution of music has become glutinous, even the top-class virtuosi have no time to think afresh about the compositions in their limited repertoires. Repetition upon the heels of repetition has rendered their performances more or less predictable. I would know in advance that Artur Rubinstein would enliven his playing by the familiar lightness of touch, with a wrong note as dazzling and as unexpected as a shooting star. I could be certain that Brendel's impressive anonymity remained undisturbed by an impulsive outbreak of temperament. Ogden's strong and masculine account of the D minor Concerto of Brahms would sound as a tonal photostat of his preceding performance of the same work. And so on and so forth.

A solo performer of music to-day gets through more concerts in a month or two than Schnabel or Backhaus or Busoni were called on to cope with in six months or even a year. We need only listen to a recording of Schnabel playing Beethoven to realize what has passed out of music, speaking generally, because of overdone professional routine. Schnabel was actually taken to task by critics because, so they alleged, he lacked a really virtuoso technique. But Schnabel himself once said to me: "A masterful technique can easily master your imagination." He never *performed*, never seemed conscious of the presence of an audience.

I first heard Schnabel playing Beethoven's Opus 111 Sonata. It was as though he were sitting at the keyboard as a medium through which Beethoven spoke or manifested himself. I wrote, in this paper, nearly a column about the Sonata leaving myself space enough only to report that Schnabel had played it. Next day, Schnabel rang me up; I had not met him then. He told me, over the telephone, that he had taken my notice as a rare compliment to his playing because "apparently my performance revealed Beethoven not Schnabel". I wonder what Herbert von Karajan would think of a notice which discussed Bruckner to the length of a column, ending with a brief, if admiring, reference to his conducting. If the glut of concerts to-day puts a blighting strain on the freshness of musical conception among performance on solo instruments, how much more burdensome must the strain be on conductors. The soloist, at any rate, has merely to control a passive instrument, piano or fiddle. The conductor is obliged, before he can even begin to think of interpretation, to unify or harmonize a mass of humanity, all of them, at one time or other, ambitious soloists, violinists, brass blowers, timpanists, and the rest, some of them bored by music, some of them eager to perform, some happily married, some unhappily, men (and women, in English orchestras) in good or poor health, one or two of them convinced that they could conduct as convincingly as the "maestro" now handling the baton.

The conductor is faced with the ordeal of welding this variable assembly of humans into a responsive, sympathetic performing instrument – yes, an instrument – upon which he is hoping to play with the freedom and intimacy of communication of Rubinstein at his piano. Only a Toscanini, a Furtwängler, a Beecham, a Bruno Walter, may ever achieve orchestral unity complete, and only then if he is in day-by-day charge of the players, a "permanent" conductor. Few orchestras, in this year of 1974 are blessed with the pervasive presence of a permanent conductor. Consequently, there is a scarcity of commanding conductors.

Before the aeroplane began to carry performing musicians the world over, in Berlin to-day, in London tomorrow, in New York the day after, it was easy to name a great company of conductors, each a master of an ensembled orchestra – Toscanini, Klemperer, Furtwängler, Mengelberg, Beecham, Harty, Weingartner, Sabata, Krauss . . . can we name six conductors to-day, even three, of this stature? "She shall have music wherever she goes" was an old nursery phrase, or words to much the same effect, and addressed as a compliment and blessing.

Years ago Constant Lambert wrote about "the appalling popularity of music". The present age, he avowed, "is one of over production. Never has there been so much food (of music) and so much starvation . . . never has there been so much music-making, and so little musical experience of a vital order." O Constant, thou shouldst be living at this hour!

A Visitation in Time of Need

20th January 1972

My most memorable performance in the concert hall or opera house? An impossible question to answer precisely. So, to ease the problem, I shall classify events memorable. For example: for pure musical delight, ravishing the senses, Horowitz at his height during the 1930s, when he enchanted from the keyboard a gem-like flame and sparkle. Or Beecham conducting Mozart, producing felicitous patterns of tone which gave delight, and wounded, yet hurt not. Or Schnabel for profound musical thinking, as he identified himself with Beethoven's Opus 111. Or Furtwängler for tragic intensity, in "Tristan and Isolde". But there are performances which go beyond an immediate music-making and get into our consciousness, stimulating awareness to life, illuminating the sometimes darkening corridors of existence (and I am not afraid of the corny word "corny").

In late summer, 1947, I returned to England after seven years of wartime in Australia. I went to the first Edinburgh Festival, and there was Bruno Walter conducting the Vienna Philharmonic Orchestra in Mahler's "Das Lied von der Erde". It was Walter's renewal of his love and connection with the Vienna orchestra. Hitler had expelled him from Germany and Austria – to say the least – considering him not fit company for a pure Aryan civilization faithfully represented by himself, Goering, Goebbels, and the rest.

For years I had argued the case for Mahler as a composer of genius, encouraged and taught in the beginning by Samuel Langford, in my 'prentice years on the "Manchester Guardian". Critics on the whole in England had in those years no time for Mahler.

Here I was, the native returned, in a beautiful city, with Bruno Walter and the Vienna Philharmonic still alive, bringing back to me vivid impressions of lost happy hours of fully-realized living in a departed Vienna. And the woman singing in "Das Lied" was a Lancashire lass, born in Blackburn or thereabouts. She came to the platform, with the tenor Patzak, and as she sat, quite still, in the first movement, in which she had no part, her face seemed to feel the waves of the music passing over it. She was, as Mahler himself might have said, lost to the world, in "der Welt abhanden gekommen".

Then she sang "The Lonely One in Autumn" – "Der Einsame im Herbst" – with Bruno Walter and the Vienna Philharmonic silver-pointing the wonderful tints of the orchestration. It was all so perfect and rapt, silence and the brown leaf; imagination evoked and stirred poignantly, without self-pity.

In "The Farewell" I was given my unique experience. The singer intoned the recitative telling of the setting sun, as she waited for the symbolic "friend" – "Ich stehe hier und harre meines Freundes." Voiceless, but none the less wondrous word-speech. Finally, in "The Farewell", the singer's heart seemed to throb in her throat at the passionate cry "O Schönheit, O ewigen Liebens – Lebens – trunkene Welt!" A cry for vanishing beauty, as singer and orchestra pressed out the bitter-sweet of the music. It was a moment of vision; yet, as we thrilled and participated in it, mind and senses, we knew that it was all passing from us, even as, paradoxically, it was entering our consciousness for good and all. But though we might call out, like Faust, "Verweile doch, du bist so schön" – "Stay, thou art so fair" – it was a perishable consummation in the universe of fact and phenomena. Memory retains only a reflection, an echo from the distant irony of awareness!

The singer, of course, was Kathleen Ferrier. She broke down emotionally at this performance, at the first Edinburgh Festival, unable to enunciate the closing words, "Ewig, ewig" – "Ever, ever." I didn't then know Kathleen but as Walter and the orchestra were acknowledging applause (she had vanished from our view), I took courage and forced my way into the artists' room, where I introduced myself to this beauteous (unself-consciously beauteous) creature. As though she had known me all her life she said: "I have made a fool of myself, breaking down like that."

When Walter came into the room she went to him, apologizing. He took her hands, saying: "My child, if we had *all* been artists like you, we should every one of us have broken down." A generous response. Possibly Diderot would not have agreed, for he maintained that at the back of the artist's mind there should always be a disinterested spectator watching and controlling technique and expression. But Kathleen's breakdown was on the side of the angels all right.

Through this concert I came to know Kathleen Ferrier. The astounding fact is that she, by nature akin to Gracie Fields, a grand Lancashire lass, as humorous, as sensitive, capable of unbuttoned talk and laughter, should have got instinctively to the heart of Mahler, a man and composer at the extreme to her, and to the English, in psychology, nerves, bloodstream, and all the rest of his make-up. She had the blessed gift of what I can only call spiritual reception; that is to say, whenever she found the wavelength to a composer she, while remaining Kathleen Ferrier to our sensory view, became a vessel of communication, a medium.

She has, since her death, been surpassed in vocal technique by other singers of her school. None has shared her warm responsive nature. The whole woman of her sang, sang the music sounded by the composer through her being. Not every composer found her on his wavelength. At Edinburgh, in 1947, grace as well as Mahler descended on her, on Bruno Walter, on the matchless Vienna Philharmonic Orchestra, and – praise whatever gods there be – on at least one music critic present.

Maybe I have evaded the question – this was not strictly, or exclusively, a musical event. It was a contribution to my more or less permanent self, to a man at the time in need of such a visitation. It was an experience that enriched my nature, quickened the antennae of consciousness of a man trying, as they say, "to believe". And, as I write that foregoing sentence, I seem to hear Kathleen's voice, her Lancashire voice, saying "Come off it."

A Critic's Vintage

1967

During the recent squabble about criticism of the theatre and its uses nobody, as far as I know, put forward the view that the critic himself is, or should be, a performer, an entertainer of his public. He is not merely a reporter of what happens at a first night, a play or actor "taster" or referee, an unpaid publicity man and agent. His judgment of the quality of a play, production or performance, may be delivered with the wisdom of a Solon or Solomon; but it will count for little if it is not immediately readable, not only to those who are involved in the production and the audience present at the event written about. The critic must, if he is worth his salt, be able, by his *writing*, to engage the attention of those of his readers who were, in fact, *not* present at all.

Each of us, of course, has his own notions concerning the functions of the critic. Frankly, I write criticism, and read it, entirely for the pleasure I get from well-written impressions of an engaging mind and temperament. I read Hobson or Wardle or Philip Hope-Wallace in order to observe and imaginatively experience the reactions of a fine sensibility while it is under the influence of a play, book, composition or performance. If a "judgment" or appraisal is nothing but magisterial or pedantic, even if I agree with it, the criticism leaves no lasting effect on my memory. But I sit up and take notice if a C. E. Montague, discussing "on the night" a performance of "Measure for Measure", digresses from an assessment of the players to say: "We are to think of Isabella as one of those great quiet souls who seem to make their own calm, like ships shedding oil in the midst of tempest and trouble. Then, when the mind is penetrated with the sense of that austere serenity, we are to see the contained spirit leap up in an instant to the free height and heat of tragic passion."

The critic working for a daily newspaper is constantly obliged to equate the job of public guide and adviser and that of his private egoistical wish to express himself as an artist. He tries to be informative about the worthwhileness of productions and performance. Often, if he is honest, he is astonished that his "assessments" are taken so seriously by the public; because frequently, between that short space of time separating the fall of the curtain to his "deadline" for putting his copy in the hands of the avid sub-editor, he himself is not too sure of his opinions as objective truth. He "gets by" many times by sheer professional virtuosity as writer or journalist. If the critic happens to have a well-stored mind; if he has behind him a long and varied experience; if he is gifted with imaginative understanding and love of his subject; and if also he is able to express himself in language stimulating mind and sense, then, I think, he will go far towards fulfilling the only purpose he can pursue, if he has any humour in him – the purpose of giving pleasure to his readers and, even more important, to himself.

As a music critic, I am constantly being asked if I play any instrument myself. It is an irrelevant question, irrelevant to the matter of a music critic's qualifications. Why, indeed, should a music-critic be expected to play an instrument? Nobody of the theatre public expects Philip Hope-Wallace to play Hamlet, or Kenneth Tynan the First Grave Digger. The critic's instrument is, indeed, his *language*. Few people have ever mastered this difficult instrument. A child can play the piano and produce effects recognizable as the music of Beethoven. Thousands of folk can perform on some musical instrument or other; precious few can write a page of English that signs itself.

Concerning the crucial questions, "How far is a critic's opinion reasonably true to objective fact? How far is it not much more than a matter of personal taste?" – my own experience has taught me that it is vain of criticism to attempt to escape from the influence of one's particular cultural environment, and from the natural reactions of one's temperament. Myself, I confess that I have failed, more or less, to discover the touchstone necessary to arrive at the objective truth about a composition. I am forced more and more to rely on my personal antennae. The wider my studies, the deeper my experience of music, the stronger and more insistent my temperamental urges become, the less interest I take in productions which do not appeal to my "sensitised plate". My knowledge and standards assure me that so-and-so's new symphony is excellent of its kind. But frankly, I can't enjoy it, or get inside it, because of a taste (and no narrow one) cultivated in a certain way, in a certain cultural environment, and by reason of a temperament that simply cannot find every wavelength in the world. Unlike Oscar Wilde's auctioneer, I am incapable of valuing and appreciating all schools of art. By critical discipline I can admire the work which my temperament shrinks from – the craftsmanship, the organization of form and so on. I can't write well of it, though – if the spirit eludes me.

It is inevitable and natural that the day comes when all of us, especially if we are critics, are charged with having closed our minds. There is often something in the accusation. After thirty or forty years of harvesting, the mind might easily be so fully stored that there is little room left in it. It takes years to get to the bottom of even one great creative genius, to know his language inside out. And there is no fool so foolish as the old fool who goes about slapping his thighs saying he's as young as ever he was, ready for everything. The dilettante is even worse, as he rushes here and there to be "with it". Wisdom in criticism is content to realize that a man's tastes and antennae, his standards and aesthetic responses, have been produced, cultivated and developed in a certain soil and period. He cannot extend the base of his pyramid. If he is sensible he will consolidate the gains of his impressionable years. Vintage implies, even with critical judgments, some lengthy cellarage. In every period the critic's vision is best focussed in a certain way. It can achieve definition only when the object, the art-work, is situated or presented at a certain point. At a rehearsal of one of Schoenberg's most esoteric works, one of the woodwind players lost his way, and afterwards went to the composer and apologized. But Schoenberg had apparently listened to the rehearsal with satisfaction. "But do you mean to say, Meister", asked the woodwind player courageously, "do you mean to say that even *you* don't always know when your music is being performed wrongly?" "No," answered Schoenberg, "no, not always. But my grandchildren will." Verb. sap. – for critics and for one and all.

My dear Neville,

Into the stuffy precincts of music criticism you bring a breath of fresh air. A window flies open; we see a cricket pitch green in the sun, and beyond it a wide world of literature and art, men and manners, solitude and talk.

Music is written by and for the whole man, not the specialist; and in you it has found not only an acute listener, but a man of Falstaffian zest – though indeed not an eagle's talon in the waist. "Prode, arguto, facondo . . . Voi siete un uom di mondo."

And now you tell us you are seventy! Well, well, you must be right: so good a journalist makes sure of his facts. Conceding the unlikely claim, we wish you many more years of happy activity – and ourselves no fewer to continue your faithful readers.

Desmond Shawe-Taylor

Neville Cardus's Own Books About Music

ed: *The Musical Criticisms* of Samuel Langford. OUP, 1929.

Ten Composers. Jonathan Cape, 1945. Republished as *A Composers' Eleven*, Jonathan Cape, 1958.

Autobiography. Collins, 1947. Republished in paperback, Hamish Hamilton, 1985.

Second Innings: more autobiography. Collins, 1950.

ed: *Kathleen Ferrier: A Memoir*. Hamish Hamilton, 1954.

Talking of Music. Collins, 1957.

Sir Thomas Beecham: a Memoir. Collins, 1961.

Gustav Mahler: his Mind and his Music, Vol. 1. Gollancz, 1965.

The Delights of Music. Gollancz, 1966.

Full Score. Cassell, 1970.

Index